Christ's
Way to
Spiritual
Growth

Christ's
Way to
Spiritual
Growth

Philip G. Samaan

REVIEW AND HERALD® PUBLISHING ASSOCIATION
HAGERSTOWN, MD 21740

Unless otherwise noted, Bible texts in this book are from the New King
James Version. Copyright © 1979, 1980, 1982, Thomas Nelson, Inc., Publishers.
Texts credited to NIV are from the *Holy Bible, New International Version.*
Copyright © 1973, 1978, 1984, International Bible Society. Used by permission
of Zondervan Bible Publishers.
Bible texts credited to Phillips are from J. B. Phillips: *The New Testament
in Modern English*, Revised Edition. © J. B. Phillips 1958, 1960, 1972. Used by
permission of Macmillan Publishing Co.
Bible texts credited to RSV are from the Revised Standard Version of the
Bible, copyright © 1946, 1952, 1971, by the Division of Christian Education of
the National Council of the Churches of Christ in the U.S.A. Used by permission.
Verses marked TLB are taken from *The Living Bible*, copyright © 1971 by
Tyndale House Publishers, Wheaton, Ill. Used by permission.

This book was
Edited by Gerald Wheeler
Designed by Patricia S. Wegh
Cover photo by Stock Market
Typeset: 10/11 Times

PRINTED IN U.S.A.

05   6 5 4

R&H Cataloging Service
Samaan, Philip. G.   1949-
    Christ's way to spiritual growth.

    1. Spiritual life—Seventh-day Adventist
authors.   2. Seventh-day Adventists—Revival and
reformation.   I. Title.

                    248.486732

ISBN 0-8280-0946-5

DEDICATED

to Jesus Christ
the Model for true spirituality

BOOKS BY PHILIP G. SAMAAN

Christ's Way of Reaching People
Christ's Way to Spiritual Growth

To order, call **1-800-765-6955**

For more information on Review and Herald products,
visit us at www.rhpa.org

CONTENTS

INTRODUCTION

Ever since the publication of my last book, *Christ's Way of Reaching People,* I have increasingly sensed the need to write a sequel to it on the spiritual life of Christ. The enthusiastic response that the first book evoked in the hearts of many people has encouraged me to do so. It is indeed gratifying to see their insatiable interest in following the example of Christ in personal witnessing, as well as everything else involved in emulating Him. And when it comes to the crucial subject of spirituality, we desperately need Christ's way to satisfy the spiritual hunger we find in us and all around us.

It is finally dawning on us that even the best human approaches cannot meet the deep desires of our souls. We futilely grope for spiritual fulfillment in human inventions, searching desperately for some way out of our spiritual dilemma. But no matter how many contraptions we may contrive, how many possessions we may acquire, or how high the positions we may attain, at the core of our being there still awaits our spiritual need to enjoy meaningful relationships with our Creator and fellow human beings.

Eugene Peterson, professor of spiritual theology at Regent College, explains that such spiritual hunger in our secular age results from our desperate need for intimacy and transcendence. That, as he puts it, all the great accomplishments of secularism have only produced an "epidemic of loneliness and boredom" and that "we are surprised to find ourselves lonely behind the wheel of a BMW or bored nearly to death as we advance from one prestigious job to another."[1]

We live in a throwaway age. And our age of the disposable does not limit itself to things, but extends to relationships as well. Desperate to find happiness, we make more money to buy more new things. We inhabit and refurbish newer and bigger houses. And for lack of commitment, we discard a spouse in order to acquire a new one, just as we trade in our car for a newer model. Or we abandon our children and our parents and use our friends until we think we no longer have use for them.

Even our relationship with God reflects the same attitude, for we think we may use Him and discard Him at will. In our restlessness we hop from place to place, from job to job, from one thing to the next, from relationship to relationship, and from god to god. Yet with all of these changes and acquisitions, we still do not experience true happiness and serenity. Laurence Shames described it as "dodging emptiness by courting novelty" in his book *The Hunger for More.*[2]

But what is novel today may become ordinary tomorrow, and all our long-sought acquisitions can swiftly vanish before our eyes. I had an old acquaintance who suffered a heart attack and died when he heard the jolting news that all his investments had abruptly disappeared with the 1987 stock market crash. It is a sad thought that worrying about our riches, amassed to supposedly provide us with happiness and fulfillment, may actually deprive us of life itself.

It is also sad to see retired individuals languishing in nursing home facilities without the fellowship of friends and relatives. They may have been avid workaholics, consumed with proving themselves successful to the neglect of nurturing meaningful relationships with God, loved ones, and friends. Although they had hoped to make up for this lack in their retirement years, now their children are similarly obsessed with their own affairs. And their friends may have dispersed elsewhere. A life of intemperance and stress now may make them more vulnerable to disease and infirmity.

Surrounded by total strangers, they long for some relative or old friend to surprise them by showing up to see them. Researchers once asked a group of retired executives what they regretted most not doing in their lives. Their most common response was that they wished they had spent more time with their loved ones and friends.

Genuine relationships of love and trust and joy is what Eugene Peterson means by "intimacy" and "transcendence." The first results from our human relationships, and the second from our divine relationship. "We long for a human touch, for someone who knows our name. We hunger for divine meaning, someone who will bless us."[3]

Regrettably, such human intimacy and transcendence is no longer common even in the family circle, and it is especially rare in our society as a whole. Recent studies show that, on the average, an American father spends less than a minute a day in meaningful contact with his child. While it is hard to understand, unfortunately it is true. We find ourselves so caught up in things—television, tasks, technology—that we neglect genuine human relationships.

The media is increasingly commenting on the nation's spiritual crisis and its interest in and hunger for spiritual solutions. More and more leaders have become convinced that the solutions to our baffling problems do not lie in more programs, but in old-fashioned values and spiritual awakening. A number of recent popular books reveal the need for values and spirituality in modern life. Among such works are *The Culture of Disbelief*, by Yale University professor Stephen Carter, and *The Spirit of Community*, by Amitai Etzioni of George Washington University.

The amazing popularity of William J. Bennett's best-seller *The Book of Virtues* is an unmistakable indication that we hunger for spiritual values and old-fashioned virtues. Bennett, a former secretary of education, in a recent article in *Newsweek* addressed the burning issue of epidemic crime and rampant violence threatening our nation. "Over the last three decades violent crime has increased by more than 500 percent," he writes. "America leads the industrialized world in rates of murder, rape, and violent crime." Moreover, the causes for such moral tragedy lie in the fact that "during the last quarter century, many parents, schools, churches, and communities sidestepped their obligations and passed off their parental, familial, and communal responsibility to government. But government, no matter how sincere, cannot do this job."[4]

How much can any leader or government, no matter how well-intentioned they may be, do to surmount the monumental crises of our society? And crime, for instance, is only one of the many other uncontrollable problems confronting us. Statistic after statistic shows that it is becoming the problem we fear the most. Senseless violence and random shootings surround us. People increasingly dread being assaulted as they peacefully mind their own business. No one feels immune from this plague, for it no longer restricts itself to urban areas, but is reaching suburban and rural regions as well.

It is finally dawning on us that government can only do so much to alleviate such fears. In our desperation, we are increasingly groping for spiritual and supernatural answers. In its cover story on belief in angels, *Time* magazine reported that "in the face of war, hunger, AIDS, drugs, sorrow and fear, only a force more potent than any earthly power could provide peace." Then it cited Peter Kreeft, a philosophy professor at Boston College, who asserted that in such desperate times "people seek supernatural solutions to their problems." He added that "we want to reassure ourselves of our spiritualism."[5]

Truly our fundamental problems are not economical, societal, or environmental, but are of spiritual origin at the core. Western culture has accustomed us to think that our greatest problems are external, and thus we often attempt externally superficial solutions. We do this because "we are not skilled in the inner life, where the real root of our problem lies."[6] Although we may have acquired more insight into our inner problems, we still have not developed the necessary skills to effectively deal with them.

Once a young college student sought my advice about a problem she was experiencing with her family. She had a luxurious home and her family took care of all her financial and material needs. The girl had everything anyone could desire in life and more. What could possibly be bothering her?

Earlier that summer, as she prepared to get used to the idea of living away from home for the first time, she suddenly realized that from now on she would be on her own. That she was never to live with her parents as before. The thought overwhelmed her that she was about to leave without really knowing her father and mother. Life had been quite hectic for both parents as they tried hard to acquire all the things they thought would make their family life fulfilling.

Yet they were quite surprised and helpless when she expressed her need to spend some time with them in order to get to know them before leaving. Although she was grateful for all that they had done for her, at the same time she felt that they were almost like strangers to her. What she really needed was to get close to them, to get to know them as persons. Her father distractingly asked if she needed any other help for college. He suggested that she see a good counselor or join some helpful program when she arrived on campus.

This superficial parent-daughter relationship probably reflected the parents' own marriage and family relationships. Perhaps they had lacked an authentic and meaningful relationship all along, and what relationships they did have were "choked with cares, riches, and pleasures of life" (Luke 8:14), to use Christ's words. In such cases family relationships only mirror societal relationships as a whole.

Pastor Bill Hybels sketches the following scenario: "The husband gets all wrapped up in his job, hoping to shore up his sagging self-esteem by being impressive at work. The wife is wrapped up in the kids, and she may have a job as well. And so they pass each other in the driveway, the hallway, and the walk-in closet. They sleep in the same bed and occasionally sit at the same table, but there's not much intimacy between them. They are cohabiting, but they are not nurturing one another. They are not involved in a vital, refreshing, authentic relationship."[7]

More and more people are realizing that real satisfaction does not come from things, but from genuine experiences of transcendence and intimacy with a personal God and other people. In their spiritual thirst they try, in whatever available ways, to see beyond their self-centeredness and to seek the things that satisfy their soul hunger.

They cannot understand why, despite all the scientific, technological, and other advancements of the world around them, they still feel such inner emptiness. In spite of today's unparalleled advancements, they remain desperately fearful and helpless as their world unravels before their very eyes. Shirley Dobson expressed their situation well when she said that "people feel a desperation and are crying out to God as their only hope."[8]

God placed an emptiness in each human soul that can be satisfied only with His infilling. A vacuum, or "depressurized space," sucks in whatever surrounds it. The human soul is like that depressurized space, and unless it sucks in Christ, it "becomes a junk receptacle, filled with whatever is nearest," Calvin Miller explains. "There is some force in the universe that does not like empty boxes."[9] Vacuums get filled. What about the empty boxes of our inward beings? Are they filled with Christ or with the world?

Yes, the subject of spirituality is in vogue today. "Whether it's middle age or the coming millennium or a bad case of the blues, many Americans are on a quest for spiritual meaning," reports *Newsweek* in a recent cover story.[10] Usually people do not think of following Christ's way to spiritual life, but in their own way they are groping for anything that seems spiritual. Peterson explains that their great interest in spirituality often is a symptom of a spiritual sickness. "A person who has healthy digestion does not talk about it. Neither does a person who has a healthy soul," he argues. "The frequency with which the word *spirituality* occurs these days is more likely to be evidence of pathology than health."[11]

However, such spiritual sickness needs the correct cure—the reliable remedy of our Redeemer. Unfortunately counterfeit ways to spiritual fulfillment are exploiting today's great spiritual need. The so-called spirituality in Eastern religions, in the New Age movement, in popular psychology, and in other human-centered movements, is but a false and misleading substitute. We need to redirect the present interest in spirituality to Christ and firmly anchor it in His Word. His way to spiritual life is the only thing that can ultimately fill such a spiritual void.

Christ's way of spirituality calls for submission, self-denial, and sacrifice. Instead of popularity, it seeks purity of character. It challenges us to radical discipleship, not rationalized disobedience. Not some easy religion to stroke our egos, but it is Christ's voice calling us to sanctification. Commenting on the popularity of some churches flooded by baby boomers, *Newsweek* observed that they seek "support, not salvation, help rather than holiness." Thus for them a "group affirmation of self is at the top of the agenda, which is why some of the least demanding churches are now in greatest demand."[12]

Jesus said: "Whoever desires to come after Me, let him deny himself, and take up his cross, and follow Me" (Mark 8:34). Christ did not merely teach such spiritual disciplines, but more important, He lived them. He did not just preach spirituality—He practiced it. Jesus indeed walked what He talked. In other words, if we had lived during Christ's time and heard Him teach the multitude about love, we would have witnessed Him actually treat others with love. As a result He lived a totally integrated spiritual life in contrast to the fragmented lives of the other so-called spiritual leaders of His day.

Likewise, in our day we have those who profess spirituality but do not practice it. Sometimes one senses that such leaders have some sort of a split personality. Although they wax eloquent and seem sincere in what they say, when one actually interacts with them, they come across as different persons, almost detached from their public pronouncements. Thomas Kelly explains that such experience reflects "an inner lack of integration of our lives." That is because "we are trying to be several selves at once, without all our selves being organized by a single, mastering life within us."[13]

That mastering and unifying life is the life of Christ. His life centered in and was unified with His Father. It focused on honoring and pleasing God in every aspect of existence. His whole being—physically, mentally, and spiritually—comprised that genuinely integrated spiritual life. Such is the Model we need to proclaim and practice in our daily lives. "When once the gaze is fixed upon Him [Christ], the life finds its center."[14]

Christ's integrated and wholistic spiritual life has amazing drawing power. And the key to all that Christ did was His constant communion with His Father. This intimate spiritual relationship motivated everything about Him and His ministry. He would withdraw in solitude to be with His Father. As His Father's life made a profound impact on Him, so His own life transformed others.

It is interesting to note that Eastern Christianity does not have a speculative and abstruse type of spirituality, but rather focuses on living in everyday situations. It places the emphasis on how spirituality affects relationships, on mutual giving of oneself to God and to others. Eastern Orthodoxy has no such thing as theoretical spirituality, but only a spiritual experience fashioned in the crucible of life.[15]

However, we need to put in a note of caution here. There exists a subtle and an inherent danger in the flurry of our activities for Christ. Activities for the sake of themselves, and not for the sake of Christ. Tragically, they can shift our focus away from Christ. The archdeceiver can actually make our profession and service to Christ the chief rival to our love and devotion to Him.

Therefore, in our fervor to do the works of Christ we must, first of all, focus on Christ, and make sure that we have His spirit in all that we do in His service. We need to closely follow His way to true spirituality and allow such an experience to transform everything we do for Him. After all, we must possess what we profess and perform. Our duty to Christ must ever be linked to our devotion to Christ. For "when once the gaze is fixed upon Him, the life finds its center. . . . Duty becomes a delight and sacrifice a pleasure. To honor Christ, to become like Him, to work for Him, is the life's highest ambition and its greatest joy."[16]

This humble volume is dedicated to our Lord and Saviour Jesus Christ, the model for true spirituality. May we follow His way to spirituality and become one with Him, as He was one with the Father. And may we ever delight ourselves in Him, tasting and seeing that He is good. Thus abiding in Christ, we may walk in the same spiritual path He did. In emulating Christ's example in spirituality, we are becoming Christlike (see John 17:21, 23; Ps. 42:1; 37:4; 34:8; 1 John 2:6).

Christ Himself gives us this powerful promise: "A disciple is not above his teacher, but every one when he is fully taught will be like his teacher" (Luke 6:40, RSV). This is what true spirituality is about: to become like Jesus, our master teacher, through the infilling of His Spirit. And we are to make it our lifework to seek such spirituality.[17] Is this our first and foremost priority in our lives? Do we sense in our souls that it is our most compelling need right now?

Such spirituality in Christ and through the Holy Spirit is what, I believe, Ellen White alluded to as "true godliness," or "primitive godliness." She urges us to diligently seek it above all else. "A revival of true godliness among us is the *greatest* and *most* urgent of *all* our needs. To seek this should be our *first* work."[18]

May we be ever so submissive and teachable, giving Christ full rein in leading us in this spiritual journey. And thus He may completely possess us and truly make us like Him—for His honor and glory. "Christ is sitting for His portrait in every disciple. Every one God has predestined to be 'conformed to the image of His Son' (Rom. 8:29). In every one Christ's long-suffering love, His holiness, meekness, mercy, and truth are to be manifested to the world."[19] Let us explore Christ's way to spiritual growth together.

---

[1] Eugene H. Peterson, "Spirit Quest," *Christianity Today,* Nov. 8, 1983, p. 28.

[2] Laurence Shames, *The Hunger for More—Searching for Values in an Age of Greed* (New York: Random House, 1989), p. 136.

[3] *Ibid.*

[4] William J. Bennett, "Raising Cain on Values," *Newsweek,* Apr. 18, 1994, p. 23.

[5] Nancy Gibbs, "Angels Among Us," *Time,* Dec. 27, 1993, p. 58.

[6] Thomas R. Kelly, *A Testament of Devotion* (London: Hodder and Stoughton, 1957), p. 105.

[7] Bill Hybels, *Too Busy Not to Pray* (Downers Grove, Ill.: InterVarsity Press, 1988), p. 100.

[8] Cited in Timothy Jones, "Great Awakenings," *Christianity Today,* Nov. 8, 1993, p. 23.

[9] Calvin Miller, *The Table of Inwardness—Nurturing Our Inner Life in Christ* (Downers Grove, Ill.: InterVarsity Press, 1984), p. 26.

[10] Barbara Kantrowitz, "In Search of the Sacred," *Newsweek,* Nov. 28, 1994, p. 52.

[11] Peterson, p. 27.

[12] Kenneth L. Woodward, "A Time to Seek," *Newsweek,* Dec. 17, 1990, p. 56.

[13] Kelly, p. 105.

[14] Ellen G. White, *Education* (Mountain View, Calif.: Pacific Press Pub. Assn., 1952), p. 297.

[15] George A. Maloney, ed., *Pilgrimage of the Heart—A Treasury of Eastern Christian Spirituality* (San Francisco: Harper and Row Pub., 1983), p. 232.

[16] White, *Education,* p. 297.

[17] _____, *Selected Messages,* book 2 (Washington, D.C.: Review and Herald Pub. Assn., 1958), p. 356.

[18] *Ibid.,* book 1, p. 121. (Italics supplied.)

[19] _____, *The Desire of Ages* (Mountain View, Calif.: Pacific Press Pub. Assn., 1940), p. 827.

CHAPTER

ONE

BECOMING LIKE CHRIST

"I would be like Jesus" we sang as we concluded our church service. It seemed like many of us were only going through the motions of mouthing the poignant words as we anticipated going home. Then I noticed the way the teenager sitting next to me sang the hymn. Clearly he seemed caught up in its meaning and spirit as he interspersed the words with sincere petitions: "Jesus, I would be like You," and "Yes, help me to be like You." Worshiping with him was a spiritual blessing I will not easily forget.

Walking out of the sanctuary together with him, I told him that I was indeed blessed by his sincere spirit of worship. "You really want to be like Jesus, don't you?" I commented.

"My life had been crowded with many competing ambitions," he explained, "but ever since I committed my life to Christ, becoming like Him has been my greatest joy and highest ambition." His words rang with an unmistakable conviction.

Should not it be our heartfelt testimony too? And should not Christlikeness be the greatest driving ambition of our lives? That was the magnificent testimony of the apostle Paul when he said that he counted everything as "loss" and "rubbish" when he compared it all to the "surpassing greatness of knowing Christ" (Phil. 3:7, 8, NIV).

Prizing to know his beloved Master, Paul yearned to become more and more like Him. He was Spirit-driven to put self to death so that Christ might form within. Thus he could triumphantly declare, "I have been crucified with Christ; it is no longer I who live, but Christ who lives in me" (Gal. 2:20, RSV). Christ formed and living within

19

is all that really mattered to him. And should not it be all that matters to us as well?

At the conclusion of a captivating discussion about the atom in a chemistry class, I could not resist saying "Praise the Lord for His marvelous creation" as I passed my teacher on the way out.

"If you don't mind, leave religion out of it," he quietly admonished me.

But how could I ever leave God out of His own creation? I kept wondering as I rushed on to the other classes. He is in fact the chemist who not only knows all about the atom but invented it in the first place! Yes, Christ is the creative genius who made the vast universe from the minutest atom to the most splendid galaxies.

All around us we see people frantically searching for idols, role models, or heroes to imitate. An innate need relentlessly propels us to look up to someone bigger than ourselves, someone to trust and to emulate. But unfortunately, all too often, human beings overlook Christ as their supreme hero and model, the one to trust, emulate, and worship.

What greater Model can we have in this world! Not only is He the creative genius, but He is the God of the universe who embodies in Himself all love, mercy, wisdom, power, glory, trustworthiness, and righteousness. "For in Him dwells all the fullness of the Godhead bodily" (Col. 2:9). In Him reside all the answers to all our predicaments, and the fulfillment to the deepest desires of our hearts. "All that can satisfy the needs and longings of the human soul, for this world and for the world to come, is found in Christ. Our Redeemer is the pearl so precious that in comparison all things else may be accounted loss."[1]

Moreover, not only is He the great giver of all good gifts, but beyond that He gives Himself. He is the source of life itself, for He gave Himself for humanity in the garden and again at Golgotha. In the garden He made us in His image, fashioned us after His likeness, and breathed into our form His *breath* of life (see Gen. 1:26; 2:7). And at Golgotha He shed His *blood* of life to restore us into His likeness (see Eph. 1:7-10). This breath and this blood of Christ ever flow into our being, offering us life abundant and life eternal.

Therefore, the grand and ultimate object of salvation is to restore the image of Christ and His likeness in us. It is the heart and essence of the gospel. And that is what Paul had in mind when he wrote about God revealing the glory and the mystery of all the ages. What was that mystery? "Christ in you, the hope of glory" (Col. 1:27, RSV). It was Paul's passionate desire for the Galatians, with whom he continued to be "in travail" until "Christ be formed in you" (Gal. 4:19, RSV).

Christ formed within needs to be our passionate desire too, our all-absorbing priority. The indwelling Christ transforms our inner being and fashions it after His own likeness. We become dead to self, but alive to Him (Rom. 6:11). He lives out His life in and through us, and we will continue until in Him we "become mature, attaining to the whole measure of the fullness of Christ" (Eph. 4:13, NIV).

As Christ forms within, it reveals that the kingdom of grace is doing its transforming work in our hearts. This reality also gives us the hope and assurance of inheriting the kingdom of glory, for "when He is revealed, we shall be like Him, for we shall see Him as He is" (1 John 3:2). Becoming Christlike is the golden thread that inextricably weaves together the realms of grace and glory in our lives. By *faith* we are becoming like Him in this world, so that by *sight* we may be like Him when we shall see Him face-to-face in the world to come.

The ancient Chinese philosopher Confucius, who lived around the fifth century before Christ, coined the phrase "the rectification of names" in his *Analects*. What he meant by his interesting phrase was the ideal that harmony would pervade society if people lived up to the meanings of their names and titles. In other words, a father is a father when he truly acts like a father, and so on. The Chinese scholar Hu Shih explains further what Confucius meant. "The rectification of names consists in making real relationships and duties and institutions conform as far as possible to their *ideal* meanings."[2]

The Scriptures constantly call for us to be authentic in our religious experience. Indeed, the most offensive thing we can do to God in our relationship to Him is religious pretense. Although we outwardly profess and pretend that we are Christians, at the core we are far away from Him. He wishes that we were either cold or hot instead of passively remaining lukewarm. Being lukewarm is so repugnant to Christ that He declares, "I will spew you out of My mouth" (Rev. 3:16).

As mentioned earlier, to be a genuine Christian is to be Christlike. That is, God desires to reveal through us what Christ is like. Are we in our innermost beings Christlike or selflike? Do others see more of our selves and less of Christ? "When we take the name of Christ we pledge ourselves to represent Him. In order for us to be true to our pledge, Christ must be formed within, the hope of glory.

The daily life must become more and more like the Christ life. . . . Christ will have *nothing* to do with pretense. He will welcome to the heavenly courts only those whose Christianity is *genuine*. The lives of professed Christians who do not live the life of Christ are a *mockery* to religion."[3]

We must ever remember we must see Christ in this world before we can see Him in the world to come. It just makes no sense to presume that we will behold Christ in heaven if we do not behold Him here. Christ will see *there* whom He knows *here*. It is as simple as that. Christ turned religious people away from entering His kingdom simply because He did not know them (Matt. 7:23). "We cannot keep Christ apart from our lives here, and yet be fitted for His companionship in heaven."[4]

In the Beatitudes, Jesus declared: "Blessed are the pure in heart, for they shall see God" (Matt. 5:8). Only our communion with Jesus can produce purity. But in such purity we have the joy of seeing Him by faith, and ultimately face-to-face. We must strive for that holiness "without which no one will see the Lord" (Heb. 12:14, RSV). Holiness is indeed Christlikeness, and only in that Christlikeness shall we ever see Christ.

To live with Christ on earth enables us to live with Him in heaven. And to know companionship with Him here will grant us companionship with Him there. We need to be familiar with Him and faithful to Him in everyday life in order to see Him face-to-face for all eternity. "To His faithful followers Christ has been a daily companion and familiar friend. They have lived in close contact, in constant communion with God. . . . In them the light of the knowledge of the glory of God in the face of Jesus Christ has been reflected. Now they rejoice in the undimmed rays of the brightness and glory of the King in His majesty. *They are prepared for the communion of heaven; for they have heaven in their hearts*."[5]

Throughout history moral philosophers, among others, have attempted to evolve the ideal human being. They have sought it through asceticism, education, culture, enlightenment, science, and technology, just to mention a few approaches. However, they have always failed because they pinned their hopes on human beings as the models to provide the needed inspiration and power for such a noble, yet impossible, accomplishment.

Confucius sought what he called the "superior man," or the

"higher type of man," through his humanistic and ethical teachings, a search often called his "greatest claim to distinction as a moral philosopher."[6] But history has repeatedly proved that it is an utter impossibility for imperfect human beings to reach perfection from within themselves. We desperately need a perfect example beyond ourselves to follow. But we can find it only in the perfect Creator, Redeemer, and Model Jesus Christ, and not in imperfect creatures. But happily, through Jesus Christ we may become superior people, a reflection of His life and character. For "to be a Christian is to be Christlike. Jesus is a perfect pattern, and we must imitate His example. A Christian is the *highest type of man,* a representative of Christ."[7]

I want to make clear that while our imitation of Christ is related to, it is not the same as our salvation by Christ. Christ came to redeem our world. If He had not died on the cross as our substitute and surety, and if He had not risen for our sanctification, then for us to attempt to imitate Him would be an exercise in futility. Thus we do not have salvation by imitation, but imitation *because of* salvation. *Christ in us* and *we in Christ.* The one has its anchor in and emanates from the other.

A truly saved person loves Christ and longs to abide with Him and be like Him. Devotion to emulate the pattern of Christ results from devotion to the person of Christ. Oswald Chambers emphasizes that "the bedrock of Christianity is personal, passionate devotion to the Lord Jesus."[8] And from such ardent devotion to Christ issues all virtues, for in being possessed by Christ we possess all else.

It is an awesome privilege that through the grace and power of God we may become like our Creator and Redeemer! Christ alone gives us the honor that we may become not just a "higher type of man" but indeed the "highest type of man," who mirrors in his life the image of his Maker!

We were in Christ when He took upon Himself our sin and death, exchanging them for His righteousness and life. "For He made Him who knew no sin to be sin for us, that we might become the righteousness of God in Him" (2 Cor. 5: 21). "He [Christ] was condemned for our sins, in which He had no share, that we might be justified by His righteousness, in which we had no share. He suffered the death which was ours, that we might receive the life which was His."[9] Such divine-human exchange provides us with our only hope of sanctification. And such oneness with Him empowers us in our pursuit of becoming like Him.

Oneness with Christ is the secret of becoming like Him. Satan knows all too well the divine plan to defeat him in this spiritual battle, and he fights it most ruthlessly. Our union with Christ is what he dreads most, for he knows that such a dynamic union will break his power. The devil had as his foremost objective after his defeat in heaven to sever forever the divine-human relationship, and to deceive people into believing that they can be their own saviors apart from Christ.

But through Calvary's cross Satan's abominable scheme backfired on him, and made it possible for humanity to be even more intimately connected with Christ than ever before. "It was Satan's purpose to bring about an eternal separation between God and man; but in Christ we become *more closely* united to God than if we had never fallen. In taking our nature, the Saviour has bound Himself to humanity by a tie that is *never* to be broken." [10]

It overwhelms us to contemplate the thought that Jesus, in His boundless desire to restore us into His likeness, irrevocably altered His own very nature for eternity. For our sake He will forever retain His humanity. And in heaven, the redeemed will gaze into His face and be struck with the realization that, for the sake of their restoration, their divine Creator will forever remain intimately identified with them. An infinite commitment impelled Him to become like us in our humanity so that we may become like Him in His divinity! Boundless love propelled our Creator and Redeemer to partake of our human nature so that we may partake of His divine nature! (See 2 Peter 1:3, 4.)

The awesomeness of it all is that, in His supreme act of condescension and incarnation, Christ did not in any way abase His own divinity or alter His eternal union with the Godhead. Roy Allan Anderson pondered the inscrutable mystery that even though the second Person of the triune God will forever retain His human nature, it will neither affect the eternal nature of the Father and the Spirit nor Their eternal relationship with the Son. [11]

Moreover, it awes us as we contemplate the thought that the acquired humanity of Christ, representing us, will forever remain a part of the triune God! The Son of God, in ever maintaining such perfect and undiminished union with the Godhead, took in His person His humanity to the very heart of that Godhead. Therefore, in Christ we will always be in the heart of the Godhead, because Christ will forever be there. "Not that we change places with God," Anderson explains, "but that God for our sakes became man. No other revelation is so unique and comprehensive as this, that in Christ Jesus God exists eternally *as man,* being both Son of God and Son of man." [12]

Ever since Christ's decisive victory at Calvary's cross, Satan has done everything possible to gain victory over us. He failed miserably in his attempt to separate Christ from His Father, and now he desperately tries to keep us from our union with Christ. Satan uses any means at his disposal to accomplish his purpose.

Then, how are we to become like Christ? How are we to reflect His image in our daily lives? The answer must be: to *become like* Christ is to *be with* Christ. And there in His presence we learn the indispensable lesson of maintaining that essential tension between distrust of self and trust in Him and what He desires to do in us. Unfortunately, sometimes we can become so preoccupied with looking at ourselves and others that we have no desire to look to Christ and let the Spirit transform us into His image.

The best of people—even our most dependable friends—can only do so much for us. They have their own struggles and problems too. It is thus essential to learn that our real help comes from Christ. We are to look to Him who cares and is alone able to accomplish His will in our lives. Before seeking human help, why not avail ourselves of divine aid? "We are to copy no human being. There is no human being wise enough to be our criterion. We are to look to the man Christ Jesus, who is complete in the perfection of righteousness and holiness." [13]

That does not mean that in trusting Jesus we distrust others. It simply reminds us that we do not place our ultimate trust in them, or in emulating their example. We need to be realistic in recognizing the frailty of the human condition, and entrust our lives to the all-sufficiency of Christ.

Even in an ideal family environment, we still need to individually look to Christ and draw our resources from Him, the ultimate source. Francis Schaeffer aptly puts it this way: "We are finite, and therefore do not expect to find final sufficiency in each other, in any human relationship, including marriage. The final sufficiency is only to be found in a relationship to God." [14] Then he sounds this sober warning: "If man tries to find everything in a man-woman relationship or friend-to-friend relationship, he destroys that which he wants and destroys the one he loves." [15]

Christ is the perfectly suited model for our human predicament, for He is the bridge between divinity and humanity. "Jesus Christ laid hold on humanity, that with His human arm He might encircle the race, while with His divine arm He grasped the throne of the Infinite." [16] He is fully divine and fully human, experiencing both the glories of heaven and the miseries of earth. "As our Example, we have One who is all and in all, the chiefest among ten thousand, One whose excellency is beyond comparison. *He graciously adapted His life for universal imitation.*" [17] Not only does He sympathize with our weaknesses, but He also saves us from our sins and empowers us to win the spiritual race. In Christ we may experience victory in reflecting His image, because we are looking unto Him, "the author and finisher of our faith" (Heb. 12:2).

A lost silver coin, marred and covered with grime, is difficult to recognize as valuable because the dirt obscures its image and superscription. Similarly, when a person created in God's image stays away from Him and imitates the world, then its grime eventually covers up His image and likeness. To many onlookers it seems that sin has completely effaced God's image, but Christ looks at the person's heart and potential.

The good news is that Christ searches untiredly for the lost. And although it is not easy to discern His image in a lost soul, His original traces are still there nevertheless. "God desires to recover that soul and to *retrace upon it His own image* in righteousness and holiness." [18] No one is irredeemable, and God's presence always brings the promise of restoration. Not only is He able to accomplish it, but He derives profound joy from doing so. For He "delights to take apparently hopeless material, those through whom Satan has worked, and make them the subjects of His grace." [19]

Christ's greatest desire is to clean away the grime in our hearts, and to retrace in our souls His image and likeness. Heaven has committed all its resources to accomplish this. Has Christ's great love and His enduring commitment to our restoration softened our hard hearts and made them pliable and moldable in His creative hands? "As wax takes the impression of the seal, so the soul is to take the impression of the Spirit of God and retain the image of Christ." [20]

May the wax, which symbolizes our lives, soften from the warmth of Christ's love. May it be pliable and workable in the creative and redemptive hands of the Master so that He may retrace on it His image and likeness.

[1] Ellen G. White, *Christ's Object Lessons* (Washington, D.C.: Review and Herald Pub. Assn., 1941), p. 115.

[2] Hu Shih, *The Development of the Logical Method in Ancient China* (Shanghai: The New China Book Company, 1917), p. 26.

[3] White, *Our Father Cares* (Hagerstown, Md.: Review and Herald Pub. Assn., 1991), p. 165.

[4] ———, *Christ's Object Lessons,* p. 414.

[5] ———, *Ibid.,* p. 421. (Italics supplied.)

[6] David S. Noss, *Man's Religion* (New York: Macmillan Pub. Co., 1984), p. 277.

[7] Ellen G. White, *Evangelism* (Washington, D.C.: Review and Herald Pub. Assn., 1946), p. 641.

[8] Oswald Chambers, *My Utmost for His Highest* (Uhrichsville, Ohio: Barbour and Co., 1963), p. 266.

[9] White, *The Desire of Ages,* p. 25.

[10] *Ibid.* (Italics supplied.)

[11] Roy Allan Anderson, *The God-Man, His Nature and Work* (Washington, D.C.: Review and Herald Pub. Assn., 1970), p. 56.

[12] *Ibid.,* p. 57. (Italics supplied.)

[13] *The Seventh-day Adventist Bible Commentary,* Ellen G. White Comments (Washington, D.C.: Review and Herald Pub. Assn., 1980), vol. 7, p. 970.

[14] Francis Schaeffer, *True Spirituality* (London: Hodder and Stoughton, 1972), p. 195.

[15] *Ibid.,* p. 196.

[16] Ellen G. White, *Messages to Young People* (Nashville: Southern Pub. Assn., 1966), p. 137.

[17] ———, *Reflecting Christ* (Hagerstown, Md.: Review and Herald Pub. Assn., 1985), p. 35. (Italics supplied.)

[18] ———, *Christ's Object Lessons,* p. 194. (Italics supplied.)

[19] ———, *Our Father Cares,* p. 230.

[20] ———, *Selected Messages,* book 1, p. 337.

Chapter Two

LOOKING UNTO CHRIST

The sunflower has always fascinated me. One may say that it lives up to its name. A certain type of this fascinating flower will open itself up and face toward the bright and life-giving rays of the sun. And it does this not just occasionally but throughout the whole day. It is also interesting to note that the sunflower, with its color, shape, and brilliance, even bears a likeness to the sun.

We can find an object lesson in the sunflower as we contemplate the vital subject of looking unto Christ the Sun of righteousness. Does the sunflower represent your Christian life and mine? Are we Sun-of-righteousness Christians or self-righteousness Christians? Son-centered or self-centered? Do we live up to our name Christians (Christlike), as the sunflower (sunlike) does to its name? Ellen White aptly utilizes this rich object lesson from nature to encourage us to turn away from self and look to Christ. "As the sunflower is constantly turning its open blossom to the sun, so let your heart, your thoughts, ever turn to Jesus, the Sun of righteousness." [1]

God has given us so many valuable object lessons in nature. Upon its pages we may trace His thoughts and learn of His salvation. The sunflower reveals to us many helpful insights about how to look up and live. In this connection, let us consider the following points of symbolic and spiritual significance regarding our relationship with the Son of God:

1. The sunflower *opens up* its blossom to the bright sun, and it *closes* it against the darkness of the night. Do we open up our lives to the light of Christ and shield them to the darkness of evil? We need

to be open-minded to the things of Christ and closed-minded to the dark things of the world. In an age of open-mindedness to everything, it is becoming increasingly vital to be closed-minded to some things. For by beholding we do indeed become changed to whatever we behold. I am increasingly convinced that open-mindedness to everything is no virtue. Christ comes to us knocking at our hearts. Why not open them wide to Him and welcome Him with open arms?

2. The sunflower *turns away* from its immediate surroundings in order to *face* the sun. The sun's life-giving rays exert a greater pull on the sunflower than anything else. Are we drawn by the matchless charms of Christ to the extent that we turn away from sin and gaze upon the Son? Is His pulling power upon our lives mightier than any other attraction? If our answer is no, then we have not really viewed the enticing yet hopeless mediocrity of the world in the light of His surpassing excellence.

For if we have *turned our eyes* upon Jesus and *looked fully* in His wonderful face, then the most dazzling things of this world will really fade into insignificance. When we become enraptured by the beauty of Christ we are drawn to Him, not because of mere duty, but because of our deep devotion. Gazing upon His brightness blinds us to the world's transitory glitter.[2]

But circumstances at times cast dark shadows that shroud our paths and seem to shield any light from our lives.

Helen Keller was one who truly saw light through darkness. "There are many shadows, but remember, where there is a shadow there must be light," she admonished. "Keep your face to the sunshine and you cannot see the shadow." Whenever we find a shadow there must be a light, for the night is but a shadow of the light. Then let that very shadow point us to the light, and as we focus on that bright light we will become blinded to the dark shadows.

3. The sunflower faithfully *follows* the sun's movement, not intermittently, but *continuously* throughout the day. Do we know and trust Christ enough to be with Him always? Do we follow our Master's movements in occasional snatches, or do we stay the whole course with Him? If we love Him, we would always want to be with Him, follow Him "wherever He goes," and like Joshua, wholly follow the Lord (see Rev. 14:4; Joshua 14:9, RSV).

4. By looking at the sunflower as it faithfully tracks the sun's movement, we have our eyes *always oriented* in the sun's direction.

When people observe us and interact with us, do we point them in the direction of Christ? Isn't this what Christian witnessing is all about? Our lives directing other lives to where the light of Christ is, and in the process becoming more and more like Christ.

5. Finally, when we look at the sunflower we notice that it actually *resembles the sun.* Its yellow color, its disk shape, and its crown of many bright petals remind us of the bright rays of the sun. By beholding we become changed. When we open up our lives to Christ and close them to evil, when we turn away from the world and gaze on Him, when we are drawn to follow Him wherever He leads, then our lives will point others in His direction as we continue to grow into His likeness.

"If you have been permitted to stand in the presence of the Sun of righteousness," Ellen White writes, "it is not that you may absorb and conceal the bright beams of Christ's righteousness, but that you may become a light to others."[3] Here are three sound suggestions from her pen for how by looking unto Christ we may become transformed into His image: (a) dwelling upon His love; (b) contemplating His character; (c) claiming His righteousness as ours by faith.[4]

May our relationship to Christ emulate the sunflower in its focus on the sun. "As the flower turns to the sun, that the bright beams may aid in perfecting its beauty and symmetry, so should we turn to the Sun of righteousness, that heaven's light may shine upon us, that our character may be developed in the likeness of Christ."[5]

Looking unto Christ involves an intentional and continuous activity of gazing with our hearts and minds at Him. As we look unto Christ, the winner of the spiritual race God set before Him, we become winners in our own spiritual race. It is axiomatic that we become changed into what we live our lives focusing on.

So many lives are blindly adrift and aimlessly tossed back and forth. They have no anchor or focus. Because humanity has rejected Christ as its focal point, it has fallen into a sorry state. Yet "when once the gaze is fixed upon Him [Christ], life finds its center."[6]

Contrary to what some may try to argue, watching immorality and violence on television day after day does lead us to become more immoral and violent. There is nothing magical about this, and it does not require exhaustive research to prove it. Instead it but illustrates the basic principle that we become what we behold, and we are what we think. Solomon understood this more than some media experts of today: "For as he thinks in his heart, so is he" (Prov. 23:7).

Yes, we are to look away from sin, self, and the subtleties of Satan. We are to fix our hearts and minds on Christ, "that by beholding we may be changed into His likeness." For as "we look to Him and think of Him, He will be formed within, the hope of glory." [7] The power of the gospel of Christ, can transform His followers into His likeness. Becoming Christlike through Christ is the personal experience everyone needs to have in preparing for heaven—"knowing for himself that Christ is formed within, the hope of glory." [8]

Satan devises whatever is necessary to obscure Jesus from our view because he knows that our only hope to behold Christ in glory is to behold Him here in the present world. He does not care about what forms within us as long as it is not Christ. Thus he cunningly uses the very blessings and spiritual activities intended to draw us closer to Christ to drive us actually further away from Him.

Christ, in showering us with His gifts and blessings, desires to keep fresh in our minds His great love for us, and to draw us closer to Himself. However, we can become so preoccupied with the gifts that we lose sight of the Giver. Let us consider the spiritual blessing of our church worship service, for instance. Sometime ago I had a striking dream in which I saw Jesus entering a church. His eyes searched the place dedicated to His worship, only to witness His people so caught up in their religious activities that they were oblivious to Him. Soon He left with sadness and disappointment written on His face. Too often we have room for all the worship programs but none for Jesus, the very object of worship.

That is why we need to be constantly and acutely aware of the fact that the best of God's people are not immune to the danger of religious activities distracting us from Christ, the heart of religion. This happened even to the well-meaning and devoted parents of Jesus. Mary and Joseph, caught up in their business of celebrating the Passover with their friends, left Jerusalem without Jesus, the Passover Lamb.

Clearly, the all-wise and all-knowing God entrusted His only Son to the most caring, conscientious, and committed set of parents from among all the Hebrews. Yet even they, because they had concentrated their attention on festivities pointing to Jesus, lost sight of Jesus Himself. The incident has an indispensable lesson for us. Let us always be vigilant in focusing on Christ. The thing that Satan works the hardest at is to distract us away from Christ by any means possible. The devoted parents of Jesus, who were the closest persons to Him, and whose primary concern was His welfare, lost sight of Him for an entire day. In fact, one day of carelessness cost them three anxious days in searching for Him.

As we reflect on Ellen White's counsel on the episode, let us ask ourselves if what she says applies to our spiritual lives right now? "Many attend religious services, and are refreshed and comforted by the word of God; but through neglect of meditation, watchfulness, and prayer, they lose the blessing, and find themselves more destitute than before they received it." For by "separating themselves from Jesus, they have shut away the light of His presence." [9]

The very blessings God intended to attract us to Him and lead us to be saved (Isa. 45:22) can at the same time needlessly cause us to look away and be lost. It is interesting to note that our trials are often our greatest blessings in disguise. Healthy Christians may not feel the need to look up to God, but when an illness leaves them flat on their backs, then they do. Ideally, this is not the way God intended it to work, but that is what often happens. "The great difficulty spiritually is to concentrate on God, and it is His blessings that make it difficult," Oswald Chambers explains. "Troubles nearly always make us look to God; His blessings are apt to make us look elsewhere." [10]

Even Bible study and Christian service can get out of hand. The archdeceiver likes it when we study Scripture in a mechanical way without spiritual discernment. He does not mind if we analyze and criticize it, and know all the facts and arguments about it. But what he fears most is that we will approach it with spiritual insight, discerning Christ as its center, the One it testifies of. He knows that when we taste the Bread of Life we will see that the Lord is good. Thus partaking of His life, we become partakers of His nature, reflecting His likeness here and in glory. "He who has the Son has life; he who has not the Son of God has not life" (1 John 5:12, RSV).

A. W. Tozer, in his classic work *The Pursuit of God,* captures this very point when he states that "the modern scientist has lost God amid the wonders of His world; we Christians are in real danger of losing God amid the wonders of His Word." [11] How more subtle can Satan be? If we take our eyes off Christ, the very words we study in the Bible can give us false security and serve as a substitute for knowing the living Word. The Jewish leaders lost the living Word in the written Word, and the same thing can happen to us today.

When we let most of our energy be absorbed in analysis and critique of the Word of God, then we are robbing it of its transcendent ability to nourish, energize, and transform us. Satan does not care if we handle the Word of Life and know much about it as long as we remain famished from not feeding on it. Some of the so-called biblical scholars dare to judge the Word of God, yet do not allow His Word to judge them and transform them.

Ellen White unmasks the disguises of Satan in his deluding power to rob our Bible study of spiritual discernment and Christ-centeredness. Let us prayerfully contemplate the striking truth of what she cautions us about: "Many a man who delights to quibble, to criticize, seeking for something to question in the Word of God, thinks that he is thereby giving evidence of independence of thought, and mental acuteness. He supposes that he is sitting in judgment on the Bible, when in truth he is judging himself. He makes it manifest that he is incapable of appreciating truths that originate in heaven, and that compass eternity. In the presence of the great mountain of God's righteousness, his spirit is not awed. He busies himself with hunting for sticks and straws, and in this betrays a narrow and earthly nature, a heart that is fast losing its capacity to appreciate God." [12]

The other area Satan cleverly uses to deceive us is our service for Christ. "Beware of anything that competes with loyalty to Jesus Christ," Oswald Chambers cautions. "The greatest competitor of devotion to Jesus is service for Him." [13] Although it sounds paradoxical, unfortunately it is true. While devotion to Christ leads to becoming like Christ, service for Christ may not necessarily always do so.

We may be exhausting ourselves to become successful in working for Christ simply because of the missing inward relationship we need to have with Him. Successful service for Christ is fine when it is Christ-centered, but it becomes spiritually dangerous when self-centered. The crucial question we must ask ourselves is Do we find ourselves more devoted to Christ's service than to Christ Himself?

During Christ's time, for example, many Jewish leaders not only lost sight of the living Word in the pages of the written Word, but also lost sight of the Lord of service in the service of the Lord. And all along they boasted that they were the closest people to God. The bottom line of their religion was their devotion to their religious performance and not their devotion to God.

We may be critical of the Jewish leaders for losing sight of their spiritual priorities. However, no disciple of Christ is immune to Satan's subtle deception. The parents of Christ were not, as we have already discovered. Neither were His disciples. Ellen White defines the problem, states five potential dangers, and then offers the appropriate remedy. The problem: Success in doing the work of the Lord may lead us to forget the Lord of the work. She does not condemn such success, but she alerts us to what it may lead to.

The potential dangers are (a) the "trusting to human plans and methods," (b) the "tendency to pray less," (c) the tendency to "have less faith," (d) "Losing sight of our dependence on God," and, (e) the "seeking to make a savior of our activity." The essential remedy to guard against the above dangers is that "we need to look constantly to Jesus, realizing that it is His power which does the work." [14]

Notice the progressive steps of the danger. It starts with trusting in our human plans and culminates in making a savior out of our successful activity for God. Whatever takes the place of God—even successful work for Him—then becomes our god. By the way, faith can also become a god. Spirituality can also become a savior to us when we are obsessed with it and pursue it instead of pursuing Christ. Real spirituality is found only in knowing Christ.[15]

No matter how noble, lofty, virtuous, or spiritual our activity is, if it supplants Christ it is in essence akin to idolatry or heathenism. For it is nothing less than self-worship. The savior of our success replaces the Saviour of our souls.

The insightful Chinese Christian writer Watchman Nee points out that God desires to take away from us not only the worldly things but even the spiritual things that threaten to replace Christ. "Before we were saved," he explains, "worldly objects and affairs usurped the place of Christ; but after being saved, *spiritual* objects and affairs now tend to occupy Christ's place." [16] When Christ Himself possesses and occupies our beings, we become truly spiritual in Him, for He becomes all and in all to us.

This spiritual problem can plague even the most committed Christian workers. Mother Teresa of Calcutta, one of the most devoted and self-sacrificing Christian servants in the world, expressed this personal concern: "Pray for me that I not loosen my grip on the hands of Jesus even under the guise of ministry to the poor." Known as the saint of the gutters, she has untiringly devoted herself to serving the poorest of the poor since at least 1950. Her total existence consists of loving acts and sacrificial service to the dying poor, lepers, orphans, outcasts, and the sick. And she does all of it for the love and sake of Christ. If she prays to God not to let her ministry weaken her firm hold on Christ, how much more we need to.

Dietrich Bonhoeffer knew what it meant to look unto Christ in all his service for Him. His mission sprang forth from his undying devotion to his Master. How he braved leaving the security of the United States to risk going back to Nazi Germany has been the source of inspiration to many. His subsequent martyrdom by the Nazis forcefully demonstrated how his passionate love and staunch loyalty to Christ eclipsed everything else. Christ was all that mattered to him. Notice how he related devotion to service: "When we are called to follow Christ, we are summoned to an *exclusive attachment* to His person. . . . Discipleship means *adherence* to Christ." [17]

---

[1] Ellen G. White, *Sons and Daughters of God* (Washington, D.C.: Review and Herald Pub. Assn., 1955), p. 151.

[2] Miller, *The Table of Inwardness,* pp. 49, 50.

[3] White, *Reflecting Christ,* p. 303.

[4] ———, *Lift Him Up* (Review and Herald Pub. Assn., 1988), p. 251.

[5] ———, *Steps to Christ* (Boise, Idaho: Pacific Press Pub. Assn., 1981), p. 68.

[6] ———, *Education,* p. 297.

[7] ———, *The SDA Bible Commentary,* Ellen G. White Comments, vol. 7, p. 970.

[8] White, *Reflecting Christ,* p. 35.

[9] ———, *The Desire of Ages,* p. 83.

[10] Chambers, *My Utmost for His Highest,* p. 22.

[11] A. W. Tozer, *The Pursuit of God* (Harrisburg, Pa.: Horizon House Publishers, 1976), p. 13.

[12] White, *The Desire of Ages,* p. 468.

[13] Chambers, p. 18.

[14] White, *The Desire of Ages,* p. 362.

[15] Miller, p. 21.

[16] Watchman Nee, *Christ the Sum of All Spiritual Things* (New York: Christian Fellowship Publishers, 1973), p. 68.

[17] Dietrich Bonhoeffer, *The Cost of Discipleship* (New York: Macmillan Publishing, 1976), p. 63. (Italics supplied.)

Chapter Three

LIKE FATHER, LIKE SON

A world religious convention gathered in the Far East some years ago. The organizers of that international event made an interesting request of each delegation. They asked each participant to bring a picture depicting the essence of his or her particular religion. It was telling to see the picture that the Christian delegation had brought along to illustrate the heart of Christianity. It was a scene of Jesus bending low to wash the feet of Judas.

Imagine yourself for a moment settling in your chair, waiting to be served during the ordinance of foot washing at your local church. You find yourself intrigued by the person coming to wash your feet. Something about his kindly face and his noble bearing rivets your attention on him as he bends down to wash your feet. He is not looking at you now, for his hands along with his head stoop low to your feet.

As he gently begins to wash your soiled feet your curiosity gets the best of you, and you discreetly ask your neighbor whom the man might be. To your utter astonishment you are informed that this person is no other than Jesus Christ! Lest you think that my imagination has run rampant, think a moment. Had you and I lived during Christ's time, He would have surely washed our feet. If He had washed the feet of His betrayer, Judas, would He not have washed ours? Of course He would have. And He is just as willing today to reach where we are and to cleanse us completely from all sin.

I invited you to imagine with me the above scene because of an experience I had as a college student. One Friday evening as I prepared for the ordinance of humility, I vividly remember praying for

Jesus to reveal Himself to me. Glancing at my friend washing my feet, I was struck with the compelling thought that if I had lived during Christ's time, I would have seen Him personally bending low to wash my feet. It is a life-transforming thought when we realize that the eternal King of the universe would abandon His glorious throne and stoop down to wash our feet!

To press this overwhelming thought further, we may also say that the Father Himself would have washed our feet, for He "was in Christ reconciling the world to Himself" (2 Cor. 5:19). In a sense, the Father in Christ shared what Christ experienced in divine acts of condescension and reconciliation. "In the person of His only-begotten Son, the God of heaven has condescended to stoop to our human nature." [1]

In Middle Eastern culture, where Jesus lived, the head of a person represents the most honorable part of the body, while the feet symbolize dishonor and abasement. Therefore, when Jesus bent His head over His betrayer and reached down to wash his feet, He showed His willingness to give His best to reach Judas at his worst. The "high and lifted up," the honored and holy Son of God, is willing to reach way down to our abyss of debasement!

"And the Word became flesh and dwelt among us" (John 1:14). This living Word, who from eternity was with God and is God—who made all things and is the source of all life, light, love, glory, grace, truth, and purity—emptied Himself and became one with sinful humanity. Can we begin to fathom this? Was not the debasement of the human race revolting enough to keep Him away? "The Sinless One must feel the shame of sin. The peace lover must dwell with strife, the truth must abide with falsehood, purity with vileness. Every sin, every discord, every defiling lust that transgression had brought, was *torture to His spirit*." [2]

The evil all around Him tortured Christ's spirit, yet He was not in any way influenced by it, nor did He seclude Himself from it. If He had wanted to withdraw from it, He would have remained in heaven. But in the power of His Father He bravely faced it, and the powerful impact He made could transform the most hardened sinner. Jesus' holiness was active and involved, and was "rooted in His union with God and His commitment to please God, and was expressed not only in rejecting evil but in actively doing good." [3]

Here we catch a glimpse of the condescension that was always there in Christ's eternal being. It also reflects what the Father is like, for again He was "in Christ reconciling the world to Himself" (2 Cor. 5:19). Don Richardson, a missionary among the Sawi tribes of New Guinea, valiantly attempted to explain to them the meaning of the gospel, but to no avail. Finally he struck on an indigenous idea from their own culture, their notion of a "peace child."

Richardson explains: "Among the Sawi, every demonstration of friendship was suspect except one. If a man would actually give his own son to his enemies, that man could be trusted! That, and that alone, was proof of goodwill no shadow of cynicism could discredit."[4] The missionary presented the Sawi people with Christ as God's peace child, who demonstrated that God can be trusted, and that reconciliation is possible between Him and the human race.

Yes, Jesus Christ is the peace child of God, who volunteered from time eternal to reconcile fallen humanity. "For God so loved the world that he gave his only Son" (John 3:16, RSV). "For if while we were enemies we were reconciled to God by the death of his Son, much more, now that we are reconciled, shall we be saved by his life" (Rom. 5:10, RSV). Christ, in condescending to redeem humanity with His life, gave the clearest picture of His Father. In beholding the Son we see the Father.

Christ manifested His spirit of divine condescension even before the incarnation when He shielded His divinity in His desire to communicate with humanity. The bush, the rock, and the pillar of cloud and the pillar of fire were some of the modest earthly forms He used in veiling His glory. And in His voluntary act of condescension, culminating with His incarnation, Christ clearly demonstrated before the universe that "the law of self-renouncing love is the law of life for earth and heaven," and this kind of love "has its source in the heart of God."[5]

Jesus fully experienced true spirituality because He was in constant relationship and union with His Father. It was the basis of His dynamic spiritual life, and the source for His relationship with all others. He desired that all His followers should possess the same relationship with His Father. The spiritual union between Them is to serve as the model for our spiritual union with Christ.

Such was the intimate spiritual relationship into which John 14:1-7 records Jesus inviting His disciples to enter. There He links believing in His heavenly Father to believing in Him, and connects the inheritance of His Father's many mansions with His eternal relationship with them. Moreover, knowing the Father and going to Him can be possible only through Christ. Yet despite all of that, Thomas was preoccupied with the mechanics of finding a way of getting himself there on his own.

Jesus again brought Thomas' attention back to the special relationship between Him and His Father. "I [very emphatic in Greek, implying I *Myself]* am the way, the truth, and the life," Jesus declared. "No one comes to the Father except through Me" (verse 6). Are we, like Thomas, in the presence of the One in whom "dwells all the fullness of the Godhead bodily" (Col. 2:9) fruitlessly searching for some other way to God? Why do we so blindly and aimlessly grope for a method of reaching God in the very presence of the One who came forth from the bosom and heart of God?

Christ is the only One who had ever seen or been with the Father. And this unique and eternal Son of the eternal Father does not merely show the way, does not simply reveal the truth, and does not only give life. Beyond all of that, He Himself in His Person is the way, the truth, and the life. All of heaven was emptied in the inestimable gift of Christ to the human race, and thus in possessing Him we possess all. Nothing is worth anything except what Christ is to us. "In the spiritual world," Nee asserts, "there is nothing but Christ, since He is God's everything."[6]

Jesus unmistakably equated knowing and seeing His Father with knowing and seeing Him. And in uttering this truth He sought to engender courage and confidence in Thomas and the other disciples. "If you had known Me, you would have known My Father also; and from now on you know Him and have seen Him" (John 14:7). Immediately after this Philip requests what Jesus had just finished granting, thus revealing that it was not easy for him to comprehend that the Christ he was looking at was in reality "the brightness of His [the Father's] glory and the express image of His [the Father's] person" (Heb. 1:3).

Philip entreated Jesus, "Lord, show us the Father, and it is sufficient for us" (John 14: 8). Did not the disciple realize that no person had ever seen the Father? Did he not understand that absolutely no one could see the Father and live? It was a most unusual request. To see the Father in all His glory would have resulted in his instant death.

But like Thomas, who stared at the Way while wondering what way led to the Father, so Philip gazed upon Him in whom "dwells all the fullness of the Godhead bodily" while requesting to see God. Philip was standing next to the One who saw God, who was with God from eternity, and who came forth from the very heart of God. "No one has seen God at any time," Jesus testified. "The only begotten Son, who is in the bosom of the Father, He has declared Him" (John 1:18).

Right there and then Philip was viewing the very express image and the very fullness of God mysteriously blended with and mercifully veiled in humanity. In beholding the face of Christ, he was indeed seeing "the light of the knowledge of the glory of God" (2 Cor. 4:6). Jesus responded patiently to Philip as to a cherished yet inattentive friend. "Have I been with you so long, and yet you have not known Me, Philip?" He wistfully asked. "He who has seen Me has seen the Father; so how can you say, 'Show us the Father'?" (John 14:9).

It is interesting to note that John was the only one among the Gospel writers to record Christ's profound dialogue with Thomas and Philip. John, who referred to himself as the disciple whom Christ kept on loving, exhibited in himself a distinct blending of volatility and sensitivity. He was more open and responsive to the love of His Master than were the other disciples. No wonder we often allude to him as the apostle of love, for he drank deeper and deeper at love's source.

"This does not mean that Jesus had favorites," Earl McQuay explains. "Apparently, John was able to receive the love of Christ more readily and more fully than the others."[7] As we read his Gospel and Epistles, it becomes apparent that his intimacy with Christ helped him not merely to record what He did but also to describe how He felt and thought. That enabled him, furthermore, to dwell more on the love of Christ, His eternal preexistence, and the mysterious interwovenness of His divinity and humanity.

That is why John was overcome with ecstatic awe in discerning that his best friend Jesus, whom he looked at, touched, and conversed with, was in reality the divine Son of God. Seeing the Son he was seeing the Father, for the Son is like the Father. Even toward the end of his life, John was still struck by the awesomeness of such firsthand experience. Hearing the living Word, seeing the face of the incarnate great I Am, and handling the Son of the living God had filled his whole life.

That is why John found himself repeating his testimony of seeing, hearing, and touching the Word of life three times at the very beginning of his First Epistle. One gets the distinct impression that many cherished memories of Jesus flooded the mind of the beloved disciple as he began to write. His voice, His looks, His gestures and movements—all lingered on in his imagination. He simply could not get over it.

"That which was from the beginning," John starts out, "which we have heard, which we have seen with our eyes, which we have looked upon, and our hands have handled, concerning the Word of life (1 John 1:1). Again, "The life was manifested, and we have seen, and bear witness, and declare to you that eternal life which was with the Father and was manifested to us" (verse 2). And again, "That which we have seen and heard we declare to you, that you also may have fellowship with us; and truly our fellowship is with the Father and with His Son Jesus Christ" (verse 3).

At a time when the Gnostic heresies sought to deny the Incarnation, John gave quite a persuasive and personal testimony of the reality and historicity of Christ's earthly life. It is his way of introducing us to his best Friend, the Son of God, so that we may all share in the intimate fellowship and profound joy that John had had with the Father and with the Son. In other words, the Father has fellowship with the Son, and the Son fellowships with John, and then John shares such fellowship with us. We are included and participate in this complete circle of divine-human fellowship!

Ray Stedman sees John's intimate description of such fellowship as an invitation to the family of God through His Son. As he ponders John's words, he vividly elucidates what the apostle was thinking and feeling. "We touched Him, he says, we felt His warm, human flesh, we looked into His human eyes, we felt the beating of His human heart. And yet, as we did, we became aware that we were listening to the heartbeat of God. In some amazing way we were looking into the eyes of God and feeling the heartbeat of God and coming into contact with the life of God." [8]

If we had been there when John penned these words, we would have asked him specific questions about the Saviour: "What was He really like?" "What kind of friendly advice did He give you?" "What other things did He say or do that you did not include in the Gospel record?" And many other such questions. After all, John had spent three and a half years with Jesus, experiencing life together with all its ups and downs.

One time as a youngster I had the opportunity of meeting a man who had reached the ripe age of 100 and was still of sound mind and body. I remember peppering him with questions about historical events that I had studied in school. He did not need to study those events, for he had lived through them, and it was quite fascinating to listen to him relive them. Imagine how John must have felt. It must have been immensely exhilarating for him to have dialogued heart-to-heart with the One who ever lived from eternity.

The consuming purpose behind John's introduction to his First Epistle (John 1:1-3) is that we may have mutual fellowship with him and with the Father and His Son. Such fellowship with us is possible only because he first enjoyed fellowship with Christ and through Christ with the Father. John Mitchell, in explaining that the essence of this First Epistle of John is "fellowship with God," emphasizes that "we cannot have *fellowship* with God apart from the Incarnate Word of God."[9]

Our human fellowship with others ultimately depends on our vertical fellowship with God. If we see that we have trouble with the first, then that indicates that we must take care of the vertical. Remember the words of Christ when He said: "I am the vine, you are the branches. He who abides in Me, and I in him, bears much fruit; for without Me you can do nothing" (John 15:5).

Imagine that we are examining a vine flourishing with luxurious branches. Yes, the branches look beautiful together, yet unless they are connected to the vine itself they will wither and die. Only in being united with the vine can they be truly connected to each other, and sharing in the common life they all mutually share with the vine. Therefore, unless we the branches have a perpendicular fellowship with Christ the true Vine, our fellowship with the other branches is lifeless and fruitless. We greatly need, first and foremost, to behold the face of Christ, hear His words, and lean on His mighty arms before we start focusing on others. The branch cannot ultimately nourish another branch without the vine first sustaining it.

Francis Schaeffer explains that such a human "bridge is not strong enough. To try to run on the bridge of human relationships that which it cannot bear is to destroy both the relationship and ourselves."[10] Moreover, "to live the spiritual life is to be related to God," Iris Cully emphasizes. With this perspective, the divine/human perpendicular relationship becomes "the basis for all human relationships."[11]

Sharing such fellowship with the Father and the Son compels us, like John, to also extend it to others, so that they may believe in Christ and fulfill His prayer that "they all may be one, as You, Father, are in Me, and I in You; that they also may be one in Us, that the world may believe that You sent Me" (John 17:21). Again Jesus stresses this mutual divine-human sharing of fellowship: "That they may be one just as We are one: I in them, and You in Me; that they may be made perfect in one, and that the world may know that You have sent Me, and have loved them as You have loved Me" (verses 22, 23).

Here we find the proper progression. The Father enjoys a loving and close fellowship with the Son, and the Son longs to share it with us. And the great impetus behind it all is the mutual fellowship of the Father and the Son, which Jesus desires to have us emulate and experience with all the members of God's family.

We do indeed have the greatest honor and the most unique privilege ever made available to humanity: to be lovingly, intimately, and eternally included in divine/human fellowship. Such glorious blessing springs forth from Christ's love for us—a love that proved stronger than death. "Greater love has no man than this," Scripture affirms, "than to lay down one's life for his friends" (John 15:13). He calls us His friends, we who only deserve to be His enemies. "I have called you friends, for all things that I heard from My Father I have made known to you" (verse 15).

Genuine friends have trusting and trustworthy relationships. They feel quite comfortable in sharing intimate and secret things with each other. Jesus wants to share with us the mysteries and confidences He and the Father mutually share together! And why? Because He includes us in His special circle of friends. "If we come to Him [Christ] in faith, He will speak *His mysteries to us personally.* Our hearts will often burn within us as One draws nigh to commune with us as He did with Enoch." [12]

Most of us have at some time or another wished that a certain remarkable person would become our friend. We would feel elated, wouldn't we, if we knew that such a person harbored the same desire of becoming our friend. I had the fortune of meeting a wonderful young woman when attending college. We took some courses together, and chatted sometimes. Though I gradually felt attracted to her, yet I could never summon up sufficient courage to ask her for a date. What held me back was the seeming ambiguity of how she felt toward me. Were our feelings toward each other mutual? I just was not sure.

Finally, with some trepidation, I risked calling her on the phone, and to my pleasant surprise she happily accepted my request. During the evening I shared with her that it had not been easy for me to invite her on this first date. And as she wondered why I was hesitant, I confided that I had not been quite sure that she would accept. Hearing that, she candidly told me that she had been hoping that I would ask her for a date. Needless to say, it felt great to know that she *too* wanted to be my friend. (By the way, this young woman is my wonderful wife today.)

Christ, the most remarkable Person, the Creator and Saviour of the world, harbors an infinite desire to be our best friend. He, in fact, said, "You did not choose Me, but I chose you" (verse 16).

Shouldn't we be overjoyed that Jesus desires friendship with us? It is really what He has had in mind for us all along. He longs to share the intimate and eternal friendship that He has with His Father with us too. We cannot imagine a greater privilege and blessing and should never take it for granted.

The term *fellowship* in Greek as well as the Semitic languages denotes the idea of mutuality in sharing partnership, communion, companionship, and friendship with others. The "great secret of fellowship," according to Stedman, is "to have things in common" in the context of "partnership and friendship" with God, where all that I have I place at His disposal. "When I do," he continues, "I discover something most remarkable. Everything that He is, is put at my disposal. Is that not marvelous?" [13]

Stedman is right. God in His great love did put Himself at our disposal in giving His only Son to humanity. And in offering His beloved Son, He did indeed give all. The gift of Christ's life embodies in it all the blessings of partnership, fellowship, communion, and friendship. Such divine-human fellowship expresses itself in love. God's love is the heart of this fellowship—the love of the Father to His Son, the love of the Son to us, and Their love through us to others.

Listen to what Jesus says: "As the Father loved Me, I also have loved you; abide in My love" (verse 9). In abiding in Christ the Vine, we naturally rest in and are sustained by His love. And as always, Christ connects what He mutually shares with us to what He mutually shares with the Father. We clearly see this in what He said in John 14:23: "If anyone loves Me, he will keep My word; and My Father will love him, and We will come to him and make Our home with him." The plural "we" and "our" clearly signify the intimate fellowship that the Father and the Son mutually enjoy, and which They desire to enjoy with us. Such loving relationship seeks togetherness with the beloved, and intends to settle down and feel at home permanently with the beloved.

Consequently, when the loving Father and Son make Their home with us, then that love overflows us and reaches out to our spiritual brothers and sisters, and through us to the world. "A new commandment I give to you," Jesus says, "that you love one another; as I have loved you, that you also love one another" (John 13:34). Then He extends such loving fellowship to embrace all: "By this all will know that you are My disciples, if you have love for one another" (verse 35). Truly it is that "when the love of Christ is enshrined in the heart, like sweet fragrance it cannot be hidden. Its holy influence will be felt by all with whom we come in contact."[14]

Thus this divine-human fellowship that expresses itself in love also manifests itself in joy. John offers two reasons for describing to us his personal experience with the incarnate Son of God. First, that we may have fellowship with him and with the Son and the Father (see 1 John 1:3). Second, that we may have full *joy.* "And these things we write you," John clinches his point, "that your joy may be full" (verse 4).

John's reasons seem to echo the words of Jesus: "These things [abiding in Christ's love and fellowship] I have spoken to you," He said, "that My joy may remain in you, and that your joy may be full" (John 15:11; see also John 16:24; 17:13). It is the inward, profound, and serene sort of joy that springs forth from His joy abiding in us. Our Lord is a joyous God. Full of joy, He wants such joy to be an integral part of our own loving fellowship with Him. He is the fountain of all joy, and in devotion to Him and communion with Him, we possess the deepest and highest joy ever possible.

Unfortunately, some who would like to come across as pious and spiritual in their relationship to God display a cold and exacting spirit devoid of any real joy. They seem to overlook the fact that joy is the natural outflow of authentic spirituality. Nehemiah said that "the joy of the Lord is your strength" (Neh. 8:10). David declared that in the presence of God is "fullness of joy," and at His "right hand are pleasures for evermore" (Ps. 16:11).

Ellen White links fellowship with the Lord with joy in the Lord.

She writes that man was "created for fellowship with God," and that only in such fellowship can he "find his real life and development. Created to find in God his *highest joy*," she continues, "he can find in nothing else that which can quiet the cravings of the heart, can satisfy the hunger and thirst of the soul." [15]

We do not experience this "highest joy" in isolation from the real world with its pressures and problems. Rather, we have it because we know that we are hid in Christ's life, and that He is in complete control of our lives despite what may come. Such joy does not depend on outward and changeable circumstances, but on being anchored in a secure and trusting union with Christ. Thus we are not constantly up and down, elated or deflated by the approval or disapproval of others. Instead, the approval of Christ means all and everything to us.

Christ was everything to Paul and Silas. He was much more precious than liberty and even life itself. The Saviour Himself was their liberty, confidence, security, and life. And although they were once severely beaten and dragged into prison in Philippi, at midnight the walls of that gloomy prison reverberated with the joyous sound of their singing (Acts 16:22-25)! This is what joyous spirituality is.

Jesus is our prime example in manifesting joy in spirituality. He exuded such joy in spite of having to struggle with many overwhelming predicaments. That joy helped Him bravely bear the cruel crucifixion. Jesus, "who for the joy that was set before Him endured the cross, despising the shame" (Heb. 12:2). "But though His life was self-denying and shadowed with pain and care, His spirit was not crushed. His countenance did not wear an expression of grief and repining, but ever one of peaceful serenity. His heart was a wellspring of life; and wherever He went He carried rest and peace, joy and gladness." [16]

The essence of true spirituality found in Christ comprises loving oneness, manifesting itself in relationship, partnership, companionship, communion, friendship, fellowship, joy, and witnessing. It all comes from God through Christ, who shared it with others. Jesus lived a life in constant loving oneness with His Father, and He certainly knew and experienced what true spirituality is all about. "You shall love the Lord your God with all your heart, with all your soul, and with all your mind" and "You shall love your neighbor as yourself" (Matt. 22:37, 39).

Jesus demonstrated in His life that spirituality was not about some abstract notion or an involved intellectual nod to some lofty idea. In His life, spirituality was an all-embracing, integrated devotion to His Father and loving service to others. He created man in His image as a total being—not as a fragmented being—thus He wants us to experience total relationships with Him and others.

In our Western society we often emphasize the cognitive to the detriment of the affective in our human relationships. We stress the mental over the emotional. Too often we carry such a lopsided emphasis over to our relationship with God. Notice that the spirituality of Jesus expressed itself in loving His Father with *all* His being, and His neighbor as Himself. "You shall love (affective) the Lord (person) your (relationship) God with all (total commitment) your heart (affective), with all your soul (spiritual), and with all your mind (cognitive)."

Here we have something that transcends the merely academic or abstract. George Maloney brings in the other emphasis—the practical emphasis of theology in Eastern Christianity—which we can apply to spirituality as well. Theology is "a mystical life seen as a continued process in love relationships and self-giving between the Trinity and the individual Christian as well as in the Christian community."[17] True spirituality is a total and balanced experience. It is not either this or that, but a spiritual experience involving the whole person with the Father, the Son, the Spirit, and others.

Additional passages in the Gospel of John show how the Son viewed His mutual oneness with the Father. We will only briefly touch on them:

1. The Father and the Son have always been *doing* things together. Moreover, the Son does nothing of Himself except what He sees His Father doing (John 5:17-20).

2. As the Father raises the dead and *gives life* to them, so does the Son (verse 21).

3. *Honoring* or dishonoring the Father is equivalent to honoring or dishonoring the Son (verse 23).

4. Just as the Father *possesses life* in Himself, so does the Son (verse 26; see also John 10:17, 18; 12:49, 50).

5. The *teaching* of the Son is the same as the Father's teaching (John 7:16; see also John 8:26, 28).

6. To *know* the Son is to know the Father, and not to know the Son is not to know the Father (John 8:19).

7. The Son and the Father are *one* (John 10:30; see also John 17:11, 21).

8. As the Father is *in* the Son, so likewise the Son is in the Father (John 10:38; see also John 14:10, 11).

9. He who *receives* the Son receives the Father who sent Him (John 13:20).

10. He who *hates* the Son hates the Father also (John 15:23).

11. As the Son *glorifies* the Father, so likewise the Father glorifies the Son (John 17:4, 5).

In this chapter we have discussed to some extent the type of fellowship the Son and the Father mutually have together. In the following chapters we will examine more specifically how we, as sons and daughters of God, may experience Christ's oneness with the Father in our own spiritual lives. How His spirituality can transform and revolutionize our spirituality, and thus its impact on other lives.

---

[1] White, *Selected Messages,* book 1, p. 292.

[2] ———, *The Desire of Ages,* p, 111. (Italics supplied.)

[3] Lawrence O. Richards, *A Practical Theology of Spirituality* (Grand Rapids: Francis Asbury Press, 1985), p. 201.

[4] Don Richardson, *Peace Child* (Glendale, Calif.: Gospel Light, 1974), p. 206.

[5] White, *The Desire of Ages,* p. 20.

[6] Nee, *Christ the Sum of All Spiritual Things,* p. 81.

[7] Earl P. McQuay, *John, Apostle of Love* (Denver: Accent Publications, Inc., 1983), p. 17.

[8] Ray C. Stedman, *Expository Studies in 1 John, Life by the Son* (Waco, Tex.: Word Books, 1980), p. 17.

[9] John G. Mitchell, *Fellowship* (Portland, Oreg.: Multnomah Press, 1974), p. 13.

[10] Schaeffer, *True Spirituality,* p. 196.

[11] Iris V. Cully, *Education for Spiritual Growth* (San Francisco: Harper and Row, 1984), p. 15.

[12] White, *The Desire of Ages,* p. 668. (Italics supplied.)

[13] Stedman, pp. 19, 20.

[14] White, *Steps to Christ,* p. 77.

[15] ———, *Education,* pp. 124, 125. (Italics supplied.)

[16] ———, *Steps to Christ,* p. 120.

[17] Maloney, ed., *Pilgrimage of the Heart,* p. 232.

Chapter Four

COMPLETE IN CHRIST—1

I woke up early this clear and breezeless morning to start working on this chapter. As I typed the title, I searched my mind for an appropriate illustration to use for the introduction, but none whatsoever came to mind at such an early hour of the morning. As I was absorbed in deep thought, all of a sudden a terrific crashing sound rudely interrupted the stillness of the morning. Parting the curtain, I quickly discovered what had just transpired. The giant sprawling willow tree in our backyard had crashed down. Curious as to what had happened to our beautiful tree, I rushed outside, only to discover that the gigantic trunk was rotted at the core.

To the onlooker the tree appeared beautiful and strong on the outside, yet its core had decayed on the inside. How well it portrays our spiritual lives when they are devoid of the spiritual life of Christ. What really matters most in spirituality is not so much how others view us, or even how we regard ourselves, but rather how God sees our inward lives.

True spirituality leaves no room for us to pretend, or for others to presume that we are what we are not. However, there must be room for God to penetrate our inner selves. God declares: "For the Lord does not see as man sees; for man looks at the outward appearance, but the Lord looks at the heart" (1 Sam. 16:7).

This is good news, isn't it? God discerns what is in the human heart far beyond what another person can see. For how else may we continue growing in Christ unless He purifies our hidden motives and opens up the dark recesses of our minds. Aren't we grateful He does?

Consider the insightful and fitting way in which Oswald Chambers conveys the message of Psalm 139:

"Thou art the God of the early mornings, the God of the late nights, the God of the mountain peaks, and the God of the sea; but, my God, my soul has *further* horizons than the early mornings, *deeper* darkness than the nights of earth, *higher* peaks than any mountain peaks, *greater* depths than any sea in nature—Thou Who art the God of all these, be my God. I *cannot* reach to the heights or to the depths; there are motives I *cannot* trace, dreams I *cannot* get at—my God, search me out." [1]

May this prayer be our heartfelt one too, so that God may have full rein in directing our spiritual growth in Christ.

Don't you think that we will have many surprises awaiting us at the coming of Christ? Have we already made up our minds as to who will and will not be ready to meet Him? God is the only one who can truly discern the human heart. Contemplate this sobering thought: "*Many* who think themselves Christians will at last be found wanting," predicts Ellen White. But on the other hand, "*Many* will be in heaven who their neighbors supposed would never enter there." And why is that? Because "man judges from appearance, but God judges the heart." [2]

So why not ask Him to search us and know our hearts (Ps. 139:23) so that He may discern what we are truly like in our innermost beings? I wonder what He would come up with. Would He see the Saviour or self formed within? If Christ is being formed within, then—praise God—we are complete in Him, but if self dominates our inner life, then pray that Christ will dethrone it and reign there instead. We will never be complete in ourselves without being complete in Him. Our eternal destiny hinges on it, for to overlook it is to court inevitable and disastrous destruction.

In the previous chapter we focused primarily on how the Father and His Son are mutually alike. Now, we will build on this base in our consideration of how we may become complete in Christ, and, born of the Spirit, how we may become sons and daughters of God. Also we will examine how Jesus often includes us in His intimate and mutual relationship with the Father, bridging in Himself the gap between the divine and the human.

Imagine for a moment Christ, through whom all things were created, walking in the Garden of Eden. He has just finished speaking the world into existence and pronouncing it "good." Yet He does not seem to be completely satisfied. He has still one more thing on His mind to create. In His grace of heart and genius of mind, He decides to begin humankind, and fashion the new race in His own image, according to His own likeness (Gen. 1:26). Humanity was the glorious and crowning act of His creation, giving Christ full satisfaction. For as He surveyed all creation He declared that "indeed it was very good" (verse 31).

Christ could have chosen to simply speak Adam into existence. However, He intended Adam's creation to be uniquely exceptional as He formed him in His image, fashioning him after His likeness, and breathing into him His breath of life (see Gen. 1:27). He planned from the very beginning to have humanity reflect His image and His likeness forever, so that He may share His life, love, joy, and fullness with the new race for eternity. It was a special honor that Christ lavishly bestowed on us in making us in His likeness, the very likeness of Divinity!

From the very beginning Christ was intimately involved in forming human beings into His likeness. The Hebrew word *yasar* ("to form") suggests the act of molding pliable clay in the skillful hands of a potter. Hence, like the potter, Christ's creative hands flawlessly fashioned the first man and deftly poured into his form the exquisite flair of the Master Sculptor.

Adam came forth from His Creator's hands in perfect form, appearing alive but for his stillness and lack of movement. Then the Lord of all life "breathed into his nostrils the breath of life; and man became a living being" (Gen. 2:7). Imagine Adam's radiant face flickering with the first smile, and gazing at the smiling face of his Creator, whose life had just surged into his form of clay! A perfect being molded in His image and likeness, complete in Him, Adam was indeed "very good."

It is told that when Michelangelo put the final touches on his sculpture of Moses, he tapped it gently on the knee and entreated it, "Now, speak to me!" But nothing happened. Michelangelo may have deftly wielded his chisel and hammer, but he could never breathe life into a lifeless form. *Only* God can! The best that humanity can produce is still imperfect, for only God can create wholeness and perfection.

Recently I saw some pictures of a royal prince moving among his subjects with his hands folded behind his back. His posture intrigued me. Curious, I asked someone acquainted with royal etiquette why the prince always kept his hands behind his back while greeting his people. The person told me that the prince did not want to shake hands with his subjects, fearing undue familiarity with them.

My thoughts raced back to Eden to contemplate another pair of princely hands, those of the Creator-Prince of life, the royal One of the universe. His hands were not protectively folded, but intimately and actively engaged with humanity. And absolutely nothing could keep the Redeemer-Prince of life from being involved with the human race, not even death itself.

One pair of hands streaked with warm blood in redemption at Golgotha. The same pair of hands sullied with wet clay at creation in the garden. One voice in Eden declaring that man's creation was indeed "very good." The same voice at Golgotha crying that fallen man's re-creation was indeed "finished." "It is finished" was "the greatest note of triumph that ever sounded in the ears of a startled universe." [3]

Christ's finished work of redemption for the sake of fallen humanity is to become complete in our lives. True spirituality is not simply good doing, but God doing His completed work in us as wrought in His Son. It is actualized in our daily lives when "God's life in us expresses itself as *God's* life, not as human life trying to be godly." [4] God, who accomplished His completed work of redemption in Christ, accomplishes it in us as well.

In the previous chapter we studied from the writings of the disciple John about the mutual oneness the Father and the Son experience together. It is significant to note that John also conveys the distinct idea that Christ wants us to experience with Him what He shares with the Father. Our Saviour longs to have the divine spirituality of the triune God become inextricably intertwined with our own human spirituality.

I can think of no greater source of encouragement and joy than to realize that the intimate relationship He experiences with His Father is in fact what He desires to share with us now and forever!

Christ frequently and explicitly declares His desires for us. Here are some of them:

1. The eternal *life* that the *Father* possesses with *Jesus* He then shares with *us*, and thus unites us to Them in that life for all eternity. "As the living Father sent Me, and I live because of the Father, so he who feeds on Me will live because of Me" (John 6:57; see also John

3:16; 6:54). Jesus wants us, deficient as we are, to join Him in this *completeness* with His Father. Christ gives us abundant and eternal life (see John 10:10, 28; 17:3).

"For in Him [Christ] dwells all the fullness of the Godhead bodily; and you are *complete* in Him, who is the head of all principality and power" (Col. 2:9, 10). God, through Christ, dealt a mortal blow to death, our ruthless enemy, and in Christ we receive His eternal life resulting from that decisive victory. "For you died, and *your* life is hidden with Christ in *God*" (Col. 3:3).

2. The *love* that the *Father* and the *Son* have for each other, and the *oneness* they enjoy together Christ wants to share with *us*. The Father loves us with the same love He has for His Son, and the Son loves us with that same love He has for His Father. They long to share Their mutual loving oneness with us. "For the Father Himself loves you, because you have loved Me, and have believed that I came forth from God" (John 16:27). Moreover, Jesus concluded His intercessory prayer in behalf of His disciples with this same idea that "the love with which You loved Me may be in them, and I in them" (John 17:26).

And the love in that oneness we clearly see in Jesus' prayer to His Father in behalf of His disciples: "I in them, and You in Me; that they may be made perfect in one, and that the world may know that You have sent Me, and have loved them as You have loved Me" (verse 23). Yes, the Father and the Son want us to know that same love and oneness They have for and with each other! And Jesus wants us, incomplete as we are, to join Him in the *completeness* of His love and oneness with His Father. We are destined to be loved with such love and united with such oneness!

3. In His same prayer for the disciples, and just before His crucifixion, Jesus entreated His Father: "As *You* sent *Me* into the world, I also have sent *them* into the world" (verse 18). You see, Jesus simply wants to share with us what He has always possessed with His Father from eternity: His life, His love and oneness, and also His mission. Just as the *Father* charged *Him* with this mission to the world, so now Jesus commissions *us* into the same world. He restated that commission to His disciples right after His resurrection when He declared to them: "Peace to you! As the *Father* has sent *Me*, I also send *you*" (John 20:21).

The apostle Paul reiterated the same sacred mission of reconciliation involving the Father, the Son, and us. He depicts the Father entreating the world through us as ambassadors for Christ. "Now all things are of God, who has reconciled us to Himself through Jesus Christ, and has given us the ministry of reconciliation, that is, that *God* was in *Christ* reconciling the world to Himself . . . and has committed to *us* the word of reconciliation" (2 Cor. 5:18, 19).

When we ask people to tell us about their profession, they often like to describe it in a way that makes it seem important and impressive. They may even base their self-worth entirely on the importance they attach to their occupation. But here Paul tells us that God shares with us the awesome occupation of His Son—the ministry of reconciling others to Him. What greater honor can we possibly imagine than that God wants us to share in and carry on the sacred work of His own Son! Absolutely nothing exists that is even faintly comparable to it.

Those who are engaged in outstanding professions will often jealously and selfishly guard them from others. But not our God. Greatly desiring to give away His ministry, He passionately wants to share with us, flawed as we are, the completeness of His Son's ministry of reconciliation. We can do no greater work on earth than the very work of Jesus Himself.

Years ago I met a real estate agent who had become recognized as the most successful salesman in his state. He was proud of the fact that he had the remarkable ability to persuade others to buy houses. In reflecting on this man's amazing success in his occupation, I thought of our glorious work with Christ of convincing others to be reconciled to God. Not just of convincing them to purchase a piece of real estate in this world, but rather of convincing them to freely possess the mansions that Christ has prepared for them in the world to come.

The gripping reality of it all is that in Christ we are engaged in the most sacred and glorious business of the whole universe. Indeed, we participate with Him in radically altering people's destinies forever!

Imagine for a moment this scene when you reach heaven. Seeing a certain individual whom Christ through you reconciled to God, you rush to him or her, shake hands, look into his or her grateful eyes, behold the transformation, and then the most exhilarating thought seizes you. This very person standing right there before you will enjoy God's perfect universe for eternity. And it happened because of Christ's witness of reconciliation through you. Can you conceive of a more impressive accomplishment? Can you fathom a more rewarding experience?

4. Such a rewarding ministry of reconciliation is possible only through union with God in Christ. He accomplished His ministry of reconciliation through Christ, and now He entrusts it to us as we abide in Christ. Thus we find that all the success we will ever have comes solely from our union with God in His Son. "I am the true vine, and My Father is the vinedresser," Jesus said to His disciples (John 15:1). "I am the vine, you are the *branches*. He who abides in Me, and I in him, bears much fruit; for without Me you can do nothing" (verse 5). Only as we adhere to Christ, rather than in focusing on the fruit, can He make us fruitful.

Notice again how our vital relationship with Christ is to reflect His own relationship with His Father. Scripture compares the children of Israel to a vine that God had plucked out of Egypt and planted in the land of Palestine. The psalmist says that He had "brought a vine out of Egypt" (Ps. 80:8). He planted the Israelites in the Promised Land to direct their attention to the coming true Vine, their only source of life and fruitfulness. However, they became so distracted by the symbol that they overlooked its reality. They thought that their mere nationalistic connection to Israel guaranteed their salvation.

Then God the Vinedresser planted Jesus the *true* Vine in the same soil of ancient Israel. And just as a vinedresser maintains his vine, so the Father sustained His Son. It is of spiritual significance to note that Jesus chose to refer to Himself as the vine, and not to other stronger and loftier trees. You see, the vine is *dependent* on supports provided by the vinedresser, so that it may cling to and intertwine itself around them in its upward growth.

Consider with me this insightful comment regarding Jesus' dependence on His Father: "Instead of choosing the graceful palm, the lofty cedar, or the strong oak, Jesus takes the vine with its clinging tendrils to represent Himself. The palm tree, the cedar, and the oak stand alone. They require no support. But the vine entwines about the trellis, and thus climbs heavenward. So Christ in His humanity was *dependent* on divine power."[5]

Norman Gulley, in reflecting on Christ's need to cling to His Father for support, includes our need to find support in Christ as well. Jesus clung to the Father, and we cling to Jesus. "The Source of man's everlasting life [was] totally sustained by His Father for life," he writes. "God's great aqueduct let down from heaven—Jesus Christ—

through whom the life of God poured out to enter dependent humans. Man can cling to Christ for life because He clung to His Father." [6]

Christ's example teaches us an absolutely essential lesson for our spiritual life and growth. We must become inextricably and upwardly intertwined around Christ just as He was around His Father. Jesus affirmed that without the Father "the Son can do nothing of Himself" (John 5:19). And we too "can do nothing" without abiding in Christ (John 15:5).

For when we abide in Christ the Vine as He in His humanity abode in His Father the Vinedresser, His life, His power, and His fruitfulness course through our lives. "The scion is engrafted into the living vine, and fiber by fiber, vein by vein, it grows into the vine stock. The life of the vine *becomes* the life of the branch." [7] Christ longs to share with us, hopeless human beings though we may be, the *completeness* of His dependency on and submission to the Father.

Abiding in and submission to Christ is the only way to become complete in Him. And thus true spirituality draws attention to Christ's spirituality, not ours, and seeks His glory, not ours. Oswald Chambers describes it as abandonment to God. "Abandon to God is of more value than personal holiness." [8] Why is it so vital? Chambers answers: "This abandon to the love of Christ is the one thing that bears fruit in the life, and it will always leave the impression of the holiness and of the power of God, never of our personal holiness." [9] Moreover, "when we are abandoned to God, *He* works through us *all* the time." [10]

5. Finally Jesus wants to share with us, imperfect as we are, the perfection of His love with His Father and His obedience to Him because He desires us to be complete in Them. Listen to what He says: "As the Father loved Me, I also have loved you; abide in My love. If you keep My commandments, you will abide in My love, just as I have kept My Father's commandments and abide in His love" (verses 9, 10).

Furthermore, the Father loves us with the same love He has for His Son. As such love manifests itself in loving obedience, both the Father *and* the Son come to dwell in our hearts. What the Son experiences with His Father He wants us also to experience in our lives. Jesus declares: "If anyone loves Me, he will keep My word; and My Father will love him, and *We* will come to him and make *our* home with him" (John 14:23). The only way we may grow and mature in our spiritual life is for the Father and the Son to make Their home with us.

Our Lord's words throb with His heart's desire to include us in His relationship with His Father. He is not exclusive in that intimate relationship, jealously guarding it just for Himself, away from any human intrusion. Instead, He opens His heart wide to lavishly share with us what He eternally enjoys with His Father: Their life, love, harmony, and their heavenly abode. Such love tirelessly seeks togetherness with us far beyond that of even the most loving parents who long to be with their children. The Father and Son even want to make Their home in our hearts here and now so that we may share in Their heavenly home.

Have we entered into this wonderful relationship They so generously share with us? Are we appreciating the abundance of Their love for us? Are we delighting ourselves in doing Their pleasure? After all, They poured out Themselves and all of heaven for our eternal happiness, didn't They? Do we find ourselves savoring Their presence and enjoying Their company? Do we really feel at home with Them?

It is tempting to work on our external behavior—which other people can observe—and neglect the inner life seen by God alone. After all, it is easier to attach ourselves to things, and become preoccupied in doing all sorts of good deeds, than to adhere to the person of Christ. But no matter what takes us away from our devotion to Christ and from feeling at home with Him, it leads us nowhere but to despair. We are complete only in Him, and in Him alone we experience our secure abode.

Let us suppose for a moment that a stranger is seeking to find where Jesus resides in our neighborhood. Wanting to know Christ's address, he or she goes from house to house knocking. "Does Jesus Christ live here?" the person inquires of the puzzled occupants.

Then before this curious stranger leaves our community, he or she knocks at *your* door and *mine* and asks the same question: "Does Jesus Christ, by any chance, live here?" How would we respond? We may tell this stranger that we are religious, that we go to church regularly, and we may even try to give the person a quick Bible study. Nevertheless, the determined stranger repeats more diligently the same probing question: "Would you please tell me if Jesus Christ lives here?"

Jesus and the Father love us and long to come to us and make Their home with us. Can others easily find Them when they knock at our hearts and homes? Do They reside there?

[1] Chambers, *My Utmost for His Highest,* p. 9. (Italics supplied.)

[2] White, *Christ's Object Lessons,* p. 72. (Italics supplied.)

[3] Chambers, p. 326.

[4] *Ibid.,* p. 264.

[5] White, *The Desire of Ages,* pp. 674, 675. (Italics supplied.)

[6] Norman R. Gulley, *Christ Our Substitute* (Washington, D.C.: Review and Herald Pub. Assn., 1982), p. 47.

[7] White, *The Desire of Ages,* p. 675. (Italics supplied.)

[8] Chambers, p. 52.

[9] *Ibid.,* p. 35.

[10] *Ibid.,* p. 52. (Italics supplied.)

Chapter Five

COMPLETE IN CHRIST—2

A literary critic met a little girl on his way to the home of the well-known John Bunyan. "Do you know where John Bunyan lives?" he asked her.

"Yes," she replied as she started showing him the way to Bunyan's residence. Walking along with the child, the man, who knew a lot about Bunyan's literary style, began to wax eloquent about allegory, metaphors, personification, etc.

Caught up in literary topics, he unwittingly turned to face his young helper, asking her if she understood what he meant. "No," she promptly answered.

Impulsively he shot back, "Then you don't know John Bunyan!"

Astonished, the little girl replied emphatically and matter-of-factly, "But I do know him. He is my father." [1]

We too know God. He is our heavenly Father, and we are His sons and daughters. We live in the same home and have the same address. And because we are born of Him and live with Him, His fatherly traits continuously rub off on us, for they run in the family, so to speak. Other people searching for God and what He is like may find Him in *our* hearts and homes. They may see a reflection of His image and His likeness in our lives and say, "Like Father, like children."

In a nutshell, this is how we may grow into such a genuine spiritual experience. It does not come about because we know many things *about* the Father, but because we know Him as a person, as *our own* Father. Because we live with Him, feel at home with Him, and reflect His characteristics because they run in His family. In no other way can we achieve spiritual growth, maturity, and perfection.

It is helpful to note the use of the terms *image* and *likeness* in connection with humanity's creation. Though Adam was very similar to God in that God created him in His own image and after His likeness, yet he was vastly different in that he was the creature and God was the Creator. We might compare Adam to the moon in its reflection of the light of the sun in that God created Adam to *reflect* the image and likeness of his Creator.

Similarly, Paul uses the term *likeness* to describe both the resemblance and the difference between Christ and us. He depicts Christ as coming to our world in the "form of a servant," in the "likeness of men" (Phil. 2:7), and more specifically, "in the likeness of sinful flesh" (Rom. 8:3). Just as being created in the likeness of God refers to our *resemblance* of Him but not our *exactness* to Him, so also Christ coming in the likeness of sinful flesh refers to His resemblance to us but not His exactness to us.

For Christ in His human form and likeness was made "to be sin for us," yet He absolutely "knew no sin" (2 Cor. 5:21). Although "tempted as we are," yet He was still absolutely "without sin" (Heb. 4:15). He was "that holy thing" who was born of Mary, the "holy child Jesus," and "the Holy One of God" (Luke 1:35, KJV; Acts 4:27, KJV; Mark 1:24, KJV). We were born wholly sinners, while He was born the holy Saviour.

Though the Creator made Adam and his children in the likeness of God, they still are and will always be fully human. And although Christ was conceived in the likeness of man, He still is and will ever be fully divine as well as human. The God/Man—both natures mysteriously and miraculously blending together. *Like* us but not the *same* as us. *Similar* to us yet *distinct* from us. That fact contains great news because it designates our help and our salvation. He is both our sympathetic Helper and our sinless Saviour. And we desperately need to have both. In the next chapter we will expand further on these concepts as they relate to our spiritual growth and sanctification in Christ.

The Son of God is the unique one who in Himself is the fullness of God. Christ does not simply bear the image of God or reflect His likeness, for He in Himself is God. He specifically said to Philip, "He who has seen Me has seen the Father" (John 14:9)—not just a reflection of the Father. "Man was to bear God's image, both in outward resemblance and in character. Christ *alone* is 'the *express* image'

(Heb. 1:3) of the Father; but man was formed in the likeness of God. His nature was in harmony with the will of God."[2]

It reassures us to know that the all-absorbing passion of Jesus Christ, our Creator and Redeemer God, is to restore in our fallen nature His image and likeness. He ardently desires that we may become complete in Him, reflecting His character and living in harmony with His will. His consuming passion is to make us whole again, to breathe into our lifeless dust His revitalizing breath, and to pour into our earthen vessels His energizing spirit.

Edward Carter depicts this integrated wholeness in a life transformed by the life of God: "The Christian is not one-half natural and one-half supernatural. He is one graced person. In his entirety he has been raised up, caught up, into a deeper form of life in Christ Jesus."[3]

We can best describe this deeper form of the spiritual life in Christ's words recorded in Matthew 5. There we find the clearest teaching on genuine spirituality, one patterned after His own spirituality. Christ not only taught it, He lived it. He was the perfect embodiment of it.

Samuel Miller captured this well when he wrote of Christ and the Sermon on the Mount: "He trusted the untrustworthy, we trust those who have good collateral. He forgave the unforgivable, we forgive those who really do not hurt us. . . . He was meek, we are ambitious. . . . He had no place to lay His head, and did not worry about it, while we fret because we do not have the latest convenience. . . . He did what He believed to be right regardless of consequences, we will determine what is right by how it will affect us. He feared God, but not the world. We fear public opinion more than we fear the judgment of God. He risked everything for God, we make religion a refuge from every risk."[4]

Scripture uses *complete* to mean "perfect," and both terms are employed interchangeably. Whenever Scripture has the latter term, we need to understand it properly. However, the former term is likely less confusing and hence more preferable, particularly in our Western way of thinking. Both the Hebrew term *tamim* and the Greek term *teleios*, translated "perfect," convey more the idea of completeness rather than the idea of perfectionism.

Literally, *tamim* means "complete, "right," "peaceful," "wholesome." And *teleios* conveys "complete," "mature," "perfect," "full grown." The Western mind, unfortunately, frequently perceives such terms to infer legalistic, static, or absolute perfection or perfectionism.

Often such misconception stems from misapplications of the biblical references to perfection, especially the classic words of Christ in the Sermon on the Mount: "Be ye therefore perfect, even as your Father which is in heaven is perfect" (Matt. 5:48, KJV). In our brief study here, we shall focus on how we, as sons and daughters of our heavenly Father, act toward Him and others from inner loving motives, culminating in our maturity or perfection in Christ.

It is essential to look carefully at this important text. The passage seems to "leap out of its setting" and to "loom larger than its context."[5] In His exhortative summary of the Sermon on the Mount, Jesus was leading people to look beyond the external manifestations of obedience, and to probe deeper beneath the inner motives of the deceitful heart. The inner motives must be genuinely actuated by God's love. Such genuine love manifested in our everyday lives is what makes us more like Him.

Few would oppose the concepts of Christ's sermon on the mount. We accept it as a guide for morality and ethical standards, yet most rarely understand or experience its intent. William Hamilton, delving deeper into it, depicts the sermon as deftly employing "knife-like probes" and skillfully wielding a "probing scalpel."[6]

How does Christ wield such sharp instruments? "He [Christ] comes turning His apparently simple and winsome words into knife-like probes," Hamilton explains, in order to "reveal our self-deception and deceit."[7] Moreover, "we have here something far different from a series of simple techniques for Christian living," he asserts. "Here is rather an undistorted mirror by which we may see our distortion, a probing scalpel that reveals our inner disease. . . . And we do not like what we see."[8]

Christ's "probing scalpel" cuts a painful revelation no matter how moral and decent we think we are, or others consider us to be. But such painful cutting leads to a profound healing.

In beholding Christ, we see a true picture of His perfection as well as one of our own hopeless condition, and that realization cuts us to the heart. We keenly sense our utter unworthiness and imperfection in His presence, yet we cling to Him as our only real value and perfection. Every one of us should feel endless gratitude to Christ because He does not turn away from us as we rightly deserve, but instead holds on to us with a grip that will never let go.

And from that position of strength in Christ, we decrease as He increases, self is dethroned and Christ enthroned. He becomes all in all to us, leading us to focus on Him and His perfection, and on how He views us rather than on how others view us. Accepted in the Beloved, secure in His person and perfection, we live only as He lives out His life in us, leading us in our joint journey to spiritual growth and perfection.

Therefore, in order to more clearly understand the concept of spiritual growth and maturity in Christ's sermon, it would be helpful to consider the following ideas:

1. The perfection that Christ had in mind was the inner righteousness that manifests itself in righteous acts. As we honestly examine our motives for what we think of as our best righteous acts, we become convicted at our very core that our own self-centeredness has tainted them. We find ourselves convicted to honestly and humbly admit that the human heart simply can never have perfect and pure inner motives, but any good things we do proceed only from their Source, the Lord our righteousness.

Even what we might perceive of in our hearts as righteous is not at the core truly righteous. Only God can really know our hearts and minds. Only His heart and mind can search the inner contents of the human heart, and probe the multiple and deceitful layers of the human mind. What the Lord Himself declared in Jeremiah captures the real inner human condition amplified in the Sermon on the Mount. "The heart is deceitful *above all* things, and *desperately* wicked; who can know it? I, the Lord, search the heart, I test the mind" (Jer. 17:9, 10).

We all can identify with this description when we are downright honest with ourselves and God. We may recall doing good things— giving a Bible study, preaching a sermon, visiting someone recovering from surgery, going on a mission project, and so on. Yet we all have a conscious or unconscious need to be noticed for what we have done. As a result we drop some word, leave certain hints, no matter how unobtrusively, to gain favor with others.

Although ever so subtle, yet it is nevertheless there, clearly indicating that we are not totally secure in being seen by God, or in having Him take all the credit. Inwardly we are still self-centered, desiring to call attention to ourselves and our performance instead of pointing others to Christ Himself and His perfection. The Sermon on the Mount speaks to everyone. Its central message excludes no one.

Haddon Robinson asserts that Jesus intended to convict His listeners of their moral bankruptcy of merely keeping the letter of the law and utterly disregarding the need to live its spirit. He goes further in admitting that even when we try to live the spirit of the law, we still fall quite short. He candidly includes himself in this. "As a seminary president, I probably pass muster, externally, but the Sermon on the Mount gets me on the inside. I know down inside what I want to be and ought to be, but I know I'm neither."[9]

We are convicted of the same thing, aren't we, when we dare to invite God to search our innermost motives for what we do? Unfortunately, we would often rather have others be impressed by our outward righteousness than to have God deal with our true inward condition. Consequently, many of us manage to gain the respect of others for our supposed spirituality. It is possible to act appropriately, anticipating the approving applause of others, without the inner regeneration. "The love of influence and the desire for the esteem of others may produce a well-ordered life. Self-respect may lead us to avoid the appearance of evil. A selfish heart may perform generous actions."[10]

2. We feel this divine conviction of our moral bankruptcy keenly when we sense our poverty of spirit. When we recognize that in our own selves and by our own righteousness we can never inherit the kingdom of heaven. Only by being overwhelmed by the abject poverty of our own spirit can we ever begin to crave His Spirit. "Pride feels no need, and so it closes the heart against Christ and the infinite blessings He came to give. There is no room for Jesus in the heart of such a person. Those who are rich and honorable in their own eyes do not ask in faith. . . . They feel that they are full, therefore they go away empty."[11]

How tragic yet true this is of those who foolishly concentrate on their external righteousness instead of focusing on their righteous Lord. He alone can create in them that poverty in spirit, that meekness of heart, that inner righteousness they so desperately need. Jesus declares that to such belong both the kingdom of heaven and the inheritance of the earth (Matt. 5:3, 5). Only they are really living for Christ and experiencing perfection in Him.

Most people today look upon poverty in spirit, meekness, and humility as evidence of weakness. The vast majority of people—even some in the church—feel sorrow and disdain for people with such divine qualities. Part of the reason, perhaps, is a reaction to what many consider as humility today. And much of it is probably nothing more than subtly concealed self-centeredness.

A story tells of a meeting convened to honor the most humble man in a particular town. At the appointed time, he came to the front to receive a ribbon. The next day people noticed him wearing the ribbon in public, and the townspeople took it back from him.

Our pride in our "humility" and the other things we desire to have people notice is usually not that obvious or simplistic. Although it may not be readily apparent, it is nonetheless pernicious, and permeates every aspect of our being. That is how things are when human nature is in control. Someone once asked Augustine how he got to know God. "Humility" was his all-encompassing reply. "Pride," he stressed, "wrests wholly from our hand any good work on which we are congratulating ourselves." [12]

Of all the spiritual maladies threatening the human soul, pride is the worst, especially in the form of so-called humility. "There is nothing so offensive to God or so dangerous to the human soul as pride and self-sufficiency. Of all sins it is the most hopeless, the most incurable," Ellen White warns. Moreover, such offensive and dangerous behavior is so subtly deceiving that "while speaking to God of poverty of spirit, the heart may be swelling with the conceit of its own superior humility and exalted righteousness." [13]

Consider this insightful diagnosis of self-centeredness, as well as the only effective remedy: "Human nature is ever struggling for expression, ready for contest," Ellen White writes, "but he who learns of Christ is emptied of self, of pride, of love of supremacy, and there is silence in the soul. Self is yielded to the disposal of the Holy Spirit. Then we are not anxious to have the highest place. We have no ambition to crowd and elbow ourselves into notice; but we feel that our highest place is at the feet of our Saviour. We look to Jesus, waiting for His hand to lead, listening for His voice to guide." [14]

It takes tremendous energy to satisfy our human craving for recognition. Why not redirect this precious energy to focus on Christ and His recognition, yielding ourselves unreservedly to Him? In Him we have already reached the highest place. Truly, "while self is all alive, we stand ready continually to guard it from mortification and insult; but when we are dead, and our life is hid with Christ in God, we shall not take neglects or slights to heart." [15]

The greatest example of humility and meekness is Christ. We will have no room left over for human pride when we focus on Christ, who "made Himself of no reputation, taking the form of a servant, and coming in the likeness of men." Moreover, He "humbled Himself and became obedient to the point of death, even the death of the cross" (Phil. 2:7, 8).

How can we ever be proud and self-centered when Jesus, the ruler of the universe, was not? "Jesus emptied Himself, and in all that He did, self did not appear. He subordinated all things to the will of His Father." [16] If He Himself showed such humility and submission to His Father, how much more we need to.

Even God's spiritual giant Daniel said about himself, "My comeliness was turned in me into corruption" (Dan. 10:8, KJV) when in a vision he beheld the Son of God. And we will be compelled to say the same thing when we behold "Christ in His self-denial, His lowliness of heart." [17] For when we have a vision of what Christ is like, we will at the same time recognize what we are really like. And consequently, "the independence and self-supremacy in which we glory are seen in their true vileness as tokens of servitude to Satan." [18]

3. The blessing of experiencing poverty in spirit and meekness of heart in Christ creates an overwhelming thirst and hunger for even more of His righteousness. For His righteousness alone can truly satiate the hunger and quench the thirst of the human soul. Steadily feeding on His Word and drinking at His well of salvation causes us to grow into His similitude and perfection. Only that will make us "pure in heart," "peacemakers," and willing to suffer persecution for His sake. The blessed work of Christ in us will lead us, as sons and daughters of God, to see Him in the kingdom of heaven.

4. As children of our heavenly Father we become the "salt of the earth" (Matt. 5:13) as Christ's life first flavors our life. And we become the "light of the world" (verse 14) as our darkness becomes light in Him who said, "I am the light of the world" (John 8:12). Paul admonished the Ephesians to "walk as children of light" because "you were once darkness, but now you are light in the Lord" (Eph. 5:8).

Salt represents our sacred ministry of infiltrating our lost world as God's agents of salvation. Among many other wonderful things, salt represents God's unconditional love flowing through us to others. It is not calculated love parceled out to the supposedly deserving. For when God's love "fills the heart, it will flow out to others, not because of favors received from them, but because love is the principle of action. . . . Cherished in the heart, it sweetens the entire life and sheds its blessings upon all around. It is this, and this only, that can make us the salt of the earth." [19]

When it comes to being light in the world, apart from Christ we are total darkness without even one ray to brighten others. We are like the moon in relation to the sun. We simply let our lives reflect the brilliant beams of the Sun of righteousness to the extent that we behold His face and avail ourselves of His life-giving brightness. The moon does not struggle in order to shine, but it simply exposes itself to the bright sun.

As children of light, the disciples were called upon to "let your light so shine before men, that they may see your good works and glorify your Father in heaven" (Matt. 5:16). And that must always be our focus—looking fully into His wonderful face and not into our good works. It is *His* light that we reflect, and thus we must not draw attention to our own good works, but give the credit and glory to God. Yes, others will see our good works, for we cannot conceal them, but they are to be amazed at what God can do in spite of us, and not what *we* can do.

The reason others glorify our Father is that we come across as unaware of what we do, yet very conscious of *His* good work. Consequently, when they look at us they clearly see how prominent Christ is, and how obscured self is in comparison. The lesson of self-forgetfulness is one of the most valuable lessons for us to learn in our pursuit of spiritual maturity. For only in forgetting self can Christ be remembered.

Haddon Robinson, commenting about the face of Stephen shining like the face of angels at his martyrdom, sheds light on this crucial lesson of self-forgetfulness. "I doubt that Stephen ever attended a face-shining seminar. I'm confident that Stephen didn't even know that his face shone." Then he concludes that "people who live in the light are not conscious of their own light. . . . [They] are more conscious of their own darkness, of His grace, and of His light than they are of how much light they reflect. But they do shine, and groping people who see them find their way to God." [20]

5. In order that the disciples may be called the sons of their Father in heaven, Jesus told them: "Love your enemies, bless those who curse you, do good to those who hate you, and pray for those who

spitefully use you and persecute you" (verse 44). How is it ever possible that even the best of humanity can ever love in that way? Such love comes only from God, who is love, for while we were still His enemies He sent His only Son to die for us (see Rom. 5:8-10). God showers this kind of love on the undeserving as well as those we would consider the good (see Matt. 5:45).

As a priest prepared Ramón Narváez, the nineteenth-century prime minister of Spain, to meet his death, the priest asked him: "Does your Excellency forgive all your enemies?"

Narváez answered candidly and matter-of-factly: "I do not have to forgive my enemies. I have had them all shot." [21]

It is human nature to hate our enemies. And though we may not kill their bodies, we slay their minds and hearts. Even at best we ignore and avoid them. To genuinely love those who hate us calls for a righteousness that can only proceed from the loving heart of Christ. "Even sinners whose hearts are not utterly closed to God's Spirit will respond to kindness; while they may give hate for hate, they will also give love for love. But it is *only the Spirit of God that gives love for hatred.*" [22]

And Jesus perfectly practiced what He preached. He loved His enemies, blessed those who cursed Him, did good to those who hated Him, and prayed for those who persecuted Him. We can exhibit this kind of divine love only if we are born of God, reflecting Christ, and are walking in the Spirit. Only then can we indeed be sons of our heavenly Father (see verse 45). Such love permeates the entire Sermon on the Mount as the truest and purest motive for good works. In all the noble things that Jesus presented, genuine love was to be their only source.

As Jesus describes this kind of extraordinary love in Matthew 5:43-47, He sums it up in verse 48, the well-known admonition to be perfect even as our heavenly Father is. Jesus leaves us with an indissoluble link between love and perfection. Good works that flow out of genuinely loving motives lead to maturity or perfection in Christ.

"This perfect or wholehearted love is perfection in action," writes Hans LaRondelle. "This gospel perfection is the revival of the principles of perfect love as proclaimed by Moses and the prophets." [23] The manifestation of this kind of love that Paul writes about in 1 Corinthians 13 is the fulfillment of the law, or, we may say, Christian perfection. Notice what else Paul says in this regard. "Owe no one anything except to love one another, for he who loves another has fulfilled the law" (Rom. 13:8). Moreover, "Love does no harm to a neighbor; therefore love is the fulfillment of the law" (verse 10).

6. We can fulfill the law only from loving motives toward God and others. They always proceed from our focus on the person of Christ, and not from some ethical behavior or lofty ideal. Here is then the badge of being true sons and daughters of God. Here we find the key to Christian perfection: belonging to God's family as His loving and loyal sons and daughters, who represent Him in their daily lives.

This genuine love that embraces all people is the clearest sign that we are indeed born of God and members of God's family. For "to be kind to the unthankful and to the evil, to do good hoping for nothing again, is *the insignia of the royalty of heaven,* the sure token by which the children of the Highest reveal their high estate." [24]

The theme of being the loving and loyal children of our heavenly Father pervades Christ's sermon. We experience Christian perfection only in the context of becoming the genuine sons and daughters of God. "Blessed are the peacemakers, for they shall be *called sons of God*" (Matt. 5:9). And "Let your light so shine before men, that they may see your good works and *glorify your Father in heaven*" (verse 16). Moreover, "But I say to you, love your enemies, bless those who curse you, do good to those who hate you, . . . that you may *be sons of your Father in heaven*" (verses 44, 45).

It is essential that we always link our experience of being such sons and daughters of God with that of being perfect in the sphere of our human existence. For "to be 'children of your Father which is in heaven' (verse 45) is equivalent to being 'perfect, even as your Father which is in heaven is perfect' (verse 48)." [25] As she commented on verse 48, Ellen White emphasized the same essential link. "Jesus said, Be perfect as your Father is perfect. If you are the children of God you are partakers of His nature, and you cannot but be like Him. *Every child lives by the life of his father. If you are God's children, begotten by His Spirit, you live by the life of God.*" [26]

Notice that Christ concludes this section at the end of chapter 5 by referring to Christian perfection as the result of being true children of our heavenly Father. Not on the basis of varying circumstances, possible consequences, or of comparing our own performance with other people's performance, but on the basis of what our heavenly Father is like, and our family resemblance of Him. "Therefore you shall be perfect, just as your *Father in heaven is perfect*" (verse 48).

Consequently, we will never feel that we are good enough or sinless, or that our righteousness is adequate because it is better than the righteousness of others. But comparing our all-deficient perfection with Christ's all-sufficient perfection leads us to be meek, submissive, and desperately longing for Him and His righteousness. When we are born of our Father, it is normal to resemble Him in our lives. It is like when we say that something runs in the family, or that it is a family tradition.

Today we use the expression "chip off the old block" and "spitting image." There is a family likeness, certain characteristics that run in the family and draw others' attention to the parents whom we belong to and resemble. As others interact with us from day to day, do they see Christ manifested in us? Do we give them cause to remark that we have a likeness to our Father in heaven? Do they declare that we reflect the image of our Father, and that we indeed are, in a spiritual sense, "chips off the old block"?

---

[1] Sakae Kubo, *Calculated Goodness* (Nashville: Southern Pub. Assn., 1974), p. 38.

[2] Ellen G. White, *Patriarchs and Prophets* (Mountain View, Calif.: Pacific Press Pub. Assn., 1958), p. 45. (Italics supplied.)

[3] Edward Carter, *Spirituality for Modern Man* (South Bend, Ind.: Fides, 1971), p. 15.

[4] Samuel H. Miller, *The Life of the Church* (New York: Harper, 1953), pp. 46, 47.

[5] William Richardson, "The Unfavorite Text," *Adventist Review,* Oct. 14, 1993, p. 8.

[6] William Hamilton, *The Christian Man* (Philadelphia: Westminster Press, 1956), pp. 35, 17.

[7] *Ibid.,* p. 35.

[8] *Ibid.,* p. 17.

[9] Haddon W. Robinson, *The Christian Salt and Light Company* (Grand Rapids: Discovery House Publishers, 1988), p. 41.

[10] White, *Steps to Christ,* p. 58.

[11] ———, *Thoughts From the Mount of Blessing* (Washington, D.C.: Review and Herald Pub. Assn., 1956), p. 7.

[12] Cited in Hamilton, p. 76.

[13] White, *Christ's Object Lessons,* pp. 154, 159. (Italics supplied.)

[14] ———, *Thoughts From the Mount of Blessing,* p. 15.

[15] *Ibid.,* p. 16.

[16] *Ibid.,* p. 14.

[17] *Ibid.,* p. 15.

[18] *Ibid.*

[19] *Ibid.,* p. 38.

[20] Robinson, p. 106.

[21] Cited in Robinson, p. 174.

[22] White, *Thoughts From the Mount of Blessing,* p. 75. (Italics supplied.)

[23] Hans K. LaRondell, "The Biblical Idea of Perfection," In *Perfection: The*

Impossible Possibility (Nashville: Southern Pub. Assn., 1975), p. 118.

[24] White, *Thoughts From the Mount of Blessing,* p. 75. (Italics supplied.)

[25] *The SDA Bible Commentary,* vol. 5, p. 341.

[26] White, *Thoughts From the Mount of Blessing,* pp. 77, 78. (Italics supplied.)

CHAPTER

SIX

COMPLETE IN CHRIST—3

If a sheep were to fall into a mud puddle, what would he do? He would push, strain, and struggle until he got out of the mud. Why? Because it is not the nature of a sheep to want to stay stuck in the mud. But if a pig were to wander into that same mud puddle, he would wallow in it for hours because it is his nature to do so."[1]

Christ is our good shepherd, and we are His sheep. We trust Him and submit ourselves to Him as we follow Him into His pastures. But although He leads and sustains us, along the way we become the bruised to be bandaged, the broken to be bound up, and the sick to be strengthened.

Obviously sheep and pigs behave quite differently. Sheep may fall in a mud hole, but they want out. Pigs relish wallowing in it. We can understand such behavior in pigs, but why do the sheep of the Good Shepherd fall into mud puddles? Why do they falter, get bruised, broken, and lost? Why do they struggle with sin, self, and Satan? After all, aren't they all new creatures in Christ? Aren't they born of the Father and led by the Spirit, and thus the sons and daughters of God?

In the previous two chapters we considered the vital connection between being true children of God and Christian growth and perfection. The question naturally arises as to the extent of human perfection in relationship to God's perfection. What range of human spirituality may we reach in relationship to Christ's spirituality?

It should be clear that for us to be perfect on earth even as our Father in heaven is perfect does not imply *absolute* perfection. God alone is absolutely perfect without the slightest variance. It is a sweeping statement that we can never make of any being except the absolutely perfect God.

Even Adam's pre-Fall perfection was relative. Adam, the original man, came forth from the Creator's hands perfect in every possible way an unfallen being could have been made perfect. Even though from the very beginning he perfectly reflected the image and likeness of his perfect Maker, yet he was ever to advance to yet higher states of perfection throughout eternity while never reaching the absolute perfection of God. For God is and will always be God, and human beings are and will always be human.

Christ, the second Adam, possessed from eternity absolute perfection, precisely as does His Father. Although at His incarnation He took upon Himself our frail and weakened physical nature, yet morally and spiritually He remained God, conceived of the Holy Spirit. Even though He shared with us hunger, fatigue, suffering, and death, yet He never shared even our inclination to sin. And although He was made in the *likeness* (not *exactness*) of sinful humanity (Rom. 8:3), He was "holy, blameless, pure, set apart from sinners" (Heb. 7:26, NIV). He lived every moment in perfect oneness and undisturbed harmony in the perfect will of His Father.

This essential tension contains glorious news for us: Christ was like us, yet He remained, thankfully, unlike us. "He assumed our human nature—its likeness, but not sameness." [2] Our Saviour shared our suffering but never our sin, our pain but never our propensities to sin, our burdens but never our bent to evil, our temptations but never our transgressions, and He even shared in our death but never in our depravity. Christ was the God-Man—fully God to be our sinless Substitute and Saviour, and fully Man to be our indispensable Example and Intercessor.

However, we must resist the temptation to become obsessed with trying to comprehend the mystery of the Incarnation. For if we let ourselves get consumed with the incarnation of the Saviour, our focus shifts away from our incarnate Saviour. We do not find our hope and salvation in resolving the mystery of His incarnation, but in resolving to submit ourselves to our incarnate Saviour. As we delve into this awesome mystery, we tread on sacred ground. And in our spiritual journey, we always move in the direction of awesome and sacred mystery, but never fully apprehend or reach it.

Some seem to think that they have comprehended the sacred mystery, or at least have come close to it. They tend not to take a balanced and seasoned view of Christ's incarnation. Instead of always moving forward in sacred mystery, they stumble into the ditches of controversy and extremism, of overemphasizing either Christ's human nature or His divine nature. Such controversial extremism inevitably leads to despair and division among God's people, and negates the gospel of Christ in their lives.

Satan uses our obsession *with* the nature of Christ to divert our attention away *from* Christ. In his subtle deceptions he will use anything to replace Christ. Do we find ourselves discussing the nature of Christ as if it is more important than Christ Himself? We need to dwell much more on Christ Himself than the fathomless mystery of His divine-human nature. For only in beholding Him, His Person, do we become changed into His image. Ellen White sounded this note of caution: "Be careful, *exceedingly careful* as to how you dwell upon the human nature of Christ."[3]

Tragically we sometimes find it easier to fight over Christ than to focus on Him, to contest Christ than to contemplate Him. For His sake and ours, we must do away with anything that may distract us from our focus on and contemplation of Christ. Not only can the study of His nature lead us away from Him, so can even our study of His gospel. For studying His gospel should never shift our attention away from the Christ of the gospel. "We are not to praise the gospel, but praise Christ," Ellen White exhorts us. "We are not to worship the gospel, but the Lord of the gospel."[4]

In the same vein we also may say that it is futile to focus on the fruits of the Vine but not on Christ the Vine Himself. Not that being fruitful is not important, for indeed it is, but only in being connected to the Vine will we produce genuine fruits of righteousness. It is not a question of whether we should be fruitful or not, but a question of how Christ wants us to be fruitful. Therefore, let us shift the emphasis from stubbornly striving to reach absolute perfection to trustingly submitting ourselves to Christ, so that *He* may make us fruitful and transform us into His likeness. Focusing on the fruit itself, the extent of its perfection or imperfection, takes our minds away from our union with the Vine, the perfect fruit giver.

Paul emphasizes the beholding of Christ that results in our essential and progressive spiritual transformation. We do not try to be transformed in order to behold Christ—rather, we first behold Christ in order to be transformed. Listen to what the apostle says about the progressive nature of such transformation: "But we all, with unveiled face, *beholding* as in a mirror the glory of the Lord, are *being transformed* into the same image *from glory to glory,* just as by the Spirit of the Lord" (2 Cor. 3:18).

We have been listening to our young daughter practicing her violin for several years now. She loves playing it, and obviously she desires to improve her mastery of that fine musical instrument. Undeniably, she has made persistent progress, but not without some struggle and setbacks. She well knows that we accept and love her through all the struggle and success of her musical experience. And no matter what level she reaches, it is totally acceptable to us that she enjoys doing her best.

It is interesting to note that in spite of our joy and acceptance of her overall progress, and in spite of her persistent practice, she never feels that she has practiced or progressed quite enough. It motivates her to strive to play better. For perfecting the art of violin performance, or of any musical instrument, never ends even for the best virtuosos. Although we say practice makes perfect, there is always room to advance further than ever before.

Ellen White makes a striking statement: "Christ has made it possible for you to *practice His life.*" [5] We are not simply to practice some aspect of religion, but the very life of Christ itself. Just as in perfecting the playing of a musical instrument we become a part of and an extension of it, so also in practicing the life of Christ we become a part of and an extension of it. The crucial question we need to ask ourselves is whether we truly love Christ, and whether we put forth as much effort in practicing the life of Christ as we do in practicing a musical instrument or anything else we love.

We all know that athletes preparing to race in the Olympics will diligently practice the sport they love as though they would abandon everything for it. And if they do it all to win a prize of some fleeting human glory, how much more should we do it all to win the prize of eternal glory? Moreover, in our spiritual race of practicing the life of Christ, we have a sure Winner who is there in the race with us from beginning to end. And in "looking unto Jesus, the author and finisher of our faith," let us "lay aside every weight, and the sin which so easily ensnares us, and let us run with endurance the race that is set before us" (Heb.12: 2, 1).

Looking unto Jesus, who perfectly won the race for us in His own sphere, should be our only impetus as we strive to win the race in our own sphere. As the committed musician and the dedicated athlete seek perfection in what they do, so we too strive for perfection in our spiritual race. In His great love God sets high ideals before us, just as we place high ideals before our children whom we love. "God's ideal for His children is higher than the highest human thought can reach." [6]

However, we must keep in mind that He who admonishes "You shall therefore be holy, for I am holy" (Lev. 11:45) also urges us to "strive" for His holiness, which He wants to "share" with us (see Heb. 12:14, 10, RSV). "Never should he [the Christian] be satisfied with an empty profession. As God is holy in *His* sphere, so fallen man, through faith in Christ, is to be holy in *his* sphere." [7]

This sounds like what Christ exhorts us to do in Matthew 5:48— to be perfect as our Father in heaven is perfect. As His beloved sons and daughters, God wants us to share in His holiness and perfection. We also "may be perfect in *our* sphere, even as God is perfect in *His.*" [8] And in our experience we simply *reflect* His holiness and perfection. As part of His family, we "cannot but be like Him" because of the vital principle that "every child lives by the life of his father." [9]

Jack Blanco, in his paraphrase of this text, gets to the essence of what Jesus was trying to convey: "You need to be different and do what your heavenly Father does. He is gracious and kind to everyone, and you should do the same." [10] In years past people expressed their expectation that certain good family traits would continue in a family. People guarded more carefully the good name, honor, and reputation of their families. "He is a good man, he comes from a good family," friends would say. "She is gracious just like her mother."

A similar example comes from Christ's sermon on the mount when He tells us to be "the light of the world" (Matt. 5:14). Of course, we can never be that light in our world unless He, the light of the whole universe, becomes the source of all our light. We are total darkness without Him, and if we presume to have light without Him, we are simply deceiving ourselves. For "many who profess to have great light are walking in sparks of their own kindling." [11]

But thanks be to God that we become light in Christ's light, and thus may brighten wherever we are. "We are to be centers of light and blessing to our *little circle,* even as He is to the *universe.* We have nothing of ourselves, but the light of His love shines upon us, and we are to reflect its brightness." [12]

Likewise, "the ideal of Christian character is Christlikeness. As the Son of man was perfect in *His life,* so His followers are to be perfect in *their life.*" [13] Christlikeness is what true spirituality is all about, and it is the lofty ideal that we perpetually pursue. In His love and through His power we may become Christlike in every progressive stage of our spiritual development.

Ellen White sheds additional light on the spiritual process of coming ever closer to Christ the pattern, but never equaling that pattern. "He [Christ] is a perfect and holy example, given for us to *imitate.* We *cannot equal the pattern;* but we shall not be approved of God if we do not *copy* it and, *according to the ability* which God has given, *resemble* it." [14] She explains, furthermore, that compared to Christ the pattern, we are deficient even when doing our very best. "We cannot gain and possess the influence that He [Christ] had; but why should we not educate ourselves to come *just as near to the Pattern as it is possible for us to do?*" [15]

In as much as a newborn baby is perfect at every level of its physical growth, so in Christ we are to be perfect at every stage of our spiritual development. A 1-month-old baby can possess only the level of perfection or maturity that can occur in only one month of growth, and not that of the one-year stage. Likewise, we cannot say that a small green apple that had only a few weeks to develop at the beginning of the summer is not perfect simply because it does not look or taste like the ripe golden apple that we will harvest in the autumn. The small green apple is perfect for its stage of development, as the ripe golden one is perfect for its stage.

Using the example of progressive growth in a plant, Ellen White illustrates spiritual development and maturity. "As its [the plant's] growth is silent and imperceptible, but continuous, so is the development of the Christian life. At *every stage* of development our life may be *perfect;* yet if God's purpose for us is fulfilled, there will be *continual advancement.* Sanctification is the work of a *lifetime.*" [16]

Therein lies the essential tension: Yes, we may be perfect at every stage of our spiritual development, yet we will continually and throughout our lives advance toward further perfection. The former one is relative perfection that we can have as our experience at every stage of our development. The latter one is absolute perfection that we will for eternity advance toward, but only God perfectly possesses it.

Striving for or pursuing such a lofty ideal is nothing less and nothing more than seeking after the person of Christ Himself. But we must be careful that in pursuing the ideals of the Person, we do not overlook the ideal Person.

Sometimes we hear people casually say that they would be willing to give all in order to have a desired outcome. But when it comes down to it, are they really willing to give all? We say that we want Christ more than livelihood or even life itself, but are we really prepared to give our lives to possess Him? That is what it does take—a life for a life. We give Him our wretched life, and in exchange He gives us His perfect life. It is true, isn't it, that the more we have of Christ, the less things we desire? And by the same token, the less we have of Christ, the more things we covet.

Therefore, in pursuing the lofty ideals Christ has set before us, we must strive to apprehend the ideal Person Himself. Christ must be all in all for us. He must be our best and most throughout our spiritual journey of becoming more like Him. "It is Christ first and last and always. He is to be with us, not only at the beginning and the end of our course, but at *every step of the way*." [17] It is precisely here that we "need to watch, to strive, to pray, that nothing may entice us to *choose* another master." [18] Our real problem at the core is not experiencing spiritual maturity, but substituting another master for the Master.

Another master can mean dwelling on self and analyzing its perfections and imperfections. Consequently, this leads us to compare our spiritual status with other human beings instead of focusing on and comparing ourselves with Christ. Thus we find ourselves critical of others, and discouraged ourselves. The archdeceiver knows that centering everything on Christ is the secret of spiritual growth and maturity. That is why it is Satan's "constant effort to keep the attention diverted from the Saviour, and thus prevent the union and communion of the soul with Christ." [19]

Dwelling on Christ in our spiritual journey is much more than merely achieving a goal—it is a whole way of life. An intriguing Toyota automobile commercial once caught my attention: "Striving for excellence is not a goal but a way of life," it declared. The message of Toyota is clear: We live to ever be striving to perfect our product, and no matter how close we come to this, we will never sit on our laurels and feel that we have arrived.

We live in a goal-oriented society. A goal has a sense of finality attached to it. However, striving for excellence has no finality, because it is actually an endless way of life. Our continuous persual after excellence helps us to apprehend it more and more, yet we will never fully reach it.

If the slogan of "striving for excellence is not a goal but a way of life" applies to Toyota engineers as they design a car, then it infinitely much more applies to those of us seeking the excellence of becoming Christlike, not as a static one-time goal, but as a dynamically continuous way of life. The very fact that continual growth is essential for our spiritual vitality clearly indicates our constant need for progress in spiritual perfection.

We may also refer to our progress in perfection as sanctification, which "is not the work of a moment, an hour, a day, but of a *lifetime.*" And such sanctification is "not gained by a happy flight of feeling, but is the result of *constantly* dying to sin, and *constantly* living for Christ." Furthermore, "so long as Satan reigns, we shall have self to subdue, besetting sins to overcome; so long as life shall last, there will be no stopping place, no point which we can reach and say, I have fully attained." [20]

We could also describe sanctification, or development in spiritual perfection, as character building. And such character building is also "the work, not of a day, nor of a year, but of a *lifetime.* The struggle for conquest over self, for holiness and heaven, is a *lifelong* struggle." [21]

Even the great spiritual giants of the Bible, those who lived nearest to God, never felt that they had fully attained complete perfection. For example, Paul, the champion of Christ caught up to the third heaven, declares: "Not that I have already attained, or am already perfected; but I press on, that I may lay hold of that for which Christ Jesus has also laid hold of me. Brethren, I do not count myself to have apprehended; but one thing I do, forgetting those things which are behind and reaching forward to those things which are ahead, I press toward the goal for the prize of the upward call of God in Christ Jesus" (Phil. 3:12-14).

Every time we think that we have apprehended that which has already apprehended us, Christ calls us to come up higher still. He appeals to us to grasp Him more fully still. This is the exciting challenge and joyful spiritual adventure that lies perpetually before us. Not only in the present world do we ever seek to draw closer and closer to God, but we will ever continue to do so in the world to come. "Heaven is a *ceaseless approaching* to God through Christ. The longer we are in the heaven of bliss, the more and still more of glory will be opened to us; and the more we know of God, the more intense will be our happiness." [22]

A German airline company adopted a succinct slogan that simply states: "Lufthansa: A passion for perfection." An almost identical slogan comes from the makers of Lexus cars: "Relentless pursuit of perfection." Both slogans cleverly imply that perfection is not a precise point to be arrived at, but a perpetual and relentless pursuit. It should be our ever-prevailing passion as we constantly look to Christ the perfecter of our faith. But this holy passion and pursuit is not so much after perfection, as it is after Christ the person of perfection.

Notice how Paul, in Philippians 3, links what he has said about pressing toward the prize in Christ with Christian maturity, or perfection, in verse 15: "Therefore let us, as many as are mature, have this mind." Or as the New International Version puts it, "take such a view of things"—the things that Paul has just alluded to in verses 12-14.

Then immediately following, in verse 16, Paul defines Christian maturity as a progressive and not absolute attainment: "Nevertheless, to *the degree* that we have already attained, let us walk by the same rule, let us be of the same mind." Paul recognized obvious degrees of attainment in our spiritual walk with Christ. Through the indwelling of the Spirit, and according to the abilities that God has given us, let us do our best in pressing on to reach higher and still higher levels of spiritual growth.

Paul never boasts of his own attainments, but always those of Christ. And that is because he always dwelled on the perfection of Christ, and consequently saw his own utter unworthiness. The "attitude of Paul is the attitude that every follower of Christ should take as he urges his way onward in the strife for the immortal crown." [23]

To dwell on Christ and to boast of His attainments, as Paul did, is the only thing that gives us courage, hope, and balance in our Christian walk. And this does not just apply to the so-called legalists or perfectionists, but to all sincere and dedicated Christians as well. The latter may become so scrupulous in striving to live a sanctified life that they focus on self, and not their Sanctifier. They may dwell on their own achievements or lack of them, and not on His all-sufficient achievements. Thus they may sadly become separated from their

Saviour, who is their only real sanctification.

"Many who are *really conscientious*, and who *desire to live for God*, he [Satan] too often leads to dwell upon their own faults and weaknesses, and thus by separating from Christ, he hopes to gain the victory. We should not make self the center, and indulge anxiety and fear as to whether we shall be saved. . . . Talk and think of Jesus. Let self be lost in Him. . . . If you will leave yourself in His hands, He will bring you off more than conqueror through Him that has loved you." [24]

Neither Paul nor any of the prophets and apostles—even the greatest among them—ever claimed full spiritual attainment. Those who lived the closest to God, and faithfully followed after His heart, never boasted that they had finished their pursuit of spiritual perfection. The nearer they came to Christ, the clearer they saw His perfection, and the more they were convinced of their imperfections. That is why they felt no confidence in their own righteousness, but constantly sought Christ's perfect righteousness.

Were they then less pure, less righteous, or less perfect than they were before by drawing ever closer to Christ? No, not at all. On the contrary, they were more so. Why? Because they became more willing to let God show them the areas of their lives that needed improvement. They did not become more sinful, but because of their close communion with God they more clearly recognized their true nature. Convicted ever more of His righteousness, yet convinced ever less of their own, they increasingly trusted in what He alone could do in their lives. It was a sure sign of their advancement in sanctification—that self was on the decrease and God was on the increase.

Earlier I shared with you the pain and progress of our daughter's violin playing. Recently I read an account of a music teacher trying to learn a new instrument, the cello. In her experience, Margarita Merriman discovered many similarities between her "musical struggles" and her "Christian aspirations." [25] Despite her continuing struggles, she was determined not to give up, and as she made the necessary sacrifices, she increasingly recognized her improving skill.

After diligently practicing a certain cello piece, Merriman's teacher pronounced her performance "very good." However, both knew that her performance still needed a lot of improvement. Why, then, did the cello teacher say that it was very good? Was the teacher simply pretending? No, she "probably meant that for me to undertake such a challenge was an accomplishment," Merriman recounts, "and that I played it as well as could be expected at my level of expertise."[26]

"In music one never attains," Merriman comments as she reflects on Paul's words in Philippians 3:12-14. "A serious musician always presses onward toward an unobtainable goal—perfection. Any musician who might brashly claim to have attained perfection would be scorned by others in the profession."[27]

She is right and encouraging when she testifies that she is not afraid of the judgment, because she is confident that just as her teacher said that she was "very good," God will pronounce the "well done, thou good and faithful servant" "if in my heart I have determined daily to do my best with His help"[28]

---

[1] Richard Lee, *Issues of the Heart* (Dallas: Word Publishers, 1990), p. 177.

[2] Gulley, *Christ Our Substitute*, p. 37.

[3] *The SDA Bible Commentary,* Ellen G. White Comments, vol. 5, p. 1128. (Italics supplied.)

[4] *Ibid.,* vol. 7, p. 907.

[5] White, *This Day With God* (Washington, D.C.: Review and Herald Pub. Assn., 1979), p. 204. (Italics supplied.)

[6] White, *The Desire of Ages,* p. 311.

[7] ———, *The Acts of the Apostles* (Mountain View, Calif.: Pacific Press Pub. Assn., 1911), p. 559. (Italics supplied.)

[8] ———, *Thoughts From the Mount of Blessing,* p. 77. (Italics supplied.)

[9] *Ibid.,* p. 78.

[10] Jack Blanco, *The New Testament—A Devotional Paraphrase to Stimulate Faith and Growth* (Collegedale, Tenn.: College Press, 1990).

[11] White, *Reflecting Christ,* p. 40.

[12] ———, *My Life Today* (Washington, D.C.: Review and Herald Pub. Assn., 1952), p. 38.

[13] White, *The Desire of Ages,* p. 311. (Italics supplied.)

[14] ———, *Testimonies* (Mountain View, Calif.: Pacific Press Pub. Assn., 1948), vol. 2, p. 549. (Italics supplied.)

[15] *Ibid.,* p. 618. (Italics supplied.)

[16] White, *Christ's Object Lessons,* p. 65. (Italics supplied.)

[17] White, *Steps to Christ,* p. 69. (Italics supplied.)

[18] *Ibid.,* p. 72.

[19] *Ibid.,* p. 71.

[20] White, *The Acts of the Apostles,* pp. 560, 561. (Italics supplied.)

[21] ———, *The Ministry of Healing* (Mountain View, Calif.: Pacific Press Pub. Assn., 1942), p. 452. (Italics supplied.)

[22] ———, *The Desire of Ages,* p. 331. (Italics supplied.)

[23] ———, *The Acts of the Apostles,* p. 562.

[24] ———, *Steps to Christ,* pp. 71, 72. (Italics supplied.)

[25] Margarita Merriman, "Meditation of a Cellist," *Adventist Review,* Nov. 11, 1993, p. 11.

[26] *Ibid.,* p. 12.

[27] *Ibid.,* p. 11.

[28] *Ibid.,* p. 12.

COMPLETE IN CHRIST—4

A man enjoyed strolling along the beach collecting small seashells carelessly flung by the waves into the shifting sand. While retrieving his shells from the sands and waves, he found himself distracted by one that had settled on a huge rock nearby. Wanting it for his collection, he reached with his hand to retrieve it, but could not because it was stuck to the rock. Although he pulled at it with both hands, try as he would, he simply could not pry it loose from the grip of the rock. Apparently it was as impossible to dislodge it as to dislodge the rock itself. They were indeed immovable.

Probably that huge rock was even bigger than what showed above the surface. Perhaps a vast mountain lurked beneath the surface of the sand. Jesus Christ is the Rock of Ages—solid, deep, lofty, vast, eternal, and immovable. In comparison with Him, we are stones, pebbles, shells—shifting and unstable. We can never become immovable unless we first become embedded into the Rock. There is no way we can be the Rock, but we can cling to Him. By tenaciously adhering to Him we become one with Him. Christ told Paul that His strength was "made perfect in weakness." Thus the apostle could testify that "when I am weak, then I am strong" (2 Cor. 12:9, 10).

Look at the life of the apostle Peter. We can say that this unstable *petros* (stone) learned along the way to cling to the solid *Petra* (Rock). It was a miraculous process accomplished only by Christ's stalwart support and Peter's submission. The disciple learned his most valuable lessons of submission in those areas he had previously felt most confident in. Peter sincerely felt that his love and loyalty to

Christ were unquestionable. He thought he was prepared to go any-where with his beloved Master, even to laying down his life for His sake if need be.

Yet he denied Christ three times (Luke 22:33, 34, 54-62). Catching a glimpse of Christ's sorrowful face full of sympathy and forgiveness, he wept bitterly for betraying his Best Friend. And in his humbled heart he desired more than anything else to please Him, and longed to have another opportunity to prove himself to Him.

Earlier in his relationship with Christ, Peter had sometimes let himself be tossed by the waves of circumstances until out of discour-agement and despair he had gone back to his fishing trade. But even there he learned a valuable lesson in fishing, an area that he had thought himself an expert in. Luke 5 records that he spent all night doing his utmost best to catch some fish, yet came up with nothing. Not only Peter, but anyone who has done his or her utmost at what he or she knows best only to experience total failure, would have been greatly disappointed.

But such utter failure aids our spiritual life. For if we fail at our best, we will then sense that our only hope lies in Jesus. We begin to distrust ourselves and to reach beyond ourselves to trust Him. That trust was evident in Peter's obedience to Christ's command to again lower his nets. Although His order did not make much sense under the circumstances, Peter's trust and love for Christ caused him to submissively say "nevertheless at Your word I will let down the net" (Luke 5:5).

Overwhelmed by Christ's great power, holiness, and love, and realizing that even his utmost best can never become a substitute for His Master's best, Peter leaves the great catch of fish and throws him-self at His knees, crying, "Depart from me, for I am a sinful man, O Lord!" (verse 8). *The Living Bible* puts it this way: "Oh, sir, please leave us—I'm too much of a sinner for you to have around."

Certainly Peter hoped that Jesus would not leave him, yet he felt unworthy in His presence. It was as if he were confessing, "Lord, how can You stand being around some unworthy person like me! But where else would I go? And You have eternal life. I need to stay close to You. Leave me, but please don't leave me!" Commenting on this encounter, Ellen White wrote: "Peter exclaimed, 'Depart from me; for I am a sinful man;' yet he *clung* to the feet of Jesus, feeling that he *could not be parted* from Him." [1]

He threw himself before the mercy of the Saviour because he experienced this essential and holy tension between his utter trust in Christ and his utter distrust of self. We should never face self-distrust alone, but must always experience it along with Christ-trust. How can anyone be lost experiencing this holy tension? Remember the story of the father who beseeched Jesus to heal his son? He too knew such tension.

Sensing his inadequacy when Jesus asked him about believing, he burst into tears, throwing himself at His mercy with the cry "Lord, I believe; help my unbelief!" (Mark 9:24). Commenting on the father's experience, Ellen White gives these heartening words full of hope: "Let these souls, in their helpless unworthiness, cast themselves upon the mercy of their compassionate Saviour. Look not to self, but to Christ. . . . Cast yourself at His feet with the cry 'Lord, I believe; help thou mine unbelief.' You can *never perish while you do this—never.*" [2]

It comforts us to know that Jesus understands how we regard Him in our hearts. He discerns clearly our inward motives, and His heart is profoundly touched when He sees that our greatest desire is to love Him and be with Him. That we will let absolutely nothing and no one come before Him. That, in spite of ourselves, we yearn to cling to Him, follow Him, and be more like Him. Isn't this really what it means to be a devoted disciple of Christ?

Dietrich Bonhoeffer, the great German theologian and Christian martyr, definitely knew what it meant to be a devoted follower of Jesus Christ. "When we are called to follow Christ, we are summoned to an *exclusive attachment to His person,*" he wrote. "Discipleship means *adherence to Christ.*" [3]

Let us again look at how Peter adhered to Christ. During the ordinance of foot washing just prior to Christ's death, he once more felt so unworthy to be in Christ's presence that he emphatically refused to allow Him to wash his feet. "You will never wash my feet," he protested.

However, the picture changed when he heard his beloved Master say something about the disciple not having a part with Him. Because whatever jeopardized Peter's relationship with Christ greatly alarmed him, he quickly overreacted, begging Him to wash not only his feet but his hands and his head as well. Although he often stumbled, in his heart Peter so prized his relationship with Christ that he was ready to submit to whatever it took to make sure he always had a part with Him.

John experienced this holy tension in the presence of His loving and holy Lord. This apostle of love and holiness, who perhaps more than anyone else was close to Christ and exemplified Christlikeness, keenly sensed his unworthiness in the presence of His Master. "The apostle [John] followed his Saviour so closely, and had such a sense of the purity and exalted holiness of Christ, that his own character appeared, in contrast, exceedingly defective."[4]

Even as he spent his final days on the isle of Patmos, he continued to feel that holy tension. Catching a glimpse of his glorified Lord "was enough to cause him to fall down as one dead."[5] Here is the personal application that we glean from John's life of continuous sanctification. His feelings, so evident in the above statements, "will *ever* be the feelings of those who know *best* their Lord and Master. The more closely they contemplate the life and character of Jesus, the more deeply will they feel their own sinfulness, and the less will they be disposed to claim holiness of heart or to boast of their sanctification."[6]

Our own spiritual journeys with our Lord teach us that the experience of Peter and John is true. It is a spiritual fact that the "closer you come to Jesus, the more faulty you will appear in your own eyes; for your vision will be clearer, and your imperfections will be seen in broad and distinct contrast to His perfect nature."[7] While it seems paradoxical that the more we see our Saviour, the more we see our sins, nevertheless, it is true.

But in what way is it true? How can it be explained? Seeing more clearly our sinfulness does not mean we have become more sinful, but that we appreciate more profoundly Christ's perfection. "A view of our sinfulness *drives us to Him* who can pardon; and when the soul, realizing its helplessness, *reaches out after Christ, He will reveal Himself in power.* The more our sense of need *drives us to Him* and to the Word of God, the more exalted views we shall have of His character, and the *more fully we shall reflect His image.*"[8]

Moreover, in this very experience of reflecting more of His image, we also acquire additional growth and maturity. That in turn reveals to us shortcomings that have been there all along but we had not previously noticed. We discern more clearly now our hidden sins and our sure need of our Saviour's forgiveness. "There will be a *continual* reaching out of the soul after God, a *continual,* earnest, heartbreaking confession of sin and humbling of the heart before Him. At *every* advance step in our Christian experience our *repentance will deepen.* We shall know that our sufficiency is in Christ alone"[9]

Thus this essential tension of trusting the Saviour more and trusting self less is precisely what leads us to becoming increasingly more like Christ. Edward Heppenstall puts it well when he explains that "it is not the most imperfect Christian who feels imperfection most but the Christian who is daily becoming more like Christ."[10]

But the spiritual consequences are vastly different when we become absorbed in outward rather than inward righteousness. It is not a question of how hard we work, but rather a question of doing the right work. Nor is it an issue of how far we go, but of whether we are going in the right direction. "When we set our own standard of external righteousness, we are capable of any evil," Haddon Robinson argues. But on the other hand, "when we are filled with His righteousness, no good is too great."[11]

Martin Weber argues that even the devil's devoted disciples can experience a counterfeit victory over sin. Is this because Satan, all of a sudden, decided to scorn sin? Of course not. In his deadly deception, he offers a clever counterfeit for every good gift from God. If he cleverly counterfeits even Jesus, and if his evil ministers transform themselves into apostles of righteousness (2 Cor. 11:13-15), why wouldn't he, then, counterfeit victory over sin? He subtly does this in order to "lure us away from the cross so that we trust in our own character attainments and thus forfeit salvation (see Gal. 5:4)."[12]

How may we know how far from or how near to Christ we are? The more we look sanctified from our own perspective, the further away we are actually from Christ, and the less sanctified we deem ourselves, the nearer to Him we are. The ones who belong to the latter group, who are sanctified in Christ, "will not set up their own opinion as a standard of right and wrong. They are not bigoted or self-righteous."[13]

Of course, the opposite is true of those who appear sanctified in their own eyes. They set up themselves as final arbiters of truth, and you had better watch out if in some way you do not agree with their opinions. They tend to be analytical, intolerant, narrow-minded, and chronically critical. With a misguided sense of righteous indignation, they seem to enjoy putting others down whom they judge as less holy than themselves. They do not project much love, mercy, kindness, joy, peace, or hope.

Regrettably, the fruits of self have replaced the fruit of the Spirit. "Some who *profess* to be servants of Christ have so long cherished the *demon* of unkindness that they seem to love the unhallowed element and to take pleasure in speaking words that *displease* and *irritate.*" [14]

However, when the Holy Spirit leads us to discern more and more of our sins, He also drives us to increasingly depend on Him. Therefore, we need not slip back into doubt, despondency, and despair. Here we must be very careful. Throughout our spiritual journey, we as the children of God "shall *often* have to bow down and *weep* at the feet of Jesus because of our shortcomings and mistakes, but we are not to be discouraged. Even if we are overcome by the enemy, we are not cast off, not forsaken and rejected of God." [15]

Not only will we bow down and weep because we recognize our own imperfections and unworthiness in the presence of our all-perfect and all-worthy Saviour, but even "*at times* a deep sense of our unworthiness will send a *thrill* of terror through the soul, but this is *no evidence* that God has changed toward us, or we toward God." [16] Therefore, we "should by faith grasp the hand of Christ, and trust Him as fully in the darkness as in the light." [17]

The "bowing down," "the weeping," and the "thrill of terror," although momentarily frightening, can drive us to the arms of Christ. Our feelings often lead us to think that either God or ourselves must have changed in our relationship to each other, but that is not true. Remember, we must never base our trust on our feelings or even on our own faith, but in Christ Himself and in Him alone. Convicted of our helplessness, yet convinced of His helpfulness, we constantly cling to Him so that He may reflect more of His image in us. "Nothing is apparently more *helpless,* yet really more *invincible,* than the soul that feels its *nothingness* and relies *wholly* on the merits of the Saviour." [18]

Kit Watts's apt illustration of erasers is quite helpful here. "There's theology in an eraser," she writes. "We try not to make mistakes, but we do." [19] Whenever we are writing something (a letter, for instance), we don't intend to make mistakes. And it is true that the more we practice writing, the less mistakes we will make. But sometimes, no matter how experienced we become in writing, we still do something wrong. Of course, that should not discourage us to the extent that we stop writing all together. We simply stay the course and do our best, grateful that erasers exist to remove our mistakes when needed.

Even now, while typing these words on my computer, I recognize that I still need to take care despite the fact that I am doing my best to write properly. However, I do not waste my energy brooding over that—rather I am thankful for the progress the Lord has helped me to make so far. And I am certain that if I stay put—one hour, one day at a time—things will eventually work out.

In striving to grow more and more into the likeness of Christ, even when doing our utmost best, we sometimes stumble. But we should not be discouraged, for we are walking in His way. The Christian life is not so much a goal as a way of walking and living with Christ. He is indeed our way of life, and as we walk in that way we sometimes make missteps—we stumble and fall. However, we must not wallow in our mistakes, but we are to look up to our Saviour, who lovingly bends over us with outstretched arms, greatly desiring to pick us up so that we may continue our walk with Him.

Christ is the good shepherd—not an exacting and cruel judge who relishes counting and marking down any misstep we make. He even sees in our problems potential spiritual progress. Taking the long look, He discerns our potential and detects the trend of our lives instead of becoming fixated with our sporadic stumblings. "The character is revealed, not by occasional good deeds and occasional misdeeds, but by the tendency of the habitual words and acts." [20]

When practicing a piece on a musical instrument, some well-meaning perfectionists will, whenever they make a mistake, go back all the way to the beginning instead of pushing ahead. Others, as they play a piece for us, wince and fret over any imperfection they may commit. Unfortunately, this often disheartens the musician as well as the audience.

Margarita Merriman, whom we cited in the previous chapter, suggests helpful spiritual insights from her rich experience of teaching music. After joining Paul in aptly urging us to follow after Christ and forget the past, she explains: "If in my practicing I were to stop at each imperfectly tuned interval, I would never reach the end of the etude or composition. Especially in public performance, a musician must not let a slip interrupt the flow. . . . In performance, to brood over a mishap is to court disaster." [21]

It should encourage us to know that Christ is there with us, leading the way when we slip and stumble in our spiritual walk. Instead of brooding over our miserable missteps, we must dwell on our merciful Master. Let our gaze into the face of our compassionate Companion be followed by the reaching out of our hand, and His hand will hold ours with a firm grip that will not let go. And grasping His loving and powerful hand, let us confidently repeat with the apostle Paul that "I know whom I have believed and am persuaded that He is able to keep what I have committed to Him until that Day" (2 Tim. 1:12).

In our relentless pursuit of perfection, let us be certain that we place our emphasis on perfecting our relationship with Christ rather than on our own human perfection. The apostle Paul declared to the Corinthians: "For I determined not to know anything among you except Jesus Christ and Him crucified" (1 Cor. 2:2). "There is nothing there apart from the personal relationship," Chambers comments. "Paul was devoted to a Person, not to a cause. He was absolutely Jesus Christ's, he saw nothing else, he lived for nothing else." [22]

We must focus only on our devotion to Christ and our relentless pursuit after Him. Christ, whom we trust to keep what we have committed to Him. The One who is able to keep us from falling, and He who is able to present us faultless before His presence (Jude 24). This is what Chambers refers to as "the discipline of spiritual tenacity." [23]

He explains that such tenacity "is more than endurance, it is endurance combined with the absolute certainty that what we are looking for is going to transpire." He further clarifies that "tenacity is more than hanging on, which may be but the weakness of being too afraid to fall off. Tenacity is the supreme effort of a man refusing to believe that his hero is going to be conquered." [24]

Looking with love and confidence to the Author and Finisher of our faith, and heroically clinging to Him, we refuse to accept that we will be anything but victorious in our victorious Hero. "Who shall separate us from the love of Christ? Shall tribulation, or distress, or persecution, or famine, or nakedness, or peril, or sword?" No, never! For "in all these things we are more than conquerors through Him who loved us" (Rom. 8:35, 37).

Such spiritual tenacity does not automatically mean that we will lead a rosy Christian life, however. I knew a fellow student in my college days who always smiled, at least whenever I ran into him. And when he caught me not smiling, he would swiftly remind me that a real Christian should always be happy. His attitude used to puzzle me and make me feel guilty for not managing to be the constantly smiling and happy Christian I needed to be.

Is a genuine Christian someone who is always smiling and

happy, and who never gets down or discouraged? Does such a Christian, in sincerely seeking to be more like Christ, ever become disappointed or unhappy? Yes, genuine Christians sometimes do. It is a part of their spiritual struggle, and a part of the process of spiritual growing and maturing. The fact that such Christians are not always happy is no proof that they are not being sanctified. Sanctification in Christ is not instantaneous, but a process that in this life continues until the day Christ appears, or till the day we die.[25]

"Darkness and discouragement will *sometimes* come upon the soul and threaten to overwhelm us, but we should not cast away our confidence. We must keep the eye fixed on Jesus, *feeling or no feeling*. We should seek to faithfully perform every known duty, and then *calmly rest* in the promises of God."[26]

Moreover, as we seek to be faithful to God in doing our best for Him, "no effort should be made to rein the mind up to a certain intensity of emotion. We may not feel today the peace and joy which we felt yesterday; but we should by faith grasp the hand of Christ, and trust Him as fully in the darkness as in the light."[27]

It is vital that we constantly remind ourselves that spiritual growth is sometimes a grueling effort, and that pursuing perfection can produce pain. "We are to grow daily in spiritual loveliness. We shall *fail often* in our efforts to copy the divine pattern. . . . But we are not to be discouraged; we are to pray more fervently, believe more fully, and try again with more steadfastness to grow into the likeness of our Lord."[28] Furthermore, "He [Christ] is a perfect and holy example, given for us to imitate. We *cannot equal the pattern;* but we shall not be approved of God if we do not copy it and, *according* to the *ability* which God has given, resemble it."[29]

While Ellen White's observation is extremely realistic, yet at the same time it kindles our hope that we can please God. Realistic because we cannot *equal* the pattern (Christ)—not even perfect angels can. For if we could equal such a pattern we would be God, and that is absolutely preposterous. Also, Ellen White's statement is hopeful. It tells us that as we trust Christ and distrust self, He can work in us until we *copy* and *resemble* Him *according* to our particular God-given abilities.

We all have our individual abilities, and all that God asks of us is to do our best in beholding and resembling His Son to the extent of those capabilities. Our understanding heavenly Father takes the particular circumstances of each person into consideration. He knows that although we love Him and do our best to please Him in all things, we still stumble in some things. How does He then relate to our failings under such circumstances?

We need to be grateful that our gracious God looks at our heart, He discerns our spirit, and He considers our disposition. Listen to these assuring words: "When it is in the heart to obey God, when efforts are put forth to this end, Jesus accepts this disposition and effort as man's best service, and He makes up for the deficiency with His own divine merit." [30] Moreover, this is how He becomes our righteousness: "Christ looks at the spirit, and when He sees us carrying our burden with faith, His perfect holiness atones for our shortcomings. *When we do our best,* He becomes our righteousness." [31]

But we *must* make sure that we are clothed with the garment of His righteousness, that He *indeed* becomes our righteousness. This alone is how we become complete in Him. We must have no confusion or illusion in this all-important matter. "When we *submit* ourselves to Christ, the heart is *united* with His heart, the will is *merged* in His will, the mind becomes *one* with His mind, the thoughts are brought into *captivity* to Him; *we live His life.* This is what it *means* to be clothed with the garment of His righteousness." [32]

Sadly, though, while doing our best for our perfect God is good enough for Him, it often is not good enough for ourselves or others. Sometimes we are perhaps harder on ourselves and others than God is. That is why it is much better to be thrown upon the marvelous mercy of God than upon the mercy of other people. Why not, then, be more patient with ourselves and others? After all, God is not through with us or them yet.

I know of parents who are so achievement-oriented with their children that they forget to value them simply for who they are. Perhaps to compensate for their own insecurities or for what they did not accomplish in their own lives, they persistently push their children beyond their human abilities. And they accept or reject their sons and daughters on the basis of what they perceive as their achievement or lack of it. But, gratefully, our heavenly Father regards us in a vastly different way.

Former president Jimmy Carter attended the U.S. Naval Academy. Once he had to go to the office of his professor, Admiral Hyman Rickover, for an evaluation interview. Young Carter felt confident as he stepped in Rickover's office, for he had a good academic record.

"How do you stand in your class?" Rickover pointedly asked.

"Fifty-nine, out of 800, sir," Carter proudly replied.

"Did you do your best?" the admiral retorted.

"No, sir," came back Carter's candid response.

"Why not?" his professor countered.

"Why not my best?" was the haunting question that dominated and inspired Jimmy Carter's life.

As a student I always tried to do my best in school. If I did my best to prepare for a test, yet still got a B, I was not dissatisfied. However, if on occasion I did not do my best beforehand yet luckily I got an A, I felt dissatisfied because I had not done my part to the best of my ability.

One young man told me that he was ready to give up on doing his best in his studies despite the fact that he has been doing quite well so far. In fact, he was getting all A's except for the one B. Bewildered, I asked him why he wanted to give up, especially considering his excellent academic record. He responded with a sigh of resignation, saying that he could never please his father no matter how hard he tried, and wondered what was the use of trying anyway.

For years his perfectionistic father had rarely affirmed his son's excellent overall academic performance. Unfortunately, the man had then focused on the B and apparently overlooked all the A's, telling his son that he did not want to see such a low grade the next time around. This exacting earthly father gave his poor son the impression that academic achievement came first before the son himself. You can imagine what kind of picture this student had of his heavenly Father. How often we forget that people live by hope and affirmation.

Why do we really strive for sanctification? Is it in order to impress an exacting God? Is it to bask in the admiration of others? Or is it rather to please our loving God because we are already saved in Christ? The first reason brings only despondency and despair. It is a dead-end road that will lead us nowhere except to certain shipwreck. The true way leads us up to Christ, our only hope. Where else can we go? And He has eternal life! His way is the way of willing submission, hope, spiritual growth, and eternal life.

When we constantly behold the beauty and excellence of Christ, sin becomes hateful to us. And when He possesses our hearts, we long to live His life, we relish being in His presence, and we yearn to increasingly reflect His image. Then we do not consider sin lightly, but we look at it in disgust as causing the most painful hurt possible to the Saviour we love.

How can we but utterly despise sin when it undermines our loving relationship with Him! How can we ever cherish sin when we cherish our Saviour! That is just impossible. "When we are clothed with the righteousness of Christ, we shall have no relish for sin; for Christ will be working with us. We may make mistakes, but we will hate the sin that caused the sufferings of the Son of God." [33]

Being clothed in the robe of Christ's righteousness is something wonderfully real and tangible. It is the totality of our lives wrapped up in His life. For when we are in Christ, He becomes for us "wisdom from God—and righteousness and sanctification and redemption" (1 Cor. 1:30). Because "when we submit ourselves to Christ, the heart is united with His heart, the will is merged in His will, the mind becomes one with His mind, the thoughts are brought into captivity to Him; *we live His life.*" [34]

Thus when we learn to live *His* life and not *ours,* He becomes all and everything to us. Not only is He our Redeemer; He Himself actually becomes our redemption. And He is not just our sanctifier, He Himself becomes our sanctification. Watchman Nee argues that for Christ to become all in all to us, we must not be satisfied to experience Him only as the doer of an act, but we must mature beyond that to experience Him as that act itself. We, therefore, must experience Christ's acts *and* His own self. [35]

"To know Him as 'er' is primary knowledge," Nee writes, but "to know Him as 'tion' is further and deeper knowledge." [36] God is trying to remove all things—secular as well as spiritual—and replace them with the Person of Christ. Prior to our conversion worldly things took Christ's place. After conversion we face the danger of spiritual things occupying His place. That is why God wants to destroy anything—whether secular or spiritual—potentially dangerous in our lives so that He can then build up Christ there. [37]

Nee is convinced that there is absolutely nothing impersonal in the religion of Christ. Everything is inescapably related to something personal. "Our patience is not a thing, ours is a Person—our sanctification is not an experience, ours is a Man—our justification is not a thing, ours is a Personality—our righteousness is not a behavior, ours is a Being." [38]

We become complete in Christ only as He possesses us and as we cleave to Him—only as He lives out His life in our lives. As we become absorbed in appreciating and appropriating Jesus, we sense our desperate need to cling to Him as our only hope. "The soul who sees Jesus by faith repudiates his own righteousness. He sees himself as *incomplete*, his repentance insufficient, his strongest faith but feebleness, his most costly sacrifice as meager, and he sinks in humility at the foot of the cross."[39]

But listen, "a voice speaks to him from the oracles of God's Word. In amazement he hears the message, 'Ye are complete in him' (Col. 2:10). Now all is at rest in his soul. No longer must he strive to find some worthiness in himself, some meritorious deed by which to gain the favor of God."[40] Nevertheless, few of us readily accept and appreciate the great news from God that we are complete in Christ. Ellen White concludes her comments on Colossians 2:10 by exclaiming at our hesitancy to appreciate such great news: "How hard it is for humanity, long accustomed to cherish doubt, to grasp this great truth! But what peace it brings to the soul, what vital life!"[41]

That vital life has everything to do with our spiritual growth and maturity. And such life proceeds from the genuine experience of being clothed with the garment of Christ's righteousness, and never from wearing a counterfeit garment. What it really comes down to is our continual abiding in Christ and constant consecration of our lives to Him. For it is "the desire of the Lord that from moment to moment we should abide in Him, and thus be *complete in Him.*"[42]

Also, those who consecrate their entire being to God, and cooperate with Christ "are *complete in Him,* and in their human weakness they are enabled to do the deeds of Omnipotence."[43]

Trees can teach us a great deal about life, growth, and maturity, and the Scriptures often use them for such object lessons. They illustrate well the dynamics of our spiritual lives. As you recall, I introduced a previous chapter about our completeness in Christ with the incident of the sudden collapse of our huge willow tree. It is fitting, then, to conclude this section with trees that powerfully depict becoming solidly anchored in Christ and beautifully reflecting His likeness.

Ellen White makes use of three types of trees to elucidate this wonderful spiritual reality: evergreen trees, the cedars of Lebanon, and the palm trees in the desert. What she writes about each one beautifully encapsulates what we have previously discussed.

As we prayerfully contemplate the following spiritual object lessons, let us invite God to search our hearts and know our thoughts, and to show us whether our lives are like the willow tree or like the flourishing and sturdy trees described below:

1. The evergreen tree illustrates genuine righteousness in Christ. During the summer season all kinds of trees wear beautiful foliage, but as the frigid winter season approaches, only evergreen trees remain clothed in their robes of green. "Thus it will be with all who are walking in *humility, distrustful* of self, but *clinging* tremblingly to the hand of Christ. While those who are self-confident, and trust in their own perfection of character, lose their *false* robe of righteousness when subjected to the storms of trial, the truly righteous, who sincerely love and fear God, wear the robe of Christ's righteousness in prosperity and adversity alike." [44]

2. The cedar of Lebanon depicts strength in Christ. The psalmist declares that "he [the righteous] shall grow like a cedar in Lebanon" (Ps. 92:12). "The Christian is likened to the cedar of Lebanon. . . . It sends strong roots deep down into the earth, and strikes down farther and still farther in search of a still stronger hold. And in the fierce blast of the tempest, it stands firm, held by its network of cables beneath. So the Christian strikes root deep into Christ. . . . Genuine Christians, like the cedar of Lebanon, do not grow in the soft surface soil, but are *rooted in God, riveted* in the clefts of the mountain rocks." [45]

3. The palm tree in the desert portrays integrity and resilience in Christ. "If the Christian thrives and progresses at all, he must do so amid strangers to God, amid scoffing, subject to ridicule. He must stand upright like the palm tree in the desert. The sky may be as brass, the desert sand may beat about the palm tree's roots, and pile itself in heaps about its trunk. Yet the tree lives as an evergreen, fresh and vigorous amid the burning desert sands. Remove the sand till you reach the rootlets of the palm tree, and you discover the secret of its life; it strikes down deep beneath the surface, to the secret waters hidden in the earth." [46]

---

[1] Ellen G. White, *The Desire of Ages,* p. 246. (Italics supplied.)

[2] *Ibid.,* p. 429. (Italics supplied.)

[3] Dietrich Bonhoeffer, *The Cost of Discipleship,* p. 63. (Italics supplied.)

[4] White, *The Sanctified Life* (Washington, D.C.: Review and Herald Pub. Assn., 1937), p. 79.

[5] *Ibid.*

[6] *Ibid.* (Italics supplied.)

[7] White, *Steps to Christ,* p. 64.

[8] *Ibid.,* p. 65. (Italics supplied.)

[9] White, *The Acts of the Apostles,* p. 561. (Italics supplied.)

[10] Edward Heppenstall, "Let Us Go On to Perfection," *Perfection—The Impossible Possibility* (Nashville: Southern Pub. Assn., 1975), p. 80.

[11] Robinson, *The Christian Salt and Light Company,* p. 184.

[12] Martin Weber, "Demons of Righteousness," *Ministry,* December 1993, p. 5.

[13] White, *The Sanctified Life,* p. 9.

[14] *Ibid.,* p. 16. (Italics supplied.)

[15] White, *Steps to Christ,* p. 64. (Italics supplied.)

[16] ——, *The Sanctified Life,* p. 90. (Italics supplied.)

[17] *Ibid.*

[18] White, *The Ministry of Healing,* p. 182. (Italics supplied.)

[19] Kit Watts, "A Short, Short List of Blessings," *Adventist Review,* Nov. 25, 1993, p. 5.

[20] White, *Steps to Christ,* pp. 57, 58.

[21] Merriman, "Meditation of a Cellist," p. 12.

[22] Oswald Chambers, *My Utmost for His Highest,* p. 24.

[23] *Ibid.,* p. 53.

[24] *Ibid.*

[25] White, *The Sanctified Life,* p. 10.

[26] *Ibid.,* p. 89. (Italics supplied.)

[27] *Ibid.,* p. 90.

[28] White, *Selected Messages,* book 1, p. 337. (Italics supplied.)

[29] ——, *Testimonies,* vol. 2, p. 549. (Italics supplied.)

[30] ——, *Selected Messages,* book 1, p. 382.

[31] *Ibid.,* p. 368. (Italics supplied.)

[32] White, *Christ's Object Lessons,* p. 312. (Italics supplied.)

[33] ——, *Messages to Young People,* p. 338.

[34] ——, *Christ's Object Lessons,* p. 312. (Italics supplied.)

[35] Nee, *Christ the Sun of All Spiritual Things,* p. 72.

[36] *Ibid.,* pp. 72, 73.

[37] *Ibid.,* pp. 68, 69.

[38] *Ibid.,* pp. 63, 64.

[39] White, *Reflecting Christ,* p. 76. (Italics supplied.)

[40] *Ibid.*

[41] *Ibid.*

[42] White, *My Life Today,* p. 15. (Italics supplied.)

[43] ——, *The Desire of Ages,* p. 827. (Italics supplied.)

[44] ——, *The Sanctified Life,* p. 11. (Italics supplied.)

[45] ——, *Our Father Cares,* p. 112. (Italics supplied.)

[46] *Ibid.*

DRIVEN BY THE SPIRIT

Orange trees and grapevines in South Africa are sometimes infested with what many refer to as the "root disease." The infected trees and vines may appear healthy, and even bear fruit, yet a tree specialist can tell that they are experiencing slow death. The farmer has to get rid of the old diseased roots and replace them with new healthy ones.[1]

The deceptively subtle aspect of this root disease is that it infects hidden parts of the tree. The trunk, the branches, the foliage, and even the fruit may appear healthy. But what about the concealed root system that anchors the tree deep into the soil and carries the life-giving moisture to all its parts? Is it healthy or unhealthy?

The inner workings of a healthy root system symbolize the inwardly transforming work of the Holy Spirit. When Nicodemus wondered about how the Spirit works, Jesus responded: "That which is born of the flesh is flesh, and that which is born of the Spirit is spirit" (John 3:6). Furthermore, "The wind blows where it wishes, and you hear the sound of it, but cannot tell where it comes from and where it goes. So is everyone who is born of the Spirit" (verse 8).

Are we born of the flesh, or are we born of the Spirit? Do we suffer from roots of bitterness, diseased roots of the flesh that insidiously and steadily destroy our spiritual lives? The only cure lies in becoming rooted and grounded in Christ through the Holy Spirit, so that the roots will be holy as well as the branches (see Rom. 11:16). According to Andrew Murray, spiritual root disease in our hidden lives is "the neglect of secret communion with Christ." It can be healed only by constantly sinking "our roots deeper into the life of Christ."[2]

But we live in a society that conditions us to impress others with appearance. To value the outward facade rather than the inward reality. To glory in the visible tree and overlook the hidden work of the roots. To be caught up in what others superficially see, and not in what God discerns. But to focus on the visible courts danger and eventual death, while to cling to the invisible is to choose eternal life. In seeking to satisfy self we sacrifice our soul, but in seeking to please God we safeguard it.

Let us use the tree to symbolize our spiritual lives. If the roots are healthy, then the tree will be. Unless we are born of and moved by the Holy Spirit, it is natural to want our branches to proudly soar higher and higher to impress others, rather than concentrating on humbly sinking our roots deeper in the soil to please God. But the Holy Spirit must be the firm anchor and solid nourishment of our souls. He must be the driving force in our inner motives.

Once in a bustling city I observed thousands of people rushing here and there, all apparently driven by something. As I contemplated that curious scene, I wondered what forces propelled that restless mass of humanity. Many of them probably scurried about because of blind ambition, while others sought fleeting fame and fortune. And, hopefully, the Spirit of God drove a few.

The apostle Paul plunges to the spiritual root of the matter when he explains that the power of the Holy Spirit is strengthening the inner being so that "Christ may dwell in your hearts through faith; that you, being rooted and grounded in love, . . . may be filled with all the fullness of God" (Eph. 3:17-19).

Here we encounter the inner drive or motivation of a truly spiritual person. For through the Holy Spirit, Jesus resides in the heart by faith, cutting away the bitter roots and grafting in their place His spiritual roots. And that is how His being flows and fills our whole being, thus solidly grounding us in His love.

To be driven by the Holy Spirit is to reveal the life of Christ in our lives, for the Holy Spirit is also the Spirit of life in Christ Jesus. "Our heart becomes the scene of a wonderful performance," Andrew Murray writes. "The Father breathing His Spirit into us and making our heart the home of Christ; and the Holy Spirit revealing and forming Christ within us, so that His very nature and character become ours; the Son imparting His life of love and leading us on to be filled with all the fullness of God." [3]

What forces really guide and compel your life and mine in the hustle and bustle of life? In the thicket of all the many pressures to perform, and in the jungle of expectation and competition, what forces egg us on? We know that we are driven. We can feel that compulsion every day. But what spirit really has hold of us? Self, or the Spirit of God? Whose expectations do we try to fulfill?

Throughout His life Jesus experienced the presence and the power of the Holy Spirit. He always availed Himself of the Spirit's power in His ministry. The Spirit directed and drove Him to please His Father in the salvation of lost humanity. Not only was the Holy Spirit involved in Christ's life on earth, but He had been involved from all eternity. He, along with the Father, participated in commissioning the Son to save our sinful world. Isaiah prophetically quotes Jesus as saying this about Himself: "From the time that it was, I was there. And now the Lord God and His Spirit have sent Me" (Isa. 48:16).

From the very beginning of Jesus' human existence till His death, the Holy Spirit intimately participated in His life. After Jesus was miraculously conceived in Mary's womb, the angel told her: "That which is conceived in her [Mary] is of the Holy Spirit" (Matt. 1:20). "Daily He [Christ] received a fresh baptism of the Holy Spirit." [4] The Father gave Him the Spirit without limit (John 3:34). Jesus performed miracles by "the Spirit of God" (Matt. 12:28). He offered Himself to the Father through "the eternal Spirit" as a perfect sacrifice in behalf of humanity (Heb. 9:14). And the Spirit of God raised Him from the dead (Rom. 8:11).

At His baptism the Holy Spirit descended upon Him in fullness, anointing and leading Him into the wilderness in preparation for His momentous mission. Matthew and Luke depict Christ as being *led* by the Spirit. On the other hand, Mark uses the stronger expression of Him being *driven* by the Spirit (see Matt. 4:1; Luke 4:1; Mark 1:12). To be driven by the Spirit implies energy, motion, action, and a thrusting forth to accomplish a certain task.

The Holy One, never needing any forgiveness, humbly submitted Himself to be baptized, thus completely availing Himself of the Spirit. Coming up from the water praying, He saw the heavens open to Him. On Him the Holy Spirit descended and remained, filling Him with His power. And His Father's voice declared, "You are My beloved Son; in You I am well pleased" (Luke 3:21, 22; 4:1; John

1:32, 33). Then immediately the Holy Spirit drove Him into the wilderness to face temptation from the devil. After defeating the devil in the Spirit, He then "returned in the power of the Spirit to Galilee" (Luke 4:14).

Let us now make some spiritual applications as we consider the various aspects of Christ's relationship with the Holy Spirit, particularly in connection with His baptism:

1. Jesus approached His baptism in an attitude of humility and submission. He opened Himself completely to His Father without any reservations. The holy Christ, who Himself "baptizes with the Holy Spirit" (John 1:33), was willing to be baptized with water as well as the Holy Spirit. Is this the spirit we have when we approach our heavenly Father? Do we go to Him with a humble and receptive heart to receive His Spirit?

2. No spiritual act should be an end in itself, and baptism was no exception in Christ's life. One such act drove Him to another. Coming out of the baptismal water, He prayed for "the witness that God accepts humanity in the person of His Son."[5] He asked that nothing would hinder His communion with His Father and His mission of redemption. Every aspect of His life rotated around His spiritual mission being empowered by the Holy Spirit.

On another occasion Jesus brought Peter, James, and John up on a high mountain to pray. Pouring out His heart in submission to His Father, He was transfigured, and He heard His Father's voice from heaven saying, "This is My beloved Son, in whom I am well pleased" (Matt. 17:1-5). Something special happens when we pray as Jesus did. Scripture records that *as* He prayed He was transfigured (Luke 9:29). It is not enough to plan to pray, or merely be with friends who pray. We just need to pray—and *as* we pray in the Spirit we become transformed. Yes, in the *process* of prayer we change—even our appearance changes to glow with the atmosphere of Christ.

Unfortunately, the disciples were not praying with Jesus, but "were heavy with sleep," only to be awakened by the glorious event taking place around them. Even then, Peter, "not knowing what he said" (verse 33), suggested that they construct tents for Jesus, Moses, and Elijah so that they might all stay and enjoy the place for a while. Notice the dramatic contrast. Jesus prayed while the disciples struggled with sleep. The Saviour wanted to leave the mountain to serve in the plains and valleys, while they wanted to construct tents to bask in the mountaintop glory. When Jesus went to pray, they fell asleep. By the time He was ready to come down, they were busy devising plans to stay up on the mountain.

We are in many ways like the three disciples who formed Christ's inner circle. Yet He is patient and loving in teaching us to be like Him. I wonder how many times Jesus takes us along so that we may share some special spiritual experiences with Him, only to watch us succumb to spiritual slumber.

Yes, it is good to be there with Jesus, but why not also pray with Him and be transformed by Him? And when we do, let us not blissfully bask in the glow of it all, but let us with Jesus descend the mountain of glory to the plains and valleys of service.

Like Peter and his two friends, we sometimes seem to be out of sync with Christ. Unlike Him, our spiritual acts sometimes tend to have no relevance to the total spectrum of spiritual life. However, Christ's acts were all interrelated to each other and integrated to the whole. In the biblical model of spirituality, God is the very center of our lives, hence all our activities rotate around that unifying center. On the other hand, the Western model of spirituality tends to place the individual at the center. Thus all aspects of life rotate around self, including the spiritual, to be guarded or discarded at will.

3. Heaven was wide open to Christ in response to His prayer, as the Father enfolded Him by His affirmations. We desperately need that same sort of spiritual experience, a sense that there is an open channel between our soul and our Saviour. That we can let go of any and all impediments that might in any way hinder the free flow of the Holy Spirit into our lives. We must clear out the clutter, remove the refuse, and smooth out the rough places so that the Holy Spirit may enter unhindered into our hearts!

Such open spiritual communication with heaven leads us to abandon ourselves to God and let ourselves be caught up in His will for us. In giving up on ourselves we offer Him free rein in our hearts, trusting Him to do whatever needs to be done with us. Knowing that He is our all-loving and wise Father, we expect Him to do for us what He deems best, and not what our flawed opinion dictates.

"The free committal of myself to God," writes Oswald Chambers, "gives the Holy Spirit the chance to impart to me the holiness of Jesus."[6] Then he admonishes: "Keep your life so constant in its contact with God that His surprising power may break out on the right hand and on the left. Always be in a state of expectancy, and see that you leave room for God to come in as He likes."[7]

4. Christ's complete committal of Himself to His Father opened the heavens and blazed a smooth highway for the Holy Spirit. The Gospels record that the Spirit descended on Christ and filled Him (Mark 1:10; Luke 4:1; John 1:32). It is clear, then, that the Holy Spirit desires nothing more than to possess us, fill us, and reside constantly in us. After all, we are His temple.

Jesus longs for us to have this experience so that He may share the intimate union and communion of the Godhead with us. Christ comes to us through the indwelling of His Spirit, and is even more near and available to us now than when He was bodily present with His disciples.[8] Yet sadly the Holy Spirit often does not feel welcome in His temple. All the clutter of evil leaves no room for Him. We do not really know and appreciate Him, and thus we do not feel at home with Him.

"Time and time again the Lord has *longed* to communicate His Spirit in rich measure, but there was *no place* for Him to *rest*," Ellen White reveals. And that was because He "was *not recognized or valued. The blindness* of mind, the *hardness* of hearts interpreted Him as something of which they should be *afraid. Some hidden evil* lurks in the heart to hinder the manifestation of the power of God, and His Spirit *cannot descend.*"[9]

The Holy Spirit, then, greatly desires to descend and rest on us in order to glorify Christ, and to accomplish *in* us that which Christ accomplished *for* us. Yet, sadly, He often finds no place available for Him to manifest God's power in us. That is because of the following reasons: (a) He is not recognized, (b) He is not valued, and (c) we have blindness of mind, hardness of heart, fear of Him, and hidden evil in the heart.

5. The affirming voice of the Father pierced the air, declaring: "This is My beloved Son, in whom I am well pleased" (Matt. 3:17). The Father and the Son have a loving relationship that gratifies the Father. It greatly pleases our heavenly Father when in trust we also submit our lives to Him. Jesus, however, showed absolute love and submission to His Father and possessed absolute perfection before Him. So no wonder His Father was very pleased with Him.

Children long to hear affirmation from the lips of their human fathers. But how may we, with all our shortcomings, hear such an assuring voice from our perfect heavenly Father? All we have to do is wholeheartedly submit ourselves to the Father as Christ did. Ephesians 1 portrays the Godhead engaged in guaranteeing our acceptance and redemption.

It was in love and pleasure that the Father adopted us as His sons and daughters in Christ, "to the praise of the glory of His grace, by which He has made us accepted in the Beloved" (verse 6). And in submission to Him we were "sealed with the Holy Spirit of promise, who is the guarantee of our inheritance" (verses 13, 14).

God loves and accepts those who love and accept Jesus. I recall an incident in my early youth when my father, commenting on a good and trusted friend I had, said to me that he too loved and accepted my friend. Somewhat surprised, I asked him why he would say that, since he barely knew the person. I have never forgotten his response: "Son, you know that I love and accept you, and whoever loves and accepts you, I love and accept too."

That is but a tiny glimpse of how our heavenly Father regards us in Jesus. Yes, He loves and accepts us the same way He does His Son. Referring to God's voice speaking love and approval to Jesus at His baptism, Ellen White affirms that God's affirmation "embraces humanity." For the Father "spoke to Jesus as our representative." And "the voice which spoke to Jesus says to every believing soul, This is My beloved child, in whom I am well pleased." [10]

Because we are loved and accepted in the Beloved, God directs all His divine and exhaustless energy to help us grow and mature as members of His family. To help us feel more at home with Him, and to feel and act like family. To increasingly carry with us our family's royal reputation. We can belong to no finer family!

The Holy Spirit longs to implant all the family traits in us as we welcome and value Him in the temple of our hearts. "The Holy Spirit is to be presented in every discourse. . . . This is the theme of *encouragement* to be kept before the people. . . . He will make us *complete* in Christ," [11] and "holy, Christlike." [12] Moreover, "the influence of the Holy Spirit is the *life of Christ* in the soul." [13]

6. The love and approval of His Father and the infilling of the Holy Spirit propelled Jesus to immediately act, to set out on His appointed mission. He did not passively ponder His spiritual experience, basking in its beauty, but upon hearing His Father's approving and empowering voice, "You are My beloved Son" (Mark 1:11), the Spirit *immedi-*

ately drove Him into the wilderness to face the devil (verse 12).

Satan introduced his first two temptations with the contemptuous question "If You are the Son of God" (Matt. 4:3, 6), hoping to undermine the Spirit's concrete confirmation and the Father's direct declaration that Jesus Christ was indeed His beloved Son.

And that is precisely Satan's subtle strategy to undermine our own spirituality. He knows that the secret of our spiritual success rests in the fact that we are *related* to God as His sons and daughters. We are born of His imperishable seed and guided by His Spirit because "as many as are led by the Spirit of God, these are sons of God" (Rom. 8:14). The devil is determined to deceive us and destroy our son and daughter relationships with our God. For only in such close family relationship with the Father, the Son, and the Spirit can we be Satan overcomers and Christlike becomers.

7. Disappointed in being so decisively defeated by Christ, Satan "departed from Him until an opportune time" (Luke 4:13). In Christ he found One whom he could not defeat. The Son of God tenaciously held on to the absolute reliability of His Father's word, and clung to the utter dependability of Their close relationship.

Even when we gain victory in Christ, Satan leaves only to regroup and devise future plans to try again at a more opportune time, hoping to dislodge us from our tenacious hold on Christ. If he dared to direct such an attack toward Christ, why would he ever hesitate to aim it toward us? Nothing stirs up the fierce fury of Satan more than to find us fighting the fight of faith, maintaining our firm grip on Christ. And nothing drives him to bitter opposition more than to see us be driven by the Spirit.

We cannot let up in our spiritual warfare, for this is the time of our greatest danger as well as our greatest opportunity. "Be sober, be vigilant," the apostle Peter counsels, "because your adversary the devil walks about like a roaring lion, seeking whom he may devour" (1 Peter 5:8). And whom does he devour? Those who venture to go it alone. Those who let go of their hold on Christ because of doubt and discouragement, reverting to being driven by self rather than the Spirit. We must remain in the Lord and in the strength of His might. Only that enables us to resist.

8. The Holy Spirit was always Christ's constant and close companion. He impelled Him from the Jordan into the wilderness. There Christ gained victory in the Spirit, delivering the devil a decisive defeat. And

now He returns "in the power of the Spirit to Galilee" (Luke 4:14). In the Spirit He goes, in the Spirit He resists and triumphs, and in the Spirit He returns in power to serve. At the very core of Satan's temptations was his attempt to entice Jesus to go it alone in His own power. But He would not yield even for a moment. He made Himself totally available to and dependent on God.

This is indeed what empowers us to resist sin. To resist without submission is to court inevitable defeat. If Jesus Himself, though much more than a match to Satan, constantly depended on God for everything, how much more we ourselves need such dependence.

James describes this dependence on God as the fundamental factor in defeating the devil. He presents us with an invariable formula for spiritual victory: "Submit yourselves, then, to God. Resist the devil, and he will flee from you" (James 4:7, NIV). Consider with me the three progressive steps in this strategy for spiritual warfare, outlined by three verbs: *submit, resist,* and *flee.* Faithfully following them in that order guarantees our spiritual victory.

The very first thing we must do, before we do anything else, is to submit ourselves to God. Who submits? We do. What do we submit? Nothing less and nothing more than our lives. To whom do we submit them? To God Himself. That was the first thing that Jesus did at His baptism, in the wilderness of temptation, and throughout His entire life and ministry. Even as He hung dying on the cross breathing His last, He uttered the words of ultimate submission: "Father, into Your hands I commend My spirit" (Luke 23:46).

The second thing we need to do is to resist the devil. Resisting Satan can come only after submitting to God, and not before. Resistance without submission guarantees sure defeat. Who does the resisting? We and God together, for He is the one to whom we submit ourselves. He is the one who resists Satan in us, through us, and with us.

A story tells how a little girl who submitted her life to Jesus resisted Satan when he knocked at the door to her heart. "As soon as Satan knocks," she said, "I ask Jesus, who is with me, to answer. Then when he sees Jesus at the door," she continued, "he says, 'Sorry, I've got the wrong address.'"

The third thing that happens when God resists through us is that Satan flees from us. Who does the fleeing? Thank God, it is Satan and not us. It is about time we see him flee more, and see God's people retreat less. Sadly, we too often flee because we have not appropriated the practical principle in our spiritual lives that we are not fit to resist unless we first submit.

Even the weakest person who submits himself or herself to God causes Satan to flee. Commenting on James 4:7, Ellen White observes that "we cannot save ourselves from the tempter's power; he has conquered humanity, and when we try to stand in our own strength, we shall become a prey to his devices." Then she adds, "Satan *trembles* and *flees* before the *weakest* soul who finds refuge in that mighty name [of the Lord]." [14]

Satan lulls to sleep those who do not strive to cling to Christ. However, as soon as the Holy Spirit awakens one from this deadly slumber, Satan tightens his deadly grip. But that person must persevere in casting self on Christ, who will send "reinforcement of those angels that excel in strength to deliver him." Satan is no match for Christ—or even one of His holy angels. And in the presence of Christ, not only will he tremble and flee, but all of his evil host will flee as well. Satan "cannot endure to have his powerful rival [Christ] appealed to, for he fears and trembles before His strength and majesty. At the sound of fervent prayer, Satan's whole host trembles." [15]

However, in our joy over his flight, we must ever remain vigilant for another fight. For he will flee from us only to find a more opportune time to attack us. How do we then remain ready for his return? We staunchly hold on to, as we would on life itself, James's sound strategy for spiritual success. Only by holding on to Christ and applying this secure strategy are we safe.

But as long as the devil exists, we will have spiritual contests to face. He desires nothing more than to confront us on *his terms* because he even "knows better than God's people the power that they can have over him when their strength is in Christ." [16] By God's grace, let us never allow him to shake us away from fighting the fight of faith in Christ on *God's terms*.

Often we foolishly overlook God's terms in defeating the devil. Too many times we tremble and flee before him. It is high time he starts trembling and fleeing himself for a change, instead of us. Terror and flight belong to the defeated devil, but never to God's children who cling to Christ and submit to the Spirit.

Such a victorious walk with Christ in the Spirit does not depend on circumstances. It rests on the sure Word of God, is anchored in the living Son of God, and is empowered by the Holy Spirit of God. "Holiness is not rapture: it is an entire surrender of the will to God; it is living by every word that proceeds from the mouth of God; it is doing the will of our heavenly Father; it is trusting God in trial, in darkness as well as in the light; it is walking by faith and not by sight; it is relying on God with unquestioning confidence, and resting in His love." [17]

9. When Jesus returned in the power of the Holy Spirit from the wilderness, He came empowered to minister. Soon afterward He stood in the synagogue to preach His prophetic message that was totally wrapped up in the Holy Spirit from beginning to end (see Luke 4:18, 19). Notice how the Spirit's anointing was to empower Him in all aspects of His ministry. Jesus said that the Spirit of the Lord was upon Him, anointing Him so that He might (a) heal the brokenhearted, (b) deliver the captives, (c) restore the sight of the blind, (d) liberate the oppressed, and, (e) preach the year of the Lord.

And that is what Peter referred to in Acts 10:38 when he said that "God anointed Jesus of Nazareth with the Holy Spirit and with power, who went about doing good and healing all who were oppressed by the devil, for God was with Him." Jesus desires that same anointing and empowering of the Holy Spirit for each one of His disciples. The Holy Spirit, who is also the Spirit of Christ and the Spirit of life in Christ, will manifest the life of Christ in our lives and witness. Jesus longs to share His intimate relationship with the Holy Spirit with every one of us.

But in order for the Holy Spirit to use us, we need to be submissive to Him so that He may form Jesus within. Mary availed herself completely of the Spirit's miraculous work of causing Jesus to be conceived and born in her life. Notice her submissive spirit to the will of God evident in her response to the angel: "Behold the maidservant of the Lord! Let it be to me according to your word" (Luke 1:38). May we be submissive like Mary, saying to God that we desire to be His humble and obedient servants. That we willingly accept whatever He desires for us according to His word, so that the Holy Spirit may cause Jesus to be spiritually formed within us.

We can be born again as the children of God in no other way. It alone allows us to walk in the Spirit, and to be filled by the Spirit. That is why Jesus explained even to the devout and learned Nicodemus the imperative of being born of the Holy Spirit. For "unless one is born of water and the Spirit, he cannot enter the kingdom of God" (John 3:5).

Even the perfect Jesus availed Himself of Spirit baptism in order to show us His example to follow. Whereas He was conceived and born of the Holy Spirit, and whereas He was Himself the Baptizer in the Holy Spirit, yet He was willing to be baptized by the Holy Spirit. Certainly, then, it was not enough for Nicodemus to be a devout Jew, born in the flesh of the seed of Abraham. He needed to be reborn of the Holy Spirit, for "that which is born of the flesh is flesh, and that which is born of the Spirit is spirit" (verse 6).

Therefore, we must start correctly in order to walk correctly, and we need to be born spiritually in order to live spiritually. True spirituality must commence with the new birth in the Holy Spirit, and must continue in daily baptism, walk, and maturation in the same Spirit. Indeed, we cannot experience genuine spirituality without the Spirit. "To believe Him [the Holy Spirit], not just when I accept Christ as Saviour," Francis Schaeffer explains, "but every moment, one moment at a time, this is the Christian life, and this is true spirituality." [18]

Many hesitate to receive God's gracious gift of the Spirit. Perhaps they associate it with something somber, and connect Him with feelings of guilt and ambiguity. That is because He is mostly unknown and misunderstood. But since He Himself is the Comforter, the source of all comfort, how can He not bring relief from the burden of guilt? How can the clear conscience He fills us with not bring us hope and joy?

It is important to note that Jesus associated the Holy Spirit not only with forgiveness and comfort but also with joy and praise. "In that hour Jesus rejoiced in the Spirit and said, 'I praise You, Father, Lord of heaven and earth'" (Luke 10:21). And in John 14:26-29 He associates Him with peace and joy. Peace, because the Holy Helper was to help the disciples in carrying out the gospel commission. Joy, because Christ was to come to them more fully in the Holy Comforter.

However, the main obstacle to our having a close relationship with the Holy Spirit is that we simply do not seek a close relationship with Jesus. He is Christ's close and special friend whom He wanted to share with His disciples. Called "the Spirit of Christ" (Rom. 8:9), He is the other Comforter and Christ's special representative to us (John 14:16).

It is not surprising, then, that Jesus introduces this subject of sending the other Comforter with the condition of loving and obeying Him. "If you love Me, keep My commandments. And I will pray the

Father, and He will give you another Helper, that He may abide with you forever, even the Spirit of truth" (John 14:15-17). Loving and obeying Christ helps us to appreciate, love, and obey Christ's Friend.

The time had finally arrived for Christ to depart His disciples. He had promised not to leave them orphans, but to be with them in the Holy Spirit (verse 18). Imagine having to bid farewell to a very dear and close friend. Not wanting to leave him or her all alone, you introduce your friend to someone like you—your best friend—to fill the void you will leave. Your friend, who appreciated and loved you, will most likely appreciate and love this new friend for your sake. In introducing us to His best Friend the Holy Spirit, Jesus desires to manifest Himself more fully to us.

Indeed, in welcoming the Holy Spirit in our hearts, we relate to Christ in even a closer way than the disciples ever experienced while He was with them in person. That is why Christ told them that it was to their advantage for Him to leave, and for the Holy Spirit to return in His place (John 16:7). Sometimes we wish that we could have been with Christ as the disciples were. That we could have walked, talked, and worked with Him.

But in receiving the Holy Spirit we find our wish fulfilled even beyond our expectations, here and now! "Cumbered with humanity, Christ could not be in every place personally. . . . By the Spirit the Saviour would be accessible to all. In this sense He would be *nearer* to them than if He had not ascended on High." [19] Furthermore, in welcoming the Holy Spirit to dwell in our hearts, we actually receive the life of Christ, and appropriate His likeness. "The Holy Spirit is the breath of spiritual life in the soul. The impartation of the Spirit is the impartation of the life of Christ. It imbues the receiver with the attributes of Christ." [20]

Among God's bountiful gifts to humanity, the supreme gift of Christ was the greatest, followed by another—the Holy Spirit. "The Holy Spirit . . . is the greatest of all gifts. . . . The Creator Himself can give us nothing greater, nothing better." [21] The second and third persons of the Godhead were the greatest gifts given to the human race, and hence it is crucially important for us to accept both. In genuinely accepting One we are consequently accepting the Other.

The Holy Spirit comes among us as Christ's personal and devoted representative. Speaking on Christ's authority, He bears witness to Him and glorifies Him (John 14:16-26; 16:13, 14). Likewise, the Holy Spirit reveals and glorifies Christ in our lives and witness. Indeed, They long to share Their mutual special relationship with us.

In order to help us appreciate how much the Father desires to give us the Holy Spirit, Jesus uses the example of any father's desire—even an evil one—to bestow good gifts on his children. If a hungry child asks his father for bread, he would certainly not give him a stone. And if he entreats him for a fish, he would definitely not give him a serpent. Or if he implores him for an egg, he would assuredly not give him a scorpion. A father would not parade good food before his famished child, only to withdraw it when he reaches for it. Worse yet, he would not instead hurl at him deadly snakes and scorpions (see Luke 11:9-13).

If even evil human fathers willingly give good gifts to their children, how infinitely more our righteous and loving heavenly Father is willing to endow us with the Holy Spirit. As His children, we who hunger and thirst for His gift of the Spirit, should we trust Him any less than a hungry child does even his ungodly father? "If you then, being evil, know how to give good gifts to your children," Jesus entreats, "how much more will your heavenly Father give the Holy Spirit to those who ask Him!" (Luke 11:13).

Moreover, if God had already gone to the extreme extent of giving us His only Son, will He not shower us with all things, including the Holy Spirit? Of course, He will. For "the Father gave His Spirit without measure to His Son, and we also may partake of its fullness." [22]

"If all were willing, all would be filled with the Spirit," [23] Ellen White assures us. Since this is what we desperately and urgently need, then why do we ignore such infilling? Why do we not "hunger and thirst for the gift of the Spirit? Why do we not talk of it, pray for it, and preach concerning it? The Lord is more willing to give the Holy Spirit to those who serve Him than parents are to give good gifts to their children. For the daily baptism of the Spirit every worker should offer His petition to God." [24]

We suppose that we appreciate and love Christ, but we do not show the same spirit toward the Holy Spirit. We think that we can feel more comfortable with Jesus than the Holy Spirit. Yet that is nothing but a curious contradiction. The Holy Helper and Comforter is certainly the one who is helpful and comforting to us. After all, He possesses the same spirit as Christ, for He is the Spirit of Christ. In essence, those who love Christ love the Holy Spirit, and those who ignore the Holy Spirit ignore Christ.

Oswald Chambers argues that we may admire and respect Christ, but indeed we cannot truly love Him without the Holy Spirit in our hearts. "The only Lover of the Lord Jesus is the Holy Ghost, and He sheds abroad the very love of God in our hearts," he writes. "Whenever the Holy Ghost sees a chance of glorifying Jesus, He will take your heart, your nerves, your whole personality, and simply make you blaze and glow with devotion to Jesus Christ." [25]

Moreover, as He commissioned His disciples after His resurrection, Christ "breathed on them, and said to them, 'Receive the Holy Spirit'" (John 20:22). He said this to prepare them for the full outpouring of the Spirit 50 days later at Pentecost. The very final words that Christ spoke to them just before He ascended to heaven concerned the Spirit. They confirmed His soon outpouring on them, empowering them to testify of Him far and near. "But you shall receive power when the Holy Spirit has come upon you; and you shall be witnesses to Me" (Acts 1:8).

And at Pentecost "there came a sound from heaven, as of a rushing mighty wind, and it filled the whole house where they were sitting. Then there appeared to them divided tongues, as of fire, and one sat upon each of them. And they were all filled with the Holy Spirit and began to speak with other tongues, as the Spirit gave them utterance" (Acts 2:1-4). Peter, full of the Spirit, exhorted the diverse multitude to repent, to be baptized in the name of Jesus, and to receive the Holy Spirit (verses 38, 39).

It was a mighty and glorious fulfillment of Christ's promise of the Holy Spirit! He who conceived Christ, guided His youthful steps, anointed and filled His life, drove and empowered His life and ministry, is the One whom Christ desires to share with us. If Christ desired His perpetual presence, we most certainly should. If the disciples needed His prevailing power, we do too. And if Christ shared the Holy Spirit with His disciples, and they in turn shared Him with others, then we too need this kind of spiritual ministry.

We are Christ's present-day disciples, and His promise of the Spirit's outpouring particularly applies to us in these last days. The Holy Spirit's outpouring awaits our reception. "This promise belongs as much to us as it did to them [the disciples], and yet how *rarely* it is presented before the people. . . . [It] is *casually* brought into our discourses, is *incidentally* touched upon, and that is all. . . .

113

This subject has been *set aside.*" [26]

Always we must keep in mind that the devil fiercely fights any opportunity that we have to receive the Holy Spirit. We must be keenly aware that he bitterly opposes any possibility for us to possess such Spirit-filled ministry. For "there is *nothing* that Satan fears so much as that the people of God shall clear the way by removing every hindrance, so that the Lord can pour out His Spirit upon a languishing church and an impenitent congregation." [27]

Thank God for the Holy Spirit. May God help us not to languish spiritually any longer. May He help us to frustrate Satan's plan by becoming ever more Christlike through the ministry of the Spirit. And may He help us appreciate and love Him enough to clear the way for the Holy Spirit to dwell in us, making us more devoted to Him and driven by Him in our lives and witness.

[1] Andrew Murray, *The Inner Life* (Pittsburgh: Whitaker House, 1984), p. 5.

[2] *Ibid.,* p. 6.

[3] *Ibid.,* p. 133.

[4] Ellen G. White, *Christ's Object Lessons,* p. 139.

[5] ———, *The Desire of Ages,* p. 112.

[6] Oswald Chambers, *My Utmost for His Highest,* p. 81.

[7] *Ibid.,* p. 25.

[8] White, *The Desire of Ages,* pp. 669, 670.

[9] *Ellen G. White Manuscript Releases* (Silver Spring, Md.: Ellen G. White Estate, 1990), vol. 4, p. 336. (Italics supplied.)

[10] ———, *The Desire of Ages,* p. 113.

[11] *Manuscript Releases,* vol. 4, p. 329. (Italics supplied.)

[12] *Manuscript Releases,* vol. 2, p. 15. (Italics supplied.)

[13] *The SDA Bible Commentary,* Ellen G. White Comments, vol. 6, p. 1112. (Italics supplied.)

[14] ———, *The Desire of Ages,* p. 131. (Italics supplied.)

[15] ———, *Testimonies,* vol. 1, p. 346.

[16] *Ibid.,* p. 341.

[17] White, *The Acts of the Apostles,* p. 51.

[18] Schaeffer, *True Spirituality,* p. 108.

[19] White, *The Desire of Ages,* p. 669. (Italics supplied.)

[20] *Ibid.,* p. 805.

[21] White, *Thoughts From the Mount of Blessing,* p. 132.

[22] ———, *The Great Controversy,* p. 477.

[23] ———, *The Acts of the Apostles,* p. 50.

[24] *Ibid.*

[25] Chambers, p. 184.

[26] White, *Testimonies to Ministers* (Mountain View, Calif.: Pacific Press Pub. Assn., 1923), p. 174. (Italics supplied.)

[27] ———, *Selected Messages,* book 1, p. 124.

CHAPTER NINE

ALONE WITH GOD

As I was returning home on the freeway the other day, the driver overtaking me in the fast lane caught my attention because he was trying to do so many things while driving. It seemed that his car was the least thing on his mind. Besides steering with his elbows, he was squeezing a cellular phone between his neck and shoulder. At the same time he was balancing a sandwich in one hand while sipping on a drink in the other. And to top it all off, his stereo was shattering his eardrums.

Seeing his car disappear in the distance, I kept thinking about the absurdity of our stressful modern life. I used to think that driving alone would relieve one from it all, but now it seems that there is no escape anywhere from all such stresses. Is there no place for people in our modern age to enjoy being alone, being still and serene in their own thoughts and reflections? Is there no quiet place to escape the tyranny of technology, the menace of mass media, and the peril of life's pressures?

We think it is tough now to escape the telephone, television, and other technology. But this may be just the tip of the iceberg. If we have not yet noticed, futuristic technology is waging total war to wield total control over every aspect of our lives. We hear a new and strange jargon of *information superhighway, scholarly skywriting, internet, black box,* and *cyberspace,* just to mention a few terms. Such things are having profound impact on the way we live as human beings.

Electronic information networking is bringing about changes of a magnitude that no one ever dreamed of in the past, or that we can yet fully foresee. No one can predict the ultimate impact this revolution will have on the individual and society. "But the experiences of people who are already using bits and pieces of the wired world in their everyday life suggest that it is likely to produce fundamental—perhaps wrenching—changes in our social fabric," reports *U.S. News & World Report* in a cover story about charting the electronic frontier. "Before long, the flow of information now coming into homes, businesses, and universities through telephone lines, cables, and myriad other connections will merge in a single two-way torrent of voice, images, motion pictures, and text." [1]

In this bewilderingly distracting world, it seems virtually impossible to be alone—to say nothing about being alone with God. It is difficult to get unplugged in our wired world, to get wired to our inner beings and get in circuit with our God. In this context, being alone is different than being lonely. To be alone is to rise above the distractions of this world and to reach beyond to its Creator. It is to enjoy the solitude and stillness of knowing that, in spite everything, He is still God. Thus we may commune with Him and our inner selves, reflecting spiritually on the real issues of life.

That is why, if we have truly experienced being alone with God, we may find ourselves surrounded by the commotion of the crowd, yet still able to enjoy our private audience with Him. But if, on the other hand, we have not experienced this, we may be encircled by our best friends and loved ones and yet feel extremely lonely. To know what it really means to be alone with God does not entail that we merely isolate ourselves from the world. Rather, to be alone with Him is what drives us to serve others, and to serve others is what compels us to be alone with God.

That is the balanced approach that Christ gives us—balance between *solitude* with God and *service* to others. Solitude leading to service and service leading to solitude. In his book *Celebration of Discipline,* Richard Foster argues that most people gravitate between two options: noise and loneliness. However, he finds a third option in solitude, which he defines as "inner fulfillment" in contrast to loneliness, which he describes as "inner emptiness." [2]

Such inner fulfillment comes from the security and serenity we have in God in our inward being. It is because of His pervading presence that regardless of whether others are present or absent we nevertheless feel fulfilled with Him. We may humanly be by ourselves, yet never alone. And that is what Jesus had in mind when He disclosed to His disciples that "indeed the hour is coming, yes, has now come, that you will be scattered, each to his own, and will leave Me alone. And yet I am not alone, because the Father is with Me" (John 16:32). They would soon forsake Him and flee (Matt. 26:56) and leave Him alone, yet with His Father He was never alone, for They were in constant communion.

Likewise, the apostle Paul expressed similar assurance in God's perpetual presence with him, even when all others had abandoned him at his trial. "At my first defense no one stood with me, but all forsook me," he acknowledges. "But the Lord stood with me and strengthened me, so that the message might be preached fully through me, and that all the Gentiles might hear" (2 Tim. 4:16, 17). Such solitude in God is not something static, for it always leads to self-sacrificing service. Strengthened by God's presence, Paul found himself driven to preach the gospel.

Solitude and service were ever linked together in the life and ministry of Jesus, and they must inextricably be linked in our lives and ministry as well. Let us not fall into the extremes of either solitude or service. We must make sure that we play neither the all-consuming role of a monk in the mountains, nor that of a missionary among the multitude. Instead, we must have both a mountain experience and a missionary experience. However, one experience is not detached from the other, but must always lead to it.

The first extreme can lure us into the pitfall of spiritual passiveness and pride. "God does not mean that any of us should become hermits or monks and retire from the world in order to devote ourselves to acts of worship. The life must be like Christ's life—between the mountain and the multitude. He who does *nothing but pray will soon cease to pray,* or his prayers will become a formal routine."[3] Furthermore, when Christians in their solitude cease to reach out to others in service, "they lose the subject matter of prayer, and have no incentive to devotion. Their prayers become personal and selfish."[4]

The second extreme can seduce us into the peril of spiritual idolatry, making a savior out of our service. "Those who are seeking to *rescue others* from vice and ruin are *especially* exposed to temptation. In constant contact with evil, they need a *strong hold upon God* lest they themselves be corrupted."[5]

Dietrich Bonhoeffer, in his book *Life Together,* insists on the indissoluble link between being alone and being in community, and presents the pitfalls of either extreme. "Let him who cannot be alone beware of community. . . . Let him who is not in community beware of being alone," he counsels. "Each by itself has profound pitfalls and perils," he cautions. "One who wants fellowship without solitude plunges into the void of words and feelings, and one who seeks solitude without fellowship perishes in the abyss of vanity, self-infatuation, and despair."[6]

Therefore, we come to the realization that aloneness with God impels us to impact our community, and solitude in His presence propels us to serve others. Jesus expressed this same balanced outlook in the context of loving God with all our being, and loving our neighbor as ourselves (Mark 12:30, 31). "It is in deep solitude that I find the gentleness with which I can truly love my brothers. The more solitary I am, the more affection I have for them. . . . Solitude and silence teach me to love my brothers for what they are, not for what they say."[7]

Pastor Bill Hybels observes that church members try to cram more and more things into their time. And all that they have left in their stressful lives is performance. Performance becomes the god we worship, because we are convinced that it is "the key to promotion, to compensation increase, to power."[8] And even when we get away on a vacation, we take advantage of that supposedly relaxing vacation and make it into what we call a *working* vacation. We leave ourselves no moment to be still and know God and ourselves.

Alarmed, Hybels asks himself, "Where does the still, small voice of God fit into our hectic lives? When do we give God the chance to lead, guide, correct, and affirm? And if this seldom happens, how can we lead authentic Christian lives?"[9]

This problem by no means limits itself to activities outside the home, but it spills over to family life as well. We find ourselves lost in our own world. Thus we senselessly sacrifice meaningful relationships at the altar of busyness, and find ourselves consumed as we passively bump into each other going in and out. And if that is the case even with our family members, then it is no wonder that we have no real communion with God. "The archenemy of spiritual authenticity is busyness, which is closely tied to something the Bible calls *worldliness*—getting caught up with this society's agenda, objectives, and activities to the neglect of walking with God."[10]

Despite all the fascinating distractions of modern technology, we still see so many people desperately lonely. They may access all the information they wish at the push of a remote control button, and they may acquire the most sophisticated pieces of modern gadgetry to amuse themselves with, yet within they continue to sense an empty void. Others try to bury their loneliness in workaholism and the struggle for position and prestige. Many are so busy expending themselves in making a living that they cannot make a life.

This is the tragic consequence of worshiping the creature rather than the Creator (Rom. 1:25). It is what happens when we bow at the shrine of gadgetry rather than serve at the altar of God, and when we love the temporary things of the world rather than the timeless things of the Word. The Word Himself who went about doing good knew how to be alone with God in spite of all His busyness. "No other life was ever so crowded with labor and responsibility as was that of Jesus; yet how often He was found in prayer! How constant was His communion with God!" [11]

Even though He constantly devoted Himself to God's work, yet at the same time He continuously sought the God of the work. He sensed His need to withdraw from His ministry to God in order to avail Himself of God's ministry to Him. Christ shared in all the sorrows, struggles, and sufferings of others, but He also sensed His need to freely unburden Himself with God. "He must turn aside from a life of ceaseless activity and contact with human needs, to seek retirement and unbroken communion with His Father. . . . Here He found comfort and joy." [12]

Jesus balanced being with God and being with others, solitude with service. Let us look at some instances that exhibited that balance in His life and ministry. This will not be a chronological or detailed study, but a gleaning of spiritual lessons from His relationship with His Father in the context of His active ministry.

1. "When Jesus heard it, He departed from there by boat to a deserted place by Himself. But when the multitudes heard it, they followed Him on foot from the cities" (Matt. 14:13). Jesus maintained constant communion with His Father in all situations, especially the crucial ones. (Even while He suffered on the cross, His enemies had to admit that "He trusted in God" [Matt. 27:43].) In Matthew 14, what caused Him to seek solitude? It was the dreadful news of John the Baptist's cruel execution at the hands of Herod. After burying his body, John's disciples "went and told Jesus" (verse 12).

Sometimes Jesus departed to a secluded place with four of His disciples or with the 12, but other times He needed to be alone by Himself with God. And this was one such time. His courageous cousin and faithful forerunner had just been wantonly beheaded, and He just wanted to be alone seeking "comfort and joy in communion with His Father." [13] Whom do we seek for spiritual strength in severe situations? Do we seek God first and foremost before scurrying everywhere else?

Notice that His private time alone with His Father took place between two important events: John's execution and the clamor of the crowds for His help. Jesus sought to be ministered to by His Father, so that He might in turn effectively minister to the multitudes. "In the hour of distress He [Jesus] turned to His Father. Himself a source of blessing and strength, He could heal the sick and raise the dead . . . ; yet He prayed, often with strong crying and tears." [14]

The multitudes interrupted such communion. When He healed their diseases and satisfied their hunger, He longed to pick up where He left off with His Father. So after sending the multitudes away (verses 21, 22), "He went up on a mountain by Himself to pray. And when evening had come, He was alone there" (verse 23). Luke 9:18 records that "He was alone praying," and His disciples joined Him as He contemplated how He "the Son of Man must suffer many things, and be rejected . . . , and be killed, and be raised the third day" (verse 22).

That is what we must do too as we contemplate critical decisions or prepare for trying circumstances (see also Mark 6:44-46). Yes, Jesus loved to sympathize with and serve the multitude, but He also loved the solitude and seclusion of the mountains. He enjoyed turning aside from a life of ceaseless activity and contact with human needs, to seek retirement and unbroken communion with His Father." [15]

2. "Now in the morning, having risen a long while before daylight, He went out and departed to a solitary place; and there He prayed" (Mark 1:35). Jesus was alone with His Father not only late in the evening, as we have already seen, but also early in the morning. It is important to conclude the day in communion with God, but it is even more vital to start the day that way as well.

Similarly, an account of an exhausting evening of healing and casting out demons precedes the passage in Mark 1, for the "whole city was gathered together at the door" (verse 33), and people told Jesus, "Everyone is looking for You" (verse 37). Jesus clearly showed how imperative it was to unwind and unburden Himself in communion with God, particularly after coming in contact with the weighty needs of the whole city. He needed such communion not only because of what He had already faced but also to prepare Himself for the many others who were "looking for Him."

There is just something special about getting up early in the morning to spend time with God. In the refreshing and restful atmosphere of the day's early hours, most of us find ourselves more able to concentrate on God, and more receptive to His Spirit. We know how energizing it is to meet the day's demands with a hearty breakfast. Thus it is with starting our day with a hearty spiritual breakfast before confronting the day's conflicts. To commence the day without being spiritually energized is to court disaster.

Indeed, this must be the very first thing we do when the Lord awakens us every morning—to thank Him for giving us another day of life, and to commit our lives completely to Him. To entrust ourselves to Him so that we may live out the fulfillment of His will for that day. The Father will awaken us to commune with Him and learn from Him as He awakened His Son morning by morning.

"From hours spent with God He came forth morning by morning, to bring the light of heaven to men. . . . In the early hours of the new day the Lord awakened Him from His slumbers, and His soul and His lips were anointed with grace, that He might impart to others." [16] And if we long to be more like Christ, then morning by morning we need to relinquish our lives to Him so that He may fashion us after His will. And like David we may say: "My voice You shall hear in the morning, O Lord; in the morning I will direct it to You, and I will look up" (Ps. 5:3).

Looking unto Christ leads to *likeness* of Christ. "Upon the vision of Christ the gaze is fixed, and the beholder grows into the likeness of that which he adores." [17] Therefore, "Consecrate yourself to God in the *morning;* make this your *very first* work. . . . This is a *daily* matter. *Each morning* consecrate yourself to God for that day. Surrender all your plans to Him, to be carried out or given up as His providence shall indicate. Thus *day by day* you may be giving your life into the hands of God, and thus your life will be *molded more and more after the life of Christ.*" [18]

3. "So He [Jesus] Himself *often* withdrew into the wilderness and prayed" (Luke 5:16). Here again, Jesus withdraws in order to be alone with God. This incident occurred right after His fame attracted

great crowds who sought teaching and healing (verse 15). This section focuses on the *frequency* of Christ's withdrawal to find solitude and solace with His Father. It was not something sporadic, but something systematic—a part of the normal course of His life.

Regularity of communion with God for our spiritual life makes every sense when we think of the necessity of breathing and eating. We must constantly breathe in the life-giving air, and yesterday's meal, no matter how ample and satisfying it was, is not sufficient for today.

We all have had the experience of wondering how we could ever feel hungry again after feasting on a lavish meal. But naturally, we do eat again and again. One breath is sufficient only for that moment, and one meal is satisfactory only for that day. The same thing applies to breathing in the Spirit of God and feeding on His life. It must be often, regular, and systematic. Today's spiritual experience is sufficient for today, but tomorrow demands a new spiritual experience.

4. "Now it came to pass in those days that He went out to the mountain to pray, and continued *all night* in prayer to God" (Luke 6:12). Here we notice His not uncommon practice of spending all night in prayer and communion with God. Of course, we cannot and ought not do this every night, but sometimes certain crucial circumstances demand major blocks of time, or even perhaps all night.

When in such special circumstances we linger long with God, we feel serendipitously energized. God's Spirit descends upon us in a special way as He fills us with His life and vigor. When we consecrate our entire being to God, we "will be constantly receiving a new endowment of physical and mental power." That is because Christ will give us "the breath of His own spirit, the life of His own life." And because "the Holy Spirit puts forth its highest energies to work in heart and mind." [19]

In our text, what special circumstance led Christ to pray all night? Notice that this particular experience took place between two crucial events. Verse 11 refers to the first one. The scribes and Pharisees had become so insanely angry at Jesus that they began planning His murder. They were so obsessed with envy and controlled by hatred that His very life was on the line. He well knew that if He continued His ministry, He would eventually be killed.

The second event appears in verse 13, when He chose the 12 apostles. He knew that it was only a matter of time before the Jewish leaders murdered Him, and He wanted to make sure that His ministry would continue through His chosen apostles.

When we face trying times or are on the verge of making life-changing decisions, we sometimes find it hard to sleep. Well, instead of fretfully tossing in bed, rehashing and rehearsing everything in our minds, why not spend that time pouring out our souls in communion with God? Such terrible times can draw us closer to Him. We can fully trust Him with all that troubles us, receiving His assurance that He understands all things and is willing to show His might on our behalf.

"We shall be tested and tried; we may be called to spend wakeful nights," Ellen White writes, "but let such times be spent in earnest prayer to God, that He may give understanding, and quicken the mind to discern the privileges that are ours." [20] Our impatience makes us expect instant results when we want something. Similarly, we may meet with God for a short while, then easily give up when things do not go our way. Instead, we need to watch and pray, and linger patiently in the Lord's presence.

Only in this way can we fortify our faith, and familiarize ourselves with our heavenly Father. We need a more firm faith in God. A faith that will sustain our souls when scorched by fiery trials. A faith that will propel us to submit our lives to God for His molding and refining. "Those who are unwilling to deny self, to agonize before God, to pray long and earnestly for His blessing, will not obtain it. Wrestling with God—how few know what it is! How few have ever had their souls drawn out after God with intensity of desire until every power is on the stretch." [21]

5. "Therefore when Jesus perceived that they were about to come and take Him by force to make Him king, He departed again to a mountain by Himself alone" (John 6:15). Jesus was becoming popular among the common people, who were convinced that He was the long-awaited Messiah who would rid them of Roman tyranny. The feeding of the multitudes, in the preceding verses, confirmed in their minds that Jesus was indeed the Promised One.

Jesus had to be careful not only among His enemies but among His friends as well. Here the approving crowd surged toward Him, not to destroy Him, but to crown Him king. And through such admirers, including His disciples, Satan was seizing again his "more opportune time" to tempt Christ to abandon His spiritual kingdom for worldly glory, to exchange the cross for a crown. The same temptation that Satan had confronted Him with in the wilderness the devil now threw at Him through His admiring friends.

To what extent does popularity go to our heads? We can become so blinded by the glittering crown of popularity that we no longer see Christ's crown of thorns and cross of sacrifice. If we cling to a temporary crown in this world, we will tragically concede the eternal crown of the world to come. Sometimes we seem so willing to worship at the shrine of popularity, and so eager for the applause of admirers, that we become incredibly willing to sell out our friends, family members, and even our faith.

Whenever we begin feeling that somehow we are indispensable or that we are God's unique gift to the church and the world, we need to contemplate the condescension of Christ. Both for the sake of our Saviour and our souls, we desperately need to rush to Christ and tarry long with Him, contemplating His thorns of shame and cross of humiliation.

6. Finally we need to notice how Christ invited His disciples to join Him in sharing His special time of solitude with His Father (see Matt. 17:1-9; 26:36-46; Mark 6:31, 32; Luke 9:10, 11). We may wonder why He included them in such sacred seasons of solitude. He wanted them to know His Father more intimately, and to understand the nature of His spiritual kingdom more clearly. Also He desired to show them an example of spiritual devotion, and thus demonstrate to them the results of true communion with God.

At the same time He made Himself vulnerable in needing their spiritual fellowship, prayer, and support. He could have opened Himself up even more if they had been willing to understand more clearly His spiritual mission. Christ especially revealed Himself to Peter, James, and John his brother, taking them up on a high mountain by themselves to witness His transfiguration (Matt. 17:1-13).

Note that Jesus brought them along even though they were not ready to fully appreciate that whole glorious event. Christ's heart was open to spiritual fellowship with Moses and Elijah as He discussed with them His spiritual mission of sacrificing Himself to save humanity. And if the disciples had been spiritually prepared, He would have entered into profound communion with them. We cannot help wondering about the many times Christ would have loved to open His heart to us and share with us His divine secrets if we only had been more in tune with Him.

He again took the same three disciples to be alone with Him as

He sought communion with His Father in Gethsemane (Matt. 26:36-46). There He longed to have them pray and share with Him this most excruciating time as He awaited the cross. Would they be more prepared to enter into such blessed fellowship than at the time of His transfiguration? But, alas, this time they all fell asleep.

Jesus longed to have them share the privileged and holy experience with Him. It is true that "the human heart longs for sympathy in suffering." And such "longing Christ felt to the very depths of His being." For "in the supreme agony of His soul He came to His disciples with a yearning desire to hear some words of comfort from those whom He had so often blessed and comforted." [22]

If Jesus Himself needed to be alone with God, to commune with Him and unburden Himself to Him, then obviously we need it even more. And if He felt the need to have spiritual fellowship and community with others, then we may too. Of course, no one but Jesus can give us real peace, comfort, and joy. And we must seek that spiritual communion with Him first and foremost in the process of realizing spiritual fellowship with others.

Sadly we will often go to anyone and try anything before we first seek Jesus. Why do we bear our heavy burdens rather than seek the heavenly burden bearer? No one else can relieve us of our burdens as He can—and we cannot help to ease the burdens of others unless we go to Him first. He offers us the invitation: "Come to Me, all you who labor and are heavy laden, and I will give you rest" (Matt. 11:28).

Jesus must first get us alone with Him. There, in His presence, we see Him as He is, and we see ourselves as we really are. He uncovers all our hiding places of noise and fear and gently removes our masks of ignorance and pretension. "The only way we can be of use to God is to let Him take us through the crooks and crannies of our own characters. It is astounding how ignorant we are about ourselves!" Therefore, "we have to get rid of the idea that we understand ourselves, it is the last conceit to go. The only One who understands us is God. The greatest curse in spiritual life is conceit." [23]

Last fall I had the chance to travel to beautiful northern Michigan. It was certainly a relaxing and memorable weekend to unwind and commune with God, especially after a hectic summer. The perfect calmness of the place, broken occasionally by the singing of birds and the rustling of leaves in the gentle breeze, particularly struck me. Often we become so conditioned to noise and so accustomed to stress that we do not realize what we are really missing unless we get away to such a quiet place.

Incessant loud music and blaring television are but two examples of how we erect walls around ourselves so that we might not have to face our fears and commune with our souls. All that noise distracts us from dealing with the real issues of our lives. Loneliness drives us to noise, and noise, in turn, forces us into loneliness—a vicious and empty circle for sure.

Trying to preempt a headache, I once asked a store clerk to lower the deafening volume of the jarring music. Reluctantly she consented, with the comment that she really needed that music to help her make it. Then, noticing me leaving, she cranked up the volume even higher than before. Like many others, it was her way of trying to cope with her life from day to day.

Likewise, as I made pastoral visits I found noisy television sets quite distracting to any kind of meaningful conversation. When I would gently request that they lower the volume a bit, they would frequently turn them off completely. So accustomed were they to the constant noise that they seemed quite unaware that their sets were actually on in the first place.

We all have our own particular distractions that keep us from communing with our hearts. They are why Jesus needs to get us alone and away from all false defenses, so that we may see ourselves from His perspective. "There are whole tracts of stubbornness and ignorance to be revealed by the Holy Spirit in each one of us and it can only be done when *Jesus gets us alone*," Chambers explains. "Are we alone with Him now, or are we taken up with little fussy notions . . . ? Jesus can expound nothing until we get through all the noisy questions of the head and are *alone with Him.*"[24] Sometimes during our spiritual journey we try to keep what we may think of as a safe distance between God and us. Because we do not feel that we can become totally comfortable or vulnerable in His presence, we sometimes imagine that we can somehow preserve some of our defenses intact. Yes, we think we can be open with God in some things but not in everything. You see, we imagine that we can shield from His scrutiny some corners of our inner being, safeguarding them for ourselves.

Such defensiveness runs rampant in the human family, being inherited from our first parents. God created Adam and Eve to enjoy mutual communion with their Creator, but after they fell, they hid from Him, covering themselves with fig leaves. Such flimsy covering represents our childish pretensions before the all-knowing and all-loving God. We may get by pretending with our fig leaves before other people, but not before God. We cannot selectively decide what we will or won't reveal to Him.

But why do we play such spiritual games anyway? After all, God already knows us more intimately than we could ever know ourselves, and yet He still loves us. Playing such games only retards our spiritual growth and leaves us with ambiguous feelings about where we really are in our relationship with God. Our spiritual relationship will start growing only when we open up ourselves completely to Him, trustingly placing ourselves at His disposal to do with us as He sees best for us.

Henri Nouwen explains that "as long as we have only a vague inner feeling of discontent with our present way of living, and only an indefinite desire for 'things spiritual,' our lives will continue to stagnate in a generalized melancholy." Moreover, resigning ourselves to this stagnated spiritual condition "prevents us from searching for the life of the Spirit." Then Nouwen suggests that "our first task is to dispel the vague, murky feeling of discontent and to look critically at how we are living our lives. This requires honesty, courage, and trust. We must honestly unmask and courageously confront our many self-deceptive games." [25]

However, the business of unmasking and confronting our spiritual games can never happen unless we first allow God to get our attention and take us off by ourselves with Him. "It is in our secret chamber, face-to-face with the Lord, that we find ourselves. This is where the unadulterated reality of the Christian life is defined," Robert Folkenberg clarifies. "In the real-heart encounter with God, we drop the facade—the pretense—and come face-to-face with the condition of our own souls. It is in this setting that real personal growth happens." [26]

Expressing his fear that all of us face the real danger of substituting our work for God for our walk with God, Folkenberg challenges us to seek solitude with God no matter how "fierce the rat race that surrounds us" may be. Without this quality time with God, he warns, "we will degenerate into the mechanical, the perfunctory, the routine—playing church, but remaining complete strangers to the real power of God." [27]

Yes, we need to work, but we also need to walk. And without taking time to walk with God, our work for Him deteriorates into just another program. When Jesus invited His weary disciples to get away from their ministry and rest, He did not by any means denigrate their work for Him. But He knew that their service and their souls would suffer severely if they did not heed His counsel: "Come aside by yourselves to a deserted place and rest a while" (Mark 6:31).

And why did He offer them this invitation at that particular time? Because they had just come from an extensive and exhausting missionary journey. And because He desired to fellowship with them—but it was impossible for them to, "for there were many coming and going, and they did not even have time to eat" (verse 31).

The description sounds like the stressful situations we find ourselves in as we try to serve the Lord, doesn't it? A lot of coming and going, and no time to scratch our heads, no time to even eat our meals. And incidentally, no time for spiritual meals, either. Yes, we desperately need to steal away to a secluded place to be alone with the Saviour. Heeding Christ's invitation, "they [the disciples] departed to a deserted place in the boat by themselves" (verse 32). May we heed that invitation too.

Christ knew that they "needed to come apart from the scenes of their busy activity, to commune with Christ, with nature, and with their own hearts." [28] In His love and compassion for them, He knew that getting away from their service to Him to solitude with Him would not in any way undermine that service. He was, in fact, helping them to be refreshed by His Spirit, to be energized by His presence in order for them to regroup, and thus carry out His work even more efficiently and effectively.

While studying the above passage in my college spiritual formation class, one of my students related a story: Two friends took out their chain saws and went out to a forest to spend the day cutting a supply of firewood for the winter. Tom, in his determination to be efficient, labored nonstop all day. John, on the other hand, worked hard, yet he enjoyed taking a few breaks to sharpen his saw while at the same time relaxing and viewing the beautiful scenery.

When it came to the end of the day, Tom was uptight and totally exhausted. However, John was his usual cheerful self—tired, yes, but not totally fatigued and stressed out. And to Tom's surprise and frustration, he had not cut as much wood as his friend. John had been more efficient and effective because he took time to recoup his energy through diverting his mind from the routine task in order to sharpen his tool. Cutting with a sharpened chain saw all day was certainly less taxing and more efficient than continuously laboring with a dull one.

May we in our service for our Saviour take time to seek solitude with Him, so that our souls may be energized by His Spirit, and our spiritual saws may be sharpened for greater service.

[1] William F. Allman, "Pioneering the Electronic Frontier," *U.S. News & World Report,* Dec. 6, 1993, pp. 58, 57.

[2] Richard J. Foster, *Celebration of Discipline* (San Francisco: Harper and Row, 1988), p. 96.

[3] White, *Steps to Christ,* p. 101. (Italics supplied.)

[4] *Ibid.*

[5] ———, *The Ministry of Healing,* p, 509, 510. (Italics supplied.)

[6] Dietrich Bonhoeffer, *Life Together* (New York: Harper and Row, 1952), pp. 77, 78.

[7] Thomas Merton, *The Sign of Jonas* (New York: Harcourt and Brace, 1953), p. 261.

[8] Hybels, *Too Busy Not to Pray,* p. 98.

[9] *Ibid.,* p. 98, 99.

[10] *Ibid.,* p. 100.

[11] White, *The Desire of Ages,* p. 362.

[12] *Ibid.,* p. 363.

[13] ———, *Steps to Christ,* p. 94.

[14] ———, *Gospel Workers* (Washington, D.C.: Review and Herald Pub. Assn., 1948), p. 256.

[15] ———, *The Desire of Ages,* p. 363.

[16] ———, *Christ's Object Lessons,* p. 139.

[17] ———, *Education,* p. 192.

[18] ———, *Steps to Christ,* p. 70. (Italics supplied.)

[19] ———, *The Desire of Ages,* p. 827.

[20] ———, *With God at Dawn* (Washington, D.C.: Review and Herald Pub. Assn., 1949), p. 200.

[21] ———, *The Great Controversy* (Mountain View, Calif.: Pacific Press Pub. Assn., 1911), p. 621.

[22] ———, *The Desire of Ages,* p. 687.

[23] Chambers, *My Utmost for His Highest,* p. 12.

[24] *Ibid.,* p. 13. (Italics supplied.)

[25] Henri J. Nouwen, *Making All Things New* (San Francisco: Harper and Row, 1981).

[26] Robert S. Folkenberg, "Time With God," *Adventist Review,* Mar. 4, 1993, p. 12.

[27] *Ibid.*

[28] White, *The Desire of Ages,* p. 360.

TASTE AND SEE—1

At her college graduation party Jane received a gift from a young engineering professor. Arriving home that evening, she opened the present and discovered it was a book. One glance at the uninteresting title was enough to cause her to lay it aside unopened for months. Engineering was not exactly the most fascinating subject to her.

Sometime later she and the professor fell in love and became engaged. One evening as they were happily pondering their wedding plans and future lives together, he asked her what she thought of the book he had given her at her graduation. All of a sudden she remembered how she had dismissed it from her mind. Embarrassed for neglecting it, she determined to show better appreciation for the gift of her soon groom-to-be.

Arriving home that evening, she could hardly wait to find the book. And looking at more than the title this time, she was pleasantly surprised to discover that the author was no other than the professor himself, and that he had written in it a note of dedication to her. Needless to say, Jane did not sleep much that night. Gripped by the whole experience, and utterly fascinated by the book her lover had written and dedicated to her, she simply could not lay it down until she had read the last page.[1]

Delighting ourselves in the Lord, who loved us and gave Himself for us, propels us to delight ourselves in His Word, and anything else related to Him. In loving Him, we love what He loves, and shun what He shuns. As we look upon Him, we come to view things from His perspective, in a brand-new way. Jesus incontestably possesses our hearts and our warmest affections. For when we are His, "our thoughts are with Him, and our sweetest thoughts are of Him. All we have and are is consecrated to Him. We long to bear His image, breathe His spirit, do His will, and please Him in all things."[2]

If we search through all our mail and happily find a letter from a loved one, we lay everything else aside and tear that letter open, devouring its contents. We find ourselves totally absorbed in the sentiments and details it brings. Probably we read it more than once to make sure that we miss out on nothing. Is this because of the stationery, handwriting, or sentence structure? No, it's because of the writer himself or herself.

That is the reason we love the Written Word—because we love the living Word. Tasting and seeing that the Lord is good, we delight ourselves in Him who poured out His love in the sacred pages of Scripture, breathed His Spirit into it, and lovingly autographed it for us with His own blood.

When I committed my life to Christ at the age of 10, I found myself driven with great desire to spend time with my best friend Jesus—praying and studying His word. Waking up long before dawn, I would sit at my desk voraciously reading my Bible. Not wanting to let go of this precious experience, I would study for hours learning about Jesus, the Person I loved and admired the most. I will never forget the look on my parents' faces when they would find me—an expression of gratitude mixed with concern. Gratitude for my spiritual interest, yet concern for my lack of sleep.

The impetus for our delighting in the Lord is His delight in us. "Let Israel rejoice in their Maker; let the people of Zion be glad in their King," the psalmist urges God's people. Then he follows his call by giving the reason for it: "For the Lord *takes delight in his people; he crowns the humble with salvation*" (Ps. 149:2-4, NIV). Our loving Lord takes delight in us just as loving parents find great pleasure in their loving children.

Jesus took delight in His relationship with His Father. He was the source of Christ's greatest joy. Speaking prophetically through the psalmist, Christ thus addressed Him: "You will show me the path of life; in Your presence is *fullness of joy;* at Your right hand are *pleasures forevermore*" (Ps. 16:11).

Not only did He taste that His Father was good, but it was His very food, His very life to do His will (John 4:34). Christ wants us to experience the same devotion and delight He and the Father mutually enjoy together. "He [Christ] studied the word of God, and His hours of *greatest happiness* were found when He could turn aside from the scene of His labors . . . to hold communion with God . . ."[3]

The biblical concept of tasting and seeing that the Lord is good (Ps. 34:8) and of delighting ourselves in Him (Ps. 37:4) is not one that we usually associate with devotional life. Normally we approach the devotional life from the perspective of a sense of duty, even of drudgery. Inevitably this leads to a meaningless relationship with God, or we abandon it altogether. If the Lord is good—and He is— then why is it so difficult for us to delight ourselves in Him? Here are a few reasons to consider.

First, it requires that we invest quality time in such a relationship. Most of us are keen on investing in things other than relationships. Second, we are more inclined to be task-oriented than people-oriented. Tasks and accomplishments drive our lives rather than relationships to others, including God. Third, we find ourselves surrounded by just too many distractions. We become so devoted to them that they divert all our attention from Him. Fourth, whatever knowledge we have of Christ tends to be head knowledge rather than heart knowledge. We go through the motions of knowing *about* Him, but do not know Him *personally*.

Of course, we do find ourselves talking about our relationship with Christ, and of our obedience to Him, but we find neither passion nor pleasure in the experience. The heart has grown rather cold and callous. "The joy of the Lord is [my] strength" (Neh. 8:10) does not exactly describe the spiritual song lived out in our daily lives.

On the other hand, our joy and delight in the Lord will reveal that our love for Him is real and our spirituality genuine. But when such love fades and such joy vanishes, then we know that self-centeredness has sapped the vitality out of our spiritual lives. One of the signs of the end, according to Christ, is that "the love of many will grow cold" (Matt. 24:12). Here He is describing those who previously loved Him and rejoiced in their relationship with Him. But in focusing on self, they destroyed that spiritual relationship.

Ellen White writes that "He [in Matt. 24:12] speaks of a class who have fallen from a *high state of spirituality*." Then she searchingly asks, "Where is the fervor, the devotion to God, that corresponds to the greatness of the truth which we claim to believe?" Finally she candidly answers her question: "The love of the world, the love of some darling sin, has *weaned the heart* from the love of prayer and of meditation on sacred things. A formal round of religious services is kept up; but where is the love of Jesus? *Spirituality is dying.*" [4]

Hannah Smith commented that the general public does not have the impression that Christians experience genuine joy in their lives. She was once told, "You Christians seem to have a religion that makes you miserable. You are like a man with a headache. He does not want to get rid of his head, but it hurts him to keep it. You cannot expect outsiders to seek very earnestly for anything so uncomfortable." [5]

But that is a far cry from what Jesus desired for all His followers. Said He, "These things I have spoken to you, that My joy may remain in you, and that your joy may be full" (John 15:11). We can never find genuine joy and permanent pleasure except in Christ, the inexhaustible source. The reason that others fail to discern our joyous experience in the Lord is that we have not ourselves tasted and seen that He is indeed good.

God could say that David was a man after His own heart (1 Sam. 13:14) because they enjoyed a heart relationship together. It becomes quite obvious from reading the Psalms that David possessed that joy and delight in the Lord. He said that his soul panted for Him as the deer thirsts for cool flowing water in a desert (Ps. 42:1, 2) and that his flesh longed for Him as he longed for cool water in a dry and hot land (Ps. 63:1). We cannot help sensing that he did indeed delight himself in God, and that he did taste and see that the Lord is good.

It all sounds like savoring a sumptuous meal, doesn't it? But the delicious spiritual meal that our souls hunger for is the Lord Himself. He is our real food that we taste, eat, and delight ourselves in. Enjoying such a meal with Christ does not in any way imply rushing through some mechanical activity. Rather it points to a relaxed and exuberant time involving our whole being. It also calls for appreciating the ambience, savoring the aroma and taste of every morsel, and relishing the goodness of the One who is altogether lovely.

Let us consider how Jesus explained the importance of such a crucial experience when He visited the home of Martha and Mary (see Luke 10:38-42). Martha was certainly a thoughtful and conscientious friend as she welcomed Jesus into the house and worked so hard to make Him feel comfortable. On the other hand, Mary seemed totally oblivious to all the hustle and bustle of cooking and cleaning taking place around her. She completely absorbed herself in Jesus and what He had to say from the very moment He entered the house. He was all that she could think of, and she was determined to take advantage of every moment she could be with Him.

Martha's *service* to Christ, and Mary's *solitude* with Christ— what made the difference? Martha had *many distractions,* but Mary had *one attraction.* Martha "was distracted with much serving" (verse 40) while Mary simply "sat at Jesus' feet and heard His word" (verse 39). She sat while Martha frantically raced back and forth. But where did she sit, and for what reason? That is the crucial question. Mary sat *at Jesus' feet listening to His word.* And that is all that matters when Christ is around.

Martha soon had had just enough. Exasperated, she complained to Him that Mary was not helping her, and that He was a part of the problem in allowing her sister to get away with it. Jesus answered her with love and concern: "Martha, Martha, you are worried and troubled about many things. But one thing is needed, and Mary has chosen that good part, which will not be taken away from her" (verses 41, 42).

Many things worry and trouble us when we really need only *one thing.* The many things that we spend our entire lives worrying about will eventually vanish, but the one needful thing will never be taken away. Doesn't this direct our minds back to what Jesus said in Matthew 6:33 about keeping our priorities in order? "But seek first the kingdom of God and His righteousness, and all these things shall be added to you."

There He exhorts us, first of all, to seek the *one* important thing—Himself—and then we will find *all other* things taken care of. Life is more than food, drink, and clothing. We should not let life's turmoil so distract us that it eclipses our view of the Life. Focusing on Jesus will straighten our priorities out, for "when once the gaze is fixed upon Him [Christ], the life finds its center."[6]

Hospitable Martha, in her concern to make sure that the meal tasted good and the house looked meticulous, missed enjoying communion with her special Guest. What Martha, the ideal hostess, did was important, but it was not a priority. "Here is a magnanimous gesture but a mistaken one," explains Ken Gire. "Because Jesus does not want food; He wants fellowship."[7] Tasty meals, immaculate homes, and perfect hosting—wonderful as they are—can get in the way of loving fellowship with friends.

So many things get in the way of meaningful and delightful times with God and others. And finally when we really want to do something about it, it may be too late. Attending a funeral of a friend, I overheard someone lament the fact that he had always intended to get together with the deceased individual but had never gotten around to it. Stephen Grellet wrote: "I expect to pass this way but once; any good thing therefore that I can do, or any kindness that I can show to any fellow creature, let me do it now; let me not defer or neglect it, for I shall not pass this way again."

Martha, out of courtesy, might have actually listened to Jesus at the very beginning. She might have been torn as to what to do, for she loved Jesus too, and would have enjoyed visiting with Him as well. Gradually, she found herself drawn more to the kitchen and pulled farther away from Jesus. Thus she found herself increasingly caught up in her frantic preparations. In the anxiety of the moment to serve Jesus, she began focusing on herself.

Consequently, her attitude changed not only toward her sister but also toward her Saviour. She accused Mary of laziness, and even blamed Jesus for indifference. And that is what subtly happens when performance becomes our priority. We focus on self, critically comparing our performance with the performance of others—or lack of it. And our criticism of others knows no limits. No one is immune to its attack, not even Jesus. Martha implied that the all-caring Jesus was uncaring!

Unfortunately, our performance for Christ may supersede our devotion to and love for the person of Christ. The spiritual danger is subtle and real, for our dedication to His service may crowd out our devotion to Him as a person. If we are not careful, the savior of our success may supplant the Saviour of our souls. "As activity increases and men become *successful* in doing any *work for God,* there is danger of trusting to human plans and methods. There is a tendency to pray less, and to have less faith. Like the disciples, we are in danger of losing sight of our dependence on God, and seeking to *make a savior of our activity.* We need to look constantly to Jesus, realizing that it is His power which does the work." [8]

Martha would make a very efficient and self-giving church member, to the delight of any pastor or church board. We need many like

135

her in the Master's service today—men and women who are energetic and resourceful. Although we do not want to dismiss such fine qualities in any church member, at the same time they must, first of all, be subordinated to Christ, and must issue forth from devotion to Him and delight in His person.

"The 'one thing' that Martha needed was a calm, devotional spirit. . . . She needed less anxiety for the things which pass away, and more for those things which endure forever. . . . There is a wide field for the Marthas, with their zeal in active religious work. But let them first sit with Mary at the feet of Jesus. Let diligence, promptness, and energy be sanctified by the grace of Christ; then the life will be an unconquerable power for good." [9]

One has to wonder how many times Jesus misses us when He comes by to enter into fellowship with us. Sadly, He too often finds us preoccupied with so many things, including serving Him, that we do not seize the opportunity to delight ourselves in simply being with Him. Planning to try us again, He reluctantly leaves, ardently hoping that the next time He comes by He will not only find our homes and kitchens open to Him, but, more important, our hearts.

And when He returns, will our welcome to Him be shown by sitting at His feet and listening to His voice, or will we be feverishly fretting about many things? What kind of welcome will our churches give Him when He stops by? Will our reception consist more of labor than devotion? "The church seem content to take only the first steps in conversion. They are more ready for *active labor* than for *humble devotion,* more ready to engage in outward religious service than in the inner work of the heart. Meditation and prayer are neglected for bustle and show." [10]

It is really a matter of priorities. Misplaced priorities can lead us to miss Christ. May this prayer become your and my heartfelt prayer, so that He may become our foremost priority and our supreme delight: "Forgive me for being so much distracted by my preparations, and so little attracted by Your presence. For being so diligent in my duties, and so negligent in my devotion. For being so quick to my feet, and so slow to Yours. Help me to understand that it is an intimate visit You seek from me, not an elaborate meal." [11]

The beautiful description of the love relationship of Solomon and his bride can illustrate the quality we yearn for in our love relationship with Christ. Said he to her: "Like a lily among thorns is my darling among the maidens." Responds she: "Like an apple tree among the trees of the forest is my lover among the young men. I delight to sit in his shade, and his fruit is sweet to my taste. He has taken me to the banquet hall, and his banner over me is love" (S. of Sol. 2:2-4, NIV).

The Song of Solomon here captures in such a superb way what the psalmist means by delighting ourselves in the Lord. It does not depict, by any means, the too often hectic, hurried, and stale relationship we have with Christ. On the contrary, it describes the great joy we have in each other's company. The blissful time to bask in the cool shade of such intimate fellowship, and to relish its taste for the sheer delight of it.

Remember that the Lord invites us to a spiritual banquet with Him, and we will feast at His table. Unfortunately, the way we are accustomed to hurriedly consume our meals today carries over to the way we feast with the Lord. Banqueting with Jesus is never like hastily gulping our fast food from a drive-in restaurant. It is neither like frozen dinners swallowed while glued to television nor like munching on snacks while reading the newspaper.

Visiting some countries in southern Europe, Latin America, and the Middle East has clearly shown me how sharing a meal with someone can be so relaxed, delightful, and conducive to human relationships. Somehow, in the West, we have been conditioned to think that if we take time to enjoy food and fellowship, we are wasting our time, perhaps depriving ourselves of a chance to make more money or get something important done. But this is not so. For in being so obsessed with gaining riches and temporal things, we squander life itself—this life and eternal life to come.

I have counseled numerous parents and youngsters having difficulties in their family relationships about the quality time they need to have together. I will never forget some of the responses.

"Dad, you are always gone. You never spend time with us," one says.

"Mom, you are always so busy. It is impossible to talk with you," another protests.

"I am killing myself to make a good life for you, and I wish you would start appreciating this for a change," the father answers defensively.

"We are doing all of this for you," the mother joins in.

"Dad, Mom, we do appreciate the money, the cars, the nice home and everything, but we just want to spend time with you. We want to go places together, do things together," one of the children answers back.

Too busy making a living, we cannot make a life with our loved ones and with our God.

In his book *The Table of Inwardness,* Calvin Miller uses the Latin term *otium sanctum,* translated "holy leisure," to explain how to delight ourselves in Christ amid the busyness of everyday life. It is not trying to squeeze Christ into our hectic mode of existence, but inviting Him to totally invade and rule it.[12] "Holy living is not abrupt living," Miller suggests. For "no one who hurries into the presence of God is content to remain for long. Those *who hurry in, hurry out.*"[13]

In our relationship with our Lord we are to devote ourselves to Him more than anything or anyone else. Our beloved Christ is like a luxurious fruit-laden tree under whose shade we delight to sit, and His fruit is sweet to our taste. This is tasting and seeing that the Lord is good, and this is the intimate experience that we so desperately need.

"In the midst of this maddening rush [in the world], God is speaking. He bids us come apart and commune with Him," Ellen White observes. "Many, even in their seasons of devotion, fail of receiving the blessing of real communion with God. They are in too great haste. With hurried steps they press through the circle of Christ's loving presence, pausing perhaps a moment within the sacred precincts, but not waiting for counsel. They have no time to remain with the divine Teacher. With their burdens they return to their work."[14]

Why do we hurry away from Christ's loving presence? Why do we make such hasty excursions to Him and eagerly pull away from Him? It is as if we suffer from the paradox of being unable to stay with Him, yet unable to remain away from Him. Is this because we are not accustomed to feeling comfortable in close relationships? We have an innate need to really know and be known, but we are afraid of the experience. Like our first parents, we hide from our God behind some flimsy fig leaves. But He already knows us, and in spite all that we are, He greatly loves us and longs to be close to us.

Furthermore, in our task-oriented society, we often do not feel at ease reaching out to others—even to friends and family members—unless we have a need, or we can come up with some sort of excuse or explanation. This mind-set frequently affects our personal relationship with God. We do not often seek Him simply for the joy of being with Him, but rather because we are in desperate straits. Even when we rush to Him under such circumstances, we still do it rather reluctantly and impersonally. One may compare such an encounter to that of paying bills or going to the dentist—unpleasant but essential.

But relationships require more than discussing issues and tackling problems. Do we ever feel that we miss being with God when we have not needed to seek His help for some time? For example, when it comes to our good friends, do we miss them and feel like seeing them just for the joy of being with them? Do we feel free to drop by to see them, or do we experience some unexplained reluctance to do so? When we sometimes feel reluctance, do we find ourselves pressed to furnish an excuse or fumble for an explanation in order to justify getting together with them?

Few of us feel free to see friends just for their sake, just for the joy of being with them. And that is perhaps because heart-to-heart interaction makes us uncomfortable. We would rather avoid such intimacy by distracting ourselves in discussing other safe issues. Is this possibly one reason that we prefer to entertain in our homes large groups rather than one person or family? That way we have less risk of vulnerability and closeness.

Although our loving God welcomes us with open arms when we run to Him in times of distress, He also longs to see us come to Him at all times simply because we love Him and enjoy being with Him. Genuine love is always seeking togetherness with the beloved. "We come to the Lord not because we want something from Him or even because we have something we need to share with Him," Larry Richards explains, "but simply because *we want to be with Him,* and with Him alone." [15]

But what can we do about the quality of our communion with Christ? How can such communion become a delight to dwell on rather than a drudgery to endure? How can we take our hectic time and make it holy time? How do we learn to enjoy lingering long in Christ's loving presence?

We need to earnestly pray for the Holy Spirit to reveal to us the excellence and all-sufficiency of our Lord. He is what our hearts desperately need because He alone possesses in Himself all that we have ever longed for. Christ is the only true source of love, peace, acceptance, security, friendship, riches, and eternal life. By uniting our lives with His we possess all things.

Hopefully we can all think of one ideal friend whom we greatly love and admire. A best friend with whom we have enjoyed a long and loving relationship. Take such quality friendship and multiply it by eternity, and there we have Jesus. Isn't this the kind of ideal and best friend that we have been searching for? Christ has our very best at heart, for His thoughts are only of good, and not evil. He created us for His pleasure, He sacrificed His life for our restoration, He longs to live His abundant life in us today, and He yearns to lavish on us His eternal glory at His coming.

If we can have this type of Friend, why should we hesitate to come to Him and stay with Him for the sheer delight of just being with Him? Why not hasten to be in His loving presence at every opportunity we have? It is easy to take such an ideal Friend for granted, but it is not that easy to maintain our vital relationship with Him unless we jealously and continuously guard and nurture it.

For you see, I know from personal experience. In rushing to finish this chapter about tasting and seeing the goodness of the Lord, I had to guard lest I let writing spiritual things in any way compete with my spiritual priority of sitting at the feet of Jesus. It would be quite an irony, if in the process of rushing to finish this book on Christ and spirituality, I find myself overlooking the joy of spiritual communion with Christ. May He ever remain the one attraction among the many distractions. And may He ever continue to be the joy and delight of our hearts as we taste and see that He is good indeed.

[1] Donald E. Mansell, *New Every Morning* (Washington, D.C.: Review and Herald Pub. Assn., 1981), p. 15.

[2] Ellen G. White, *Steps to Christ,* p. 58.

[3] ———, *The Ministry of Healing,* p. 52.

[4] ———, *Testimony Treasures* (Mountain View, Calif.: Pacific Press Pub. Assn., 1949), vol. 2, p. 210. (Italics supplied.)

[5] Hannah Whitall Smith, *The Christian's Secret of a Happy Life* (Westwood, N.J.: Flemming H. Revell Co., 1952), p. 15.

[6] White, *Education,* p. 297.

[7] Ken Gire, *Intimate Moments With the Savior* (Grand Rapids: Zondervan Pub. House, 1989), p. 66.

[8] White, *The Desire of Ages,* p. 362. (Italics supplied.)

[9] *Ibid.,* p. 525.

[10] White, *Testimonies,* vol. 4, p. 535. (Italics supplied.)

[11] Gire, p. 69.

[12] Miller, *The Table of Inwardness,* p. 36.

[13] *Ibid.* (Italics supplied.)

[14] White, *Education,* p. 260.

[15] Richards, *A Practical Theology of Spirituality,* p. 106.

TASTE AND SEE—2

L et us suppose that some friends invite us to eat at their home. At mealtime they want us to sample the fine whole-wheat bread they just made. However, before we can try it, we hear a detailed discourse describing all the wonderful things about the tasty loaf of bread. As our appetites quicken, we hear them winding down their lecture on the bread's ingredients, nutrients, taste, and texture—only to have them whisk it away at the end. Baffled, we wonder how useful an exercise the experience was—learning all about the fine qualities of the bread, yet stopping short of actually tasting and seeing that it was good.

While few people would actually do that to us in everyday life, in the spiritual realm it, unfortunately, occurs all too often. The bread of life contains all the spiritual nourishment ever needed for spiritual restoration. However, all too often we test this bread but never taste it, describe it but not digest it, and analyze it but not assimilate it.

The Scriptures present an intimately intertwined relationship between themselves and the living Word. Jesus Christ and the Holy Bible are both referred to as the Bread of Life. Moreover, both were conceived by the Holy Spirit, who leads us to encounter the living Word in the written Word. Both give spiritual strength and life to all who taste and see that the Lord and His Word are good.

Scripture interchangeably uses such descriptive terms as "taste," "eat," "rejoice," and "delight" to illustrate our intimate relationship with the Lord and His Word. Jeremiah said: "Your words were found, and I ate them, and Your word was to me the joy and rejoicing of my heart" (Jer. 15:16). Notice the progression in this text. God's words are, first of all, to be found, implying a desire to search for them. Second, finding such words is not enough in itself, for then we must eat them. And finally, partaking of the life-giving words brings profound joy to the heart. George Mueller accustomed himself to continue feeding on the Word until he rejoiced in God, and then he felt ready to face the new day.

David declared: "How *sweet* are Your words to my *taste,* sweeter than honey to my mouth!" (Ps. 119:103). And, "I long for Your salvation, O Lord, and Your law is my *delight"* (verse 174; see also verses 97, 111, 127, 162). And he says of God's judgments: "More to be desired are they than gold, yea, than much fine gold; sweeter also than honey and the honeycomb" (Ps. 19:10).

As we look at such biblical references, we clearly sense that the divine bread of life can be personally experienced as surely as eating our daily physical bread. Christ is ever revealing Himself in His Word, encouraging and empowering us. And we can experience it as immediately as tasting fine food, and as readily as enjoying being with a faithful friend.

Jeremiah and David clearly come across as taking their time to feast on the words of God. They are not interested merely in thinking about the words, or even hearing them. But they linger in God's presence, slowly savoring every bit and morsel of His spiritual meal, and assimilating its nutrients into every fabric of their being. Each summons every faculty to such spiritual activity. The reason they delighted themselves in the word of the Lord is that they delighted themselves in the Lord of the Word.

Jesus, in John 6, referred several times to Himself as the "bread of life" (verses 35, 48, 51). Then He added that this bread is His flesh, which when eaten gives life eternal (verses 51, 53). Said He: "For My flesh is food indeed, and My blood is drink indeed" (verse 55). Whenever we eat, it should remind us that He gave His body for us, and whenever we drink we remember that He spilled His blood for us.

Yes, we receive life from eating His flesh as we receive it from appropriating His words. "The words that I speak to you are spirit, and they are life" (verse 63). In studying Scripture we are meeting the Saviour. For in seeking His words we find ourselves "brought into communion with Christ."[1] As we feed on the Word of the Lord we are feasting on the Lord of the Word, and in receiving life from His

Word, we are receiving *His* very life.

"He who by faith receives the Word is receiving the *very life* and character of God."[2] Andrew Murray compares the word with prayer, declaring that in prayer we give ourselves to God, and go up to dwell with Him, while in the word, God gives Himself to us, and comes down to dwell with us.[3]

In Christ giving Himself to us in His Word, He also speaks to us just as He spoke to His contemporaries when He lived on earth. I used to wish that I could hear Christ's voice speaking specifically to me. But I learned in time that He indeed does. "The word of the living God is not merely written, but spoken. The Bible is God's voice speaking to us, just as surely as though we could hear it with our ears. If we realized this, with what awe would we open God's Word. . . . The reading and contemplation of the Scriptures would be regarded as an audience with the Infinite One."[4]

In childhood we first hear before we are able to speak. Similarly, if we do not listen to God speak to us, then we do not learn how to speak with Him. Unfortunately, even then we often do more talking to God than listening to Him. "To speak words that reach and touch God, affecting and influencing the power of the unseen world, depends entirely on our hearing God's voice," Andrew Murray explains. "The extent to which we listen will determine the extent to which we learn to speak in the voice and the language that God hears." Murray continues: "As the words of Christ enter our very hearts, becoming and influencing our lives, our words will enter His heart and influence Him."[5]

It is true that we are what we eat. If we eat poor food, we have poor health, but if we eat good food, we have good health. More than that, we biologically become the very food we eat and assimilate. When we feed on Jesus, He becomes our health and life. For "what food is to the body, Christ must be to the soul. Food cannot benefit us unless we eat it, unless it becomes a part of our being. . . . A theoretical knowledge will do us no good. We must feed upon Him, receive Him into the heart, so that *His life becomes our life.*"[6]

No wonder that we may find even some Bible scholars, who devote themselves to the study of the Scriptures, spiritually anemic and lacking the joy of the Lord. They squander their precious time losing sight of the Lord in His Word. Knowing the theory but not the power of the Word, they analyze but do not assimilate. Such individuals delve into but do not digest, critique but not consume, the Word.

While it helps to spend some time in analysis, we must still go beyond that to taste and see that the bread of life is good. Only here will we truly find spiritual vitality, and without it we become famished and emaciated. "We must be Christians in whom the Word is never separated from the living God Himself. We must live as Christians to whom God in heaven speaks every day and all day long."[7]

But some may say that they tried to taste the Word of God, but unfortunately found it neither good nor sweet. In fact, it was bland and boring to them. Consequently, either they have given up Bible study altogether or they just read it out of routine or duty. Why do we, then, suffer such deprivation and lack of joy in God's Word? At least five thoughts come to mind:

First of all, have we experienced Christ's love and fellowship in our lives? If we haven't, then it is understandable why we do not enjoy His Word. When we genuinely love someone, we become quite interested in knowing about that person. Likewise, we need to experience a loving relationship with the living Word in order to delight ourselves in His written Word.

Second, we tend to be impatient, expecting quick results. We give up easily unless a desired outcome is immediately forthcoming. But no project will produce worthwhile results unless we have put considerable effort into it. Things of value take time to cultivate and enjoy. We often ask whether doing something is *fun* when we really need to ask whether something is *right*. This applies particularly in the spiritual realm.

Of course, some things are fun as soon as you start them, but that must not be the main criterion. On the other hand, there are many things in life worth doing, but we do not always feel like doing them. Yet we do them because we know they are right to do. With time such worthwhile endeavors become increasingly easier and more enjoyable. Then they become *real* fun.

Most of us know from experience that it is not that easy to start and sustain a physical exercise program. Take jogging, for example. It is not initially fun, and it takes discipline to keep it up. Our sore and aching bodies tempt us to give it all up for good. However, with perseverance, such activity becomes progressively invigorating, enjoyable, and even something we actually look forward to.

Third, we are so used to tasting and consuming unspiritual foods that our spiritual taste buds become too depraved to enjoy wholesome spiritual foods. The body craves whatever we get it used to. How can we enjoy the bread of life if we have been feasting on unspiritual junk foods? How can we relish studying the Bible if we have been saturating our minds with whatever we find in the hedonistic media? Or if we have been caught up in what the world has to offer, how can we enjoy what the Word has to offer?

If we get so conditioned from childhood to consume inordinate amounts of sugar in our food, then whatever is naturally sweet is no longer sweet enough for us. We even pour more sugar on breakfast cereals whose first ingredient is sugar! Therefore, we should not be surprised and become discouraged if the word of God does not taste good initially. We need to give God time to recondition and recreate our spiritual taste buds. Each of us needs to alter our spiritual diet by eating His Word and staying away from spiritual junk foods. He will help us recover the capacity to appreciate and enjoy the wholesome spiritual food that He offers us.

Fourth, even the most tasty food does not appeal to us when we get sick. But we still must eat in order to regain our stamina and strength. I remember my childhood years when I would become ill. My mother would prepare my favorite food and bring it to my bedside. I would take a bite or two of it and then discard it. I simply did not have the appetite or the taste. Under normal circumstances I would have quickly devoured it. Now she would encourage me to eat, explaining that her food tasted as great as before, and that I especially needed to eat it on account of my illness.

It is likely that when we are spiritually sick, spiritual food does not feel appetizing to us. However, we must not go merely by feeling, but by principle. We must eat in order to regain our strength, and soon we will recover our appetite for spiritual food and it will become an integral part of our everyday lives.

Finally, we need to keep in mind that discouragement is one of the most formidable weapons Satan uses against us, especially in the area of communion with God. He knows that for us to continue such communion would break his power over us. Therefore, he tries his hardest to defeat us, realizing that if he succeeds here he would overwhelm us in many other areas as well.

Years ago when I resolved to commit myself to a devotional life, I decided to do that every morning. I chose mornings because that is the best way to begin the day, energized by a hearty spiritual breakfast. However, at times circumstances forced me to forgo my spiritual breakfast. Satan would seize on that, causing me to become demoralized and to question the depth of my commitment. A sense of failure would flood me, affecting my entire day.

One day as I sought God's help, He impressed me with the commonsense thought that while the first meal of the day is the most important one, still if you sometimes miss your breakfast, it does not mean you have to go hungry all day. You still can eat a late breakfast, lunch, or supper. Certainly eating something sometime during the day is much better than simply eating nothing. The thought was a timely spiritual insight and apt analogy! It does not mean that our entire day has to be ruined if sometimes we miss our devotional time in the morning. We definitely do not have to be spiritually famished all day, for we can take time at noon, in the evening, or sometime between to meet with God for spiritual nourishment. Now if I have to miss my devotional time in the morning (which I never like to do), then I make sure to satisfy my spiritual hunger later in the day.

How do we then taste and see that the Word of the Lord is good? Relational Bible study (RBS) is one special way that has greatly helped me along my spiritual journey. This approach to Bible study does not focus on information acquisition, but on life transformation. It concentrates on partaking of Christ's life rather than finding texts in order to prove someone is right or wrong.

I am sure the latter has its place, but our priority here is to experience Christ's life becoming our life. The ultimate purpose of God giving His Word was not merely to dispense helpful information but to invest His life in us, so that His life may in turn become ours. For only His life can quicken and transform ours, molding and fashioning them after His likeness. Jesus said: "The words that I speak to you are spirit, and they are life" (John 6:63). They contain His very spirit. And whoever by faith receives His words receives His life (John 5:24) and the semblance of His character.

To start a relational Bible study you need to follow successive steps. Such important steps help us enter and experience the spiritual atmosphere of the divine presence. To summarize them, I have used four verbs beginning with the letter P for easy recall.

1. *Pick* a passage. The first thing to do is to select a suitable biblical passage describing an incident in which God encounters people.

We focus on such episodes to discover the dynamics of the divine-human interaction. Let us look at four aspects for this rationale:

First, the Bible is brimming with stories. Apparently, that is the way God desires to reveal Himself to us. Second, stories are an easier and more attractive way to start and continue such a spiritual endeavor. Third, God comes across as more real as He reveals Himself in the context of interacting with and helping others like ourselves. And fourth, we can more readily identify with the characters in the stories, for they were in many ways like us.

The different accounts from the four Gospels offer a good place to start. And for an illustration, let us take the narrative of Jesus stilling the storm on the Sea of Galilee, as recorded in Mark 4:35-41. Here is the account in full:

"On the same day, when evening had come, He [Jesus] said to them, 'Let us cross over to the other side.' Now when they had left the multitude, they took Him along in the boat as He was. And other little boats were also with Him. And a great windstorm arose, and the waves beat into the boat, so that it was already filling. But He was in the stern, asleep on a pillow. And they awoke Him and said to Him, 'Teacher, do You not care that we are perishing?' Then He arose and rebuked the wind, and said to the sea, 'Peace, be still!' And the wind ceased and there was a great calm. But He said to them, 'Why are you so fearful? How is it that you have no faith?' And they feared exceedingly, and said to one another, 'Who can this be, that even the wind and the sea obey Him!'"

2. *Pray.* Now that we have chosen the passage, we need to pray. The Bible is a spiritual book inspired by the Holy Spirit. It reveals the very thoughts and feelings of God Himself. Therefore, in order to discern His mind and heart, we need to earnestly and humbly seek His Spirit's guidance from the very beginning. After all, He is the Bible's real author, and thus He knows the ideas He implanted in Scripture, and how to correctly communicate them to the honest seeker after truth. *"Never* should the Bible be studied without prayer. Before opening its pages we should ask for the enlightenment of the Holy Spirit, and it will be given."[8]

The apostle Paul explains that "the natural man does not receive the things of the Spirit of God, for they are foolishness to him; nor can he know them, because they are spiritually discerned" (1 Cor. 2:14). We greatly need spiritual discernment derived from prayerful Bible study, for God's wisdom seems foolish from a human perspective. "When we come to the Bible, reason must acknowledge an authority superior to itself, and heart and intellect must bow to the great I AM."[9]

It must be an honest-to-God prayer through which we open wide our hearts to Him as our most loved and trusted friend. This is a good way to start communing with Him, because we need to recognize that we no longer have any need to hide or pretend in His presence. No longer do we have to keep a safe distance, save a safe corner somewhere in our lives, or gloss over a hidden problem. We will feel a sense of liberation as we come honestly before His presence, unburdening ourselves of anything that hinders our intimate communion with Him.

He already knows our problems and defects all too well, and yet He loves us anyway and desires to meet with us. Freed from the burden of needing to impress Him, we find ourselves released to freely commune with Him because we are known and accepted in the Beloved. And our greatest recommendation to go to Him is simply our need. In fact, even when we sometimes do not have a spiritual appetite to taste and see that He is good, we can still tell Him exactly how we feel. We are simply doing His will by humbly and honestly coming into His presence in whatever condition we may be in.

He is the one who invites us: "Come to Me, all you who labor and are heavy laden, and I will give you rest" (Matt. 11:28). And Peter, who knew from firsthand experience, encourages us to humbly come to Him with *all* our cares. "Therefore humble yourselves under the mighty hand of God, that He may exalt you in due time, casting all your care upon Him, for He cares for you" (1 Peter 5:6, 7).

It should give us a great sense of freedom to know that in His presence we no longer need to play spiritual hide-and-seek games or have hidden spiritual agendas. We are simply open, vulnerable, and authentic before Him—not in order to impress Him but to help us become free and receptive to what He desires to do in our lives.

The obstructions that block the free flow of His Spirit in us get swept away. Like David, we personally and wholeheartedly invite Him to "search me, O God, and know my heart; try me, and know my anxieties; and see if there is any wicked way in me, and lead me in the way everlasting" (Ps. 139:23, 24). God most assuredly answers such humble, honest, and heartfelt prayers that give Him total freedom to break through and penetrate the innermost corners of our lives.

When we are praying such honest-to-God prayers, we should not let what prayer forms we must employ distract us, nor should we become preoccupied with what words to use. Rather we must let ourselves get caught up in talking and listening to God just as we would when conversing with someone sitting in our study or living room. Would an observer, upon hearing such a prayer, sense that we were really communicating with somebody?

Breathing such an authentic prayer is indeed the breath of the soul, and without it we will experience only spiritual weakness and suffocation. The physiological act of breathing is certainly more than exhaling carbon dioxide—it is also inhaling the life-giving oxygen. Both things are absolutely essential for survival and vitality. Likewise in our prayer life, we breathe out to God our discouragement, anxiety, and sin, and breathe in from Him His life-giving encouragement, peace, and cleansing.

That is why prayer is a two-way street. Unloading on Him our toxic burdens is essential, but not enough. We must also receive His life into ourselves. Each one of us must be still and know that He is God. As His children we need to even listen more than talk to Him. God has specific things to personally tell each one of us about our lives. Just imagine what would happen if we availed ourselves of His perfect understanding of us and acted on it.

But this is exactly what worries Satan the most—for us to be in touch with the living God, and to experience His power flashing in our lives. The devil does not worry about our prayerless Bible study; he ridicules our routine religious rituals, and he laughs at our pretentious spirituality, but he shakes with dread when our prayers open wide the heart of God and unlock the gates of heaven. Let our prayers ever continue to be the very breath of our souls, glorifying God and disappointing Satan. And let our fears vanish in the power of our God. It is about time to see Satan be the one quaking with fear for a change.

3. *Ponder.* After praying for the Holy Spirit to guide us in our study of the inspired account, we ponder it in our hearts. To ponder something is to contemplate it, to meditate and dwell on it, to consider it quietly and deeply. It is more than just casually reading the chosen passage, but rather allowing its spirit and life to thoroughly penetrate the depths of our hearts. "Merely to hear or to read the Word is not enough. He who desires to be profited by the Scriptures *must meditate* upon the truth that has been presented to him. By

earnest attention and prayerful thought he must . . . drink deep of the spirit of the holy oracles." [10]

To ponder His words is to take time to enjoy His presence. So many things in our lives beckon us incessantly to hurry, to dash about, and to clamor for instant satisfaction. But this simply does not work if we want to saturate our beings with His words, experience His presence, and receive His life. To ponder is to *linger*. It is to sit down with Him, conversing and enjoying His companionship.

Just as when we are in the company of trusted friends, we won't find ourselves fidgety and fretful, or frantically rushing in and out of their living rooms and lives. But we linger to savor their words and enjoy their presence without being detached and distracted. To be otherwise is not to be real friends. Similarly, we do not simply pause for a few moments in Christ's presence, detached and distracted, and quickly glance over His words for us, then with a sense of relief rush away. There is no friendship in this, no intimacy, no renewal of life.

God longs for us to ponder His words by being still before Him and knowing that He is our God (Ps. 46:10). Stillness is an essential ingredient for reflection and meditation. It is the only way we get to know both God and ourselves. As we place ourselves at His disposal in that sacred atmosphere of stillness, we may hear His voice striking a responsive chord in our souls.

Witnessing and participating in the divine-human resonance, He greatly rejoices that He finally has our undivided attention. Now He can fashion us after His likeness. It is precisely the position we need to be in, for we desperately need His living words to break through the world's hold on us, penetrating our souls and reshaping our lives.

"We must individually hear Him speaking to the heart. When every other voice is hushed, and in quietness we wait before Him, the silence of the soul makes more distinct the voice of God," Ellen White writes. Then as a result of such a quiet encounter with God, our lives "will breathe out a fragrance, and will reveal a divine power that will reach men's hearts." [11]

Such intimate communion with Christ is what relational Bible study is about. After all, the Bible is a book about relationships. And a sacred story from the Scriptures can provide us with a focal point so that He can pull our relationships toward Him and address us in His Word. Thus He diverts our attention from our different distractions and focuses it on Himself and His Word.

Robert Slocum explains that if we are interested in a genuine dialogue with God, to "really talk" with Him and not merely to toss some empty words at Him, then focusing on a biblical passage can provide us with the opportunity to "have something specific to discuss." "Meditation over a passage of Scripture provides the subject matter through which God speaks to me. Then, once I have listened, the same passage gives me something practical to talk to God about."[12]

4. *Project.* In other words, we must put ourselves in the sacred story we are studying, imagining that we are there with the participants. If the word *imagination* unsettles us a bit, then let us recognize the fact that such mental activity is an integral part of our daily thinking processes. Unfortunately, most of it is selfish, secular, and sinful. So why not redirect the imagination to something sacred and spiritual?

Christ's use of illustrations redirected His hearers' imagination, channeling it into something holy and heavenly. Of course, Jesus is the subject that deserves our most intense contemplation and our richest imagination. "We should take it [the life of Christ] point by point, and let the *imagination* grasp each scene."[13] We lose many fresh spiritual insights that God desires to reveal to us by dwelling on worldly things rather than "educating the *imagination* to dwell upon divine things."[14]

Human imagination is often not only unholy but also unreal. However, when we educate it to dwell on Christ, we are using this God-given ability to examine what is eternally real. For "Jesus Christ is the same yesterday, today, and forever" (Heb. 13:8), and He is as willing to make an impact on our lives today as He did on the people of yesterday. After all, we have similar needs and problems.

Someone once observed that the reason movie actors are so successful in their work is that they take something unreal and make it real by imagining it is so. On the other hand, we Christians often take what is most real, and by our lives make it seem so unreal. If actors can make unreal things seem so real, why cannot we take the real things of God and keep them that way? After all, the most real things in this world are temporary, but the things of God are eternal.

Notice what Ellen White counsels us to do as we study the teachings of Jesus to His disciples and the multitude: "Let us *in imagination go back* to that scene, and, as we *sit with* the disciples on the mountainside, *enter into* the thoughts and feelings that filled their hearts. Understanding what the words of Jesus meant to those who heard them, we may discern in them a new vividness and beauty, and may also gather for ourselves their deeper lessons." [15]

And in connection with celebrating Communion, she counsels us to imagine the sacred scenes in order to awaken "living and sacred emotions in our hearts" and to keep "fresh in memory the scenes of Calvary." For "as we receive the bread and the wine symbolizing Christ's broken body and spilled blood, we in *imagination* join the scene of Communion in the upper chamber. We seem to be passing through the garden. . . . We witness the struggle. . . . Christ is set forth crucified among us." [16]

[1] Ellen G. White, *Sons and Daughters of God* (Washington, D.C.: Review and Herald Pub. Assn., 1955), p. 304.

[2] ———, *Christ's Object Lessons,* p. 38. (Italics supplied.)

[3] Andrew Murray, *The Inner Life* (Springdale, Pa.: Whitaker House, 1984), p. 22.

[4] White, *Testimonies,* vol. 6, p. 393.

[5] Andrew Murray, *With Christ in the School of Prayer* (Springdale, Pa.: Whitaker House, 1981), pp. 164, 165.

[6] White, *The Desire of Ages,* p. 389. (Italics supplied.)

[7] Murray, *The Inner Life,* p. 90.

[8] White, *Steps to Christ,* p. 91. (Italics supplied.)

[9] *Ibid.,* p. 110.

[10] White, *Christ's Object Lessons,* pp. 59, 60. (Italics supplied.)

[11] ———, *The Desire of Ages,* p. 363.

[12] Robert E. Slocum, *Ordinary Christians in a High-Tech World* (Waco, Tex.: Word Books Pub., 1986), p. 119.

[13] White, *The Desire of Ages,* p. 83. (Italics supplied.)

[14]*The SDA Bible Commentary,* Ellen G. White Comments, vol. 6, p. 1085. (Italics supplied.)

[15] White, *Thoughts From the Mount of Blessing,* p. 1. (Italics supplied.)

[16] ———, *The Desire of Ages,* p. 661. (Italics supplied.)

CHAPTER
TWELVE

TASTE AND SEE—3

Having already picked the proper passage, prayed, pondered, and projected ourselves into the account of Jesus calming the storm, let us describe in our own words the thoughts that may have struck our minds.

In this particular event Jesus and His disciples, at the end of a full day's work, slipped away in a boat to cross to the other side of the Sea of Galilee. They were enjoying a restful and smooth voyage in the company of Jesus when all of a sudden a severe windstorm struck them. Furious waves dashed against the boat, battering and filling it with water, and threatening to destroy it and its occupants.

The disciples had tried to save themselves, and coming to the end of their rope, they seemed to have stumbled over Jesus in the darkness and confusion (suggested by the astonishment evident in their testy question). Awakening Him from His peaceful sleep, they brusquely asked Him if He even cared if they all perished. Probably they thought that everyone else had been killing himself trying to do something to weather the storm while He did not even budge. *What is the matter with Him?* they wondered. *Doesn't He care at all what happens to us?*

It was easy for the disciples to remember Jesus and be aware of His presence and power when things were going well. But when things got suddenly stormy, they resorted to their own strength. Yet Jesus, the Creator and Commander of all nature, was apparently waiting for them to ask for help. For no sooner had they asked, though rudely, than He rescued them.

He could have taken offense at their implied accusation that He did not care for them, or He could have argued with them and chastened them. Instead, He rebuked the wind and calmed the sea. Yes, Jesus is bigger than any storm, and at His word the wind and the sea obey Him.

Now we are ready to proceed to the next phase in relational Bible study: writing down answers to a series of questions regarding the passage in a special notebook. Jotting things down helps to reinforce and concretize what is in our minds and hearts. Furthermore, it will serve later on as a reminder of how the Holy Spirit had led us in our walk with Christ at a particular time and circumstance in our spiritual journey.

There are basically three questions to ask ourselves. The first pertains to Jesus, the second relates to the other character(s) in the account, and the third deals with ourselves. As you respond to the following questions, write down several things that the Holy Spirit brings to your mind.

The first question: What does this account teach me about *Jesus?*

The second question: What does it teach me about the other *character(s)?*

The third question: What does it teach me about *myself?*

As you notice, the questions are progressive in nature, beginning with Jesus and concluding with us. And wedged in between is the question about others.

The rationale for such an order is that we need to, first of all, start with Jesus so that we may see others, ourselves, and circumstances from His perspective. It does make a great difference to consider things from the vantage of Christ's viewpoint, and to see that from the very beginning. Otherwise, we may find our minds so engrossed in ourselves or so focused on others that it obscures our view.

When we concentrate on Jesus first, when we immerse ourselves in who He is and what He can do, our trust and hope in Him will grow. Then we will know that we are not alone, but that He is right there facing whatever comes our way along with us. The problems do not necessarily vanish, but now they do not overwhelm us, because we sense His powerful presence assuring us that nothing is impossible for Him. It is true that "when once the gaze is fixed upon Him [Christ], the life finds its center."[1] In the thick of our many distractions and competing priorities, our lives desperately need a center, a focal point to pull the many pieces together. For when our souls are stayed on Him, and when our sights always turn toward Him, then everything else will fade into its proper perspective.

"We need constantly a fresh revelation of Christ, a daily experience that harmonizes with His teachings. . . . Many have a twilight perception of Christ's excellence, and their hearts thrill with joy. They long for a fuller, deeper sense of the Saviour's love. Let these cherish every desire of the soul after God. The Holy Spirit works with those who will be worked, molds those who will be molded, fashions those who will be fashioned. Give yourselves the culture of spiritual thoughts and holy communings."[2]

Our minds need constant reminders of Jesus. "Memory's hall should be hung with sacred pictures, with views of Jesus, with lessons of His truth, with revealings of His matchless charms. If memory's hall were thus furnished, we would not look upon our lot as intolerable. We would not talk of the faults of others. Our souls would be full of Jesus and His love."[3] Our spirit needs to sympathize with His Spirit as we "meditate day and night upon His character." Then we will "see His beauty and rejoice in His goodness." Our hearts "will glow with a sense of His love." Also, we "will be uplifted as if borne by everlasting arms."[4]

Anchored in Christ, we grow strong in His strength. We make a spiritual impact on humanity because we have first seen divinity. That was the experience of John the Baptist, who "looked upon the King in His beauty, and self was forgotten. . . . He was ready to go forth as Heaven's messenger, *unawed by the human, because he had looked upon the Divine. He could stand erect and fearless in the presence of earthly monarchs, because he had bowed low before the King of kings.*"[5]

So, in response to our first question about Jesus, here are some possible insights that we may glean from our study of the passage. Of course, you may be impressed with some different or additional concepts from your own meditation. Therefore, consider the following points as a sample exercise to help you get started.

1. Jesus is the Creator of all nature and He is Commander of all its forces. He is still in control, and He will still have the last word in my life.

2. Jesus is bigger than the most raging storm that may burst upon me. The roaring winds and the towering waves are subject to Him. Nothing is impossible for Him, for He can handle whatever

comes my way.

3. Jesus does not "abandon ship" during a storm. He wants to navigate my turbulent life and confront my storm as He stands by me. Christ wants to be close to me in the peaceful as well as the stormy times. My Saviour wants to share my joys and shoulder my burdens.

4. Jesus is there with me even though I sometimes do not sense His presence. Too preoccupied with myself and my problems, I have not focused upon Him and what He is able and willing to do for me. Feelings are frequently fleeting, but His presence with me is a fact based on His promise that He will never leave me nor forsake me.

5. Jesus is indeed the Prince of Peace. In the midst of chaos, fear, and hopelessness, He is always calm. Absolutely nothing can make Him lose His composure. Though vicious storms rage all around Him, He possesses an inner peace that prevails over them all. That is the kind of daily companion I must have to calm my own fears and steady my way.

6. Jesus does not necessarily mind how in our desperation we reach out to Him for help, as long as we just do. He eagerly awaits our cry for aid. And the fact that the disciples finally asked Him to save them is more important to Him than the manner in which they requested that salvation. I do not need to wait for better times or more suitable opportunities to cry out to Christ. Nor do I need to have a perfect speech to address Him. I may reach out to Him at any time, in any way, and in any circumstance I may be in.

7. Jesus would rather focus on the solution than the problem. He arose to rebuke the storm, not the disciples. When Jesus knows that I sincerely desire His help, He prefers not to dwell on my trials and transgressions, but on my transformation.

If Christ fills our minds and hearts from the very outset of our relational Bible study, then we view Him and His Word from a fresh and revitalizing perspective. As the Holy Spirit brings conviction to our hearts, we are "brought into communion with Christ. Familiar truths will present themselves to your mind in a new aspect, texts of Scripture will burst upon you with a new meaning as a flash of light, . . . and you will know that Christ is leading you, a divine Teacher is at your side."[6]

Our appreciation and trust of Him revive and our love to Him rekindles when we experience a relationship with Him. Also, our love for the Bible stirs up because it reveals Christ, and because in its sacred pages we contemplate the beauty of His holiness. Joy and gratitude grip our hearts because we know that only in that holy contemplation will we become transformed into His likeness.

Ellen White captured this thought well when she affirmed that "as the student of the Bible beholds the Redeemer, there is awakened in the soul the mysterious power of faith, adoration, and love. Upon the vision of Christ the gaze is fixed, and the beholder grows into the likeness of that which he adores. The words of the apostle Paul become the language of the soul: 'I count all things but loss for the excellency of the knowledge of Christ Jesus my Lord . . .' (Phil. 3:8-10)."[7]

Such insights about Christ—what He is like and what He can do—when dwelt on can firmly establish us in Him. And thus in a position of trust and strength in Him, we find ourselves prepared to respond to the other questions. Moreover, our focus on Christ at the beginning makes the entire relational Bible study Christ-centered. Our attention on Christ is not merely to spark our interest but should pervade our total experience.

Our spiritual experience with Christ through the Holy Spirit transforms how we perceive Scripture. Currents of living water course in and through our beings, carrying freshness and vitality. "As you seek unto those living springs you will, through the Holy Spirit, be brought into communion with Christ."[8]

In response to the second question on what the biblical account teaches us about the characters in it, consider the following points as an example:

1. The disciples found it easy to feel strong and spiritual as long as they remained aware of Christ's presence near them. But when stunned by the sudden storm, they took their eyes off Him and forgot He was right there in their very midst.

2. The disciples seemed to have tried to confront the storm by themselves, and they cried out to Him only from total desperation.

3. The disciples, even though they knew that Jesus loved them very much, blamed Him anyway for not caring about them. They had focused on the storm rather than the Saviour.

4. The disciples, consequently, became exceedingly fearful, and their faith shook to the core.

5. The disciples, again becoming aware of Jesus, called out to Him. It was the redeeming feature of their stormy experience. Although it was belated, at least they finally sought Him.

In our first question we learn about Christ and what He desires to do for us. Here, in the second question, we see how He actually helped people like you and me. This builds up our faith and bolsters our confidence in what Christ says and does. For as He ministered to the disciples in the past, He will also tend us in our present need. What He has done for others He will do for us, for He is always the same.

The third question has to do with what the biblical account tells us about ourselves. What do we learn about you and me as a result of reflecting on Christ and His way of helping other human beings? Do we find ways in which we may identify with the disciples? In what ways are we like them?

We are not beyond His help, for He had already proven Himself to them, and He will prove Himself to us as well. The characters serve as our point of contact with Him.

This question about ourselves is vital, because it touches upon where we need to practice God's precepts and promises in our individual lives. How will the great insights gained in our study benefit us spiritually unless we implement them? It is true that the "reading of the Bible through and through, or the explanation of it verse by verse, will not benefit us or those who hear us unless we bring the truths of the Bible into our individual experience. . . . Then through the work of the Holy Spirit the precepts of the Word will become the principles of the life."[9]

Here is an example of some insights the Holy Spirit may help us discern about ourselves in answering the third question:

1. Like the disciples, I am shaken up by sudden storms. I lose my bearing, and it takes quite an effort to get me back on track. Greatly tempted to go it alone, I delude myself that I am capable of handling the storm on my own.

2. Like what happened to the disciples, sometimes the sunny face of Jesus gets obscured by dark clouds, howling winds, and thundering tempests. It is easier for me to see Him when things are calm and clear.

3. Like the disciples, sometimes I find myself blaming Jesus for allowing difficult things to happen to me. I feel so small in this big world, and sometimes I wonder if He knows who I am, if He is really there for me, or if He really cares about me.

Ideally the previous three questions should be sufficient. But I have discovered that quite often I need to respond to two more questions in order to make sure that I daily apply the spiritual insights I have distilled from the relational Bible study. Unfortunately, spiritual insight is not sufficient by itself—it has to propel us to action. We need to recognize that sometimes we do not allow the insights to transform our lives. And Satan does not care if we study and gain profound spiritual knowledge as long as we allow him to keep us from putting it to practice.

As a result, here are the two additional questions to further assist us in the practical application:

The fourth question: What specific things do I need to do in my life as a result of my study? This will help align what is going on in our lives with the spiritual insights gained from our study. Here we must be honest and specific in focusing on areas of need in our lives. As the Holy Spirit impresses our minds with these specific needs, we need to write them down. For example, we may be impressed with the need to do such things as:

1. To affirm and practice the presence of Jesus with me regardless of how I may feel. To claim His promises to be with me in the serene as well as in the stormy situations of my spiritual pilgrimage.

2. To make a firm commitment to turn first to Christ whenever a storm strikes me. To seek Him first though greatly tempted to rely on myself, solicit the help of others, and focus on the problem. And for that matter, to seek Him first at the beginning of every day, so that whatever may come, rain or shine, I may remain solidly anchored in Him.

3. To commit myself to stop brooding over sudden setbacks, and to stop rehearsing every reversal in my spiritual experience. To continually commit myself to concentrate on the Lord, and to repeatedly remind myself of His goodness. To learn from Jeremiah the prophet, who decided to cease dwelling on all his afflictions, and to rekindle hope in God by remembering that "through the Lord's mercies we are not consumed, because His compassions fail not. They are new every morning; great is Your faithfulness" (Lam. 3:22-23).

4. To constantly affirm in my mind that Jesus is ultimately in control. That He is more than a match to whatever problem I may face, and to confidently trust Him to work things out for the best.

We may need a final question to help us implement what the Lord impresses us to do. And this question enables us to zero in on the timing of our response.

The fifth question: When will I apply the specific things that the Holy Spirit has revealed to me? Now this calls for a decision, asks for a commitment. And the answer to the "when" must be "now." For when the voice of the Holy Spirit convicts us to do something, then that is the very time we must obey. That is the best time, the best place, and the best circumstance. Listen to the Holy Spirit: "Therefore, as the Holy Spirit says: '*Today,* if you will hear His voice, do not harden your hearts'" (Heb. 3:7, 8).

The last two questions motivate us to act promptly and specifically on what the Holy Spirit has revealed to us in our study of the Word. This is crucial, because unless what we have learned becomes incarnated in our daily lives, it will not be of much benefit to us. We need to wholeheartedly believe that what we have studied is the "Word of the living God, the Word that is our life, the Word that is to *mold* our *actions,* our *words,* and our *thoughts.* To hold God's Word as anything *less* than this is to *reject* it." [10]

Therefore, no matter how diligently we study the words of Scripture, unless we allow them to become an integral part of our being, transforming our experience, we indeed reject them. What we must do is to listen to what the words of the Bible say, receive what they give, and obey what they command.

As we began our relational Bible study with prayer, we will also want to close it with prayer. The first prayer sought to open wide our hearts and minds to God, breathing out self and breathing in the Spirit. Our closing prayer is one of praise, gratitude, and consecration to Jesus. It is a prayer of contrition, repentance, and commitment to what His Spirit revealed to us in the study. Commitment to implement immediately the specific insights revealed to us.

We must keep alive in our hearts the thought that our Lord rejoices to see us come to Him with the attitude outlined above. For "He waits with unwearied love to hear the confessions of the wayward and to accept their penitence. He watches for some return of gratitude from us, as the mother watches for the smile of recognition from her beloved child. He would have us understand how earnestly and tenderly His heart yearns over us. . . . Never has one been disappointed who came unto Him." [11]

Such prayer does not repeat stale phrases and mouth canned words. This living prayer of commitment is born and nourished in the holy process of contemplating Jesus in the relational Bible study. Consequently, "we shall have a *continual freshness* in our religious life. Our prayers will take the form of a *conversation* with God as we would talk with a friend. He will speak His *mysteries* to us *personally.* Often there will come to us a *sweet joyful* sense of the presence of Jesus. Often our hearts will burn within us as He draws nigh to commune with us as He did with Enoch." [12]

Such prayer originates in and is shaped in the heart of God, for it springs forth from our spiritual experience in the sacred account of His Word. As we have experienced this written word becoming the living Word incarnated in our hearts, we thus find access into the very presence of God. That is why the very words of the Scriptures, and the inspired insights revealed to us in them, need to be interwoven into our prayer. After all, they are His words, and His words express His will for us as well as for others whom we pray for. (We will be discussing intercessory prayer in chapter 14.)

Judson Cornwall wrote a book on the subject of using the words of God in praying to Him. "What seems to have been forgotten by some . . . is that the Bible can also become the very prayer we need to pray," he explains. "When we let the Bible become our prayer, we are praying an inspired vocabulary. I will often release deep inner feelings far better than extemporizing prayers that will come from our minds." [13]

Here are some suggestions for the prayer of consecration to conclude our relational Bible study:

My dear Father, I thank You for the Holy Spirit, who guided me in revealing Jesus in the study of this story. I am grateful for Jesus, who can deal with any storm I am facing. I am confronting a storm in my life right now. Forgive me for my lack of trust, and for trying to calm my storms in my own way. Help me now to take my eyes off that storm and focus on Christ and what He can do. Help me not to postpone this any longer. Now, I give You full control of my life to fashion me according to Your good pleasure.

My dear God, I am in so many ways like the disciples—forgetful, fearful, and self-centered—but like them, I am desperately crying out for Your help, the help that You alone can give. Lord, I believe, please help my unbelief. Take away my fear and replace it with Your abiding trust. Lord Jesus, I am so thankful that You are always the same, and that You love and care for all equally. Therefore, as You stretched forth Your mighty hands above the tumult of that Galilean storm, stretch forth those same hands again above the tumult of my life. Rebuke the howling wind, and say to my turbulent sea, "Peace, be still!"

And my Lord, if in Your love and wisdom You see that going through the storms will bring me a needed spiritual blessing, then "Your will be done." As long as I know that we will face the storm together, I will be fine. And if the storm is to rage on some more, then help me to rest in Your peace that "passes all understanding." The peace that You experienced in the middle of that Galilean storm as You rested on the pillow.

Thank You, Lord, for manifesting Yourself to me as we communed together. Thank You for making Yourself totally available to me. Break me, mold me, fashion me, and do to me whatever it takes to make me more like You. I now make myself completely available to You. Use me, in spite of myself, to lead someone to You today, for Your honor and glory. (You may include an intercessory prayer in behalf of specific persons or situations here.) In the worthy name of Jesus, I pray. Amen.

Imagine what would happen to us spiritually if we would start every day experiencing this quality encounter with God! For "no other influence can equal the sense of God's presence" to keep us spiritually strong.[14] Contemplate the great impact it would have on our families, churches, and communities. I know that having this energizing spiritual experience with Christ in His Word has made a big difference in my life and my witness. I would not face any day without it.

To be filled with Christ and to experience His presence. To be nourished, invigorated, and made strong by His living Word. To be confident that united with Him I can face whatever life brings my way. To know that He is doing His best for me with all the love, wisdom, and power that He possesses. All this cannot help making a profound and significant difference in our daily lives. It is precisely what we all need today.

I well know what I tragically lack when I neglect this consistent communion with Jesus in His Word. And you know too what I am talking about from your own personal experience. We can relate to this when we think of all the benefits that a daily physical fitness program does for us. As such physical activity becomes an integral part of our lives, we quickly recognize what we will lose when we neglect it.

As I mentioned earlier, keeping a daily journal for each relational Bible study serves as a living reminder of our enriching spiritual encounters with God. This permanent record of our communion with God records how He ministered to us, and how that affected our thoughts and feelings at those particular times and circumstances. Such vital and uplifting experiences—so real and life-transforming at the time—may fade away or be forgotten altogether unless we capture them in the pages of our journal.

For example, at times we may succumb to discouragement as our spiritual struggles and setbacks buffet us. When we feel forsaken by God, and when our minds are too stressed to sort things out, then let us retreat to our spiritual journal. Let it remind us how God has proven Himself to us in our past.

There, as we immerse ourselves in its pages, God will help us recapture the thoughts and feelings we had earlier experienced in His presence. With our hearts warmed, our minds refocused, and our faith rekindled, we are assured anew that the changeless God who led us in the past will surely guide us in our present and future circumstances. "When temptations assail you, when care, perplexity, and darkness seem to surround your soul, look to the place where you *last saw the light.* Rest in Christ's love and under His protecting care." [15]

We cannot conclude this chapter about relational Bible study without recognizing that such spiritual discipline is not just for the individual, but it also encompasses the family circle and other small groups as well.

A husband and his wife may work on the same biblical account separately, then come together to share their responses to the different questions and whatever they discovered to be of particular help to them. Let them conclude with prayers of consecration and intercession befitting what they experience with Christ in His Word. Later on, they may include their children in a gradual and simple way. This can prove to be a good early training for them, so that as they grow up such Bible study may become an integral part of their daily lives.

Today, small groups meet an essential need for nurture and fellowship in the church. Because of our rootlessness, fracture of the family, and fragmentation of the very fabric of society, many people grapple with life alone, without much sense of belonging and community. Unfortunately, this sad situation exists even in our churches. Thus, small groups are more essential than ever to fill that vacuum by providing a family atmosphere for support, growth, and discipleship.

It was Christ's way, for He entrusted the gospel to a small group of 12. If that was Christ's plan in a world of strong family and community relationships, how much more we need to follow His example today. We need it to build family and community, where individuals may find a conducive environment in which to grow and mature in Christ, building up His body for the work of ministry.

For example, if you want to start a small group to have a relational Bible study, then ask the Lord to guide you to call on the right individuals who will commit themselves to meet regularly. It is all right to start even with three to four persons, because from that small nucleus, empowered by the Holy Spirit, the group will grow. The number of participants is not as crucial as the presence of the Spirit in the relational study of the Word.

And when the number hovers around 12, experts suggest that a new group should start. Christ may have kept His small group of disciples to 12 for several good reasons. Small groups enhance communication, meet individual and group needs better, and provide greater involvement and more effective training. This not only maintains the success of the existing group but also promotes the proliferation of more such small groups. "A small group is an intentional gathering of three to twelve people who commit themselves to work together to become better disciples of Jesus Christ."[16]

Whenever you organize such a small group, share with its members what you have experienced in relational Bible study and the spiritual impact it has had on your life. Explain to them in a simple way how it is done, and then proceed to lead them into the various steps we have already explored in this chapter and the one preceding it.

When they finish this exercise, including the written responses to the questions, let them form smaller subgroups of two or three. Then invite them to share with each other, to the extent they feel comfortable and impressed to do so, some of their responses. Let these smaller groups of two or three persons conclude this part with prayers in one another's behalf, asking God to meet the needs the various individuals have expressed to one another.

Now let the subgroups reconvene in the main group. Have the facilitator invite the participants to feel free to mention some helpful things they have discovered during this time of contemplation, study, and fellowship. Because the participants have experienced something fresh and spiritually worthwhile, they will be prepared to give more than you will usually have time for. Such spontaneous and mutual sharing of spiritual insights greatly helps in enhancing an atmosphere of cohesiveness, affirmation, and oneness in Christ.

Imagine the spiritual impact this can have on any individual who sincerely seeks a more genuine relationship with Christ and others. It will affect not only individual spiritual life but also a couple's relationship with each other and the rest of their family members, and will revitalize other small groups in the church. And if individuals, families, and other small groups experience such spiritual vitality in Christ, think of the great spiritual impact it will have on their churches and communities.

So far in this chapter we have been discussing this type of Bible study in terms of biblical accounts, stories, or events. Because they comprise major portions of Scripture, it will be quite difficult to exhaust studying them all. However, other portions of the Bible consist of proverbs, promises, wise sayings, and teachings. How do we study them relationally?

We still need to experience the four P's: Pick the passage, Pray, Ponder, and Project. And we still need to keep the question about Jesus in mind, because He must always remain the central personality of the whole Bible. No matter what kind of biblical portion we may be studying, we must centralize it in Christ, so that we may discern all things from His perspective.

However, we need to modify the rest of the questions with the following ones:

The first question: What does the text *say?* We need to know what God does actually declare or proclaim through that passage. Most important, we simply need to be still and listen to the words, so that we may distinctly hear them in our minds. Sometimes we do not listen carefully to what people say to us, or we do not pay close attention to what we read. Or possibly we are already biased about the subject matter.

Our minds may get distracted so that we catch only a word here or read a word there, or our attention may get diverted to the first phrase we hear or read. Thus we often form rash and erroneous opinions of what others really mean. Unfortunately this attitude can carry over to our study of the Word of God. Therefore, before we can know what a text means, we must first know what it actually says.

The second question: What does the text *mean?* We need to know what it did mean to the people God originally addressed it to, and then what it does mean to us today. Consulting dictionaries, lexicons, and commentaries may help us get a clearer understanding, but what is of utmost importance is that we let the Holy Spirit control us in order for us to have spiritual discernment, thus arriving at the text's true meaning.

The third question: What does the text *mean to me?* What we really need is to arrive at the meaning that the real Author of the biblical text, the Holy Spirit, has in mind for us personally. Yes, it is necessary to comprehend the accurate and spiritual meaning of the text, but we must then incorporate it into our actual daily life. For unless its meaning becomes incarnated in our lives, and unless it transforms us, it has no real value to us.

Satan tempts us to be satisfied with merely spiritual insights, and will furiously fight our attempt to *personally* appropriate what we learn. "As our physical life is sustained by food, so our spiritual life is sustained by the Word of God. And *every* soul is to receive life from God's Word for *himself.* As we must eat for ourselves in order to receive nourishment, so we must receive the Word for ourselves." [17]

The fourth and the fifth questions are the same as those discussed earlier in the chapter. You may refer back to them for review. We will just mention them here:

The fourth question: What *specific things* do I need *to do* in my life as a result of my study?

The fifth question: *When* will I *apply* the specific things the Holy Spirit has revealed to me?

Let us always keep uppermost in our minds the underlying truth in responding to all these questions that "the word of God is living and powerful, and sharper than any two-edged sword, piercing even to the division of soul and spirit, and of joints and marrow, and is a discerner of the thoughts and intents of the heart" (Heb. 4:12).

In conclusion, we should consider several helpful steps contained in a statement Ellen White made about exploring one biblical verse at a time. "We should carefully study the Bible, asking God for the aid of the Holy Spirit, that we may understand His Word. We should take one verse, and concentrate the mind on the task of ascertaining the thought which God has put in that verse for us. We should dwell upon the thought until it becomes our own, and we know 'what saith the Lord.'" [18]

She is emphasizing the quality of Bible study more than the

quantity. What benefit would we receive if we were to cover large portions of it without assimilating their content? Spiritual growth demands that we receive the life and Spirit of God. We linger in His presence from the specific desire to satisfy our spiritual hunger. For "one passage thus studied until its significance is clear is of more value than the perusal of many chapters with no definite purpose in view and no positive instruction gained." [19]

Here is the summary of the progressive steps of studying one verse at a time:

1. Pray for the aid of the Holy Spirit to give us true understanding.
2. Select one Bible verse.
3. Concentrate the mind on that verse.
4. Ascertain the thought that God has for us in the verse.
5. Dwell on that thought until it becomes our own.
6. Know what God says to us personally.

---

[1] White, *Education,* p. 297.

[2] ——, *The Ministry of Healing,* p. 503.

[3] ——, *In Heavenly Places* (Washington, D.C.: Review and Herald Pub. Assn., 1967), p. 123.

[4] ——, *The Ministry of Healing,* p. 514.

[5] ——, *The Desire of Ages,* p. 103. (Italics supplied.)

[6] ——, *Thoughts From the Mount of Blessing,* p. 20.

[7] ——, *Education,* p. 192.

[8] ——, *Thoughts From the Mount of Blessing,* p. 20.

[9] ——, *The Ministry of Healing,* p. 514.

[10] ——, *Education,* p. 260. (Italics supplied.)

[11] ——, *Thoughts From the Mount of Blessing,* pp. 84, 85.

[12] ——, *Christ's Object Lessons,* p. 129. (Italics supplied.)

[13] ——, Judson Cornwall, *Praying the Scriptures* (Lake Mary, Fla.: Creation House, 1990), p.11.

[14] White, *Education,* p. 255.

[15] ——, *The Ministry of Healing,* p. 250. (Italics supplied.)

[16] Jeffrey Arnold, *The Big Book on Small Groups* (Downers Grove, Ill.: InterVarsity Press, 1992), p. 9.

[17] White, *The Desire of Ages,* p. 390. (Italics supplied.)

[18] *Ibid.*

[19] ——, *Education,* p. 189.

CHAPTER

THIRTEEN

HEALTH AND HOLINESS—1

Luke records in his Gospel that "the child [Jesus] grew and became strong; he was filled with wisdom, and the grace of God was upon him" (Luke 2:40, NIV). Also, "Jesus grew in wisdom and stature, and in favor with God and men" (verse 52, NIV). Here we have the description of Jesus' harmonious and total development physically, mentally, socially, and spiritually. Our matchless model for spiritual life is also our unequal example for physical and mental health as well.

He came to our fallen world veiled in humanity as the second Adam to succeed where the first Adam had failed, and to demonstrate what God can do with the whole being—physically, mentally, and spiritually. Through their disobedience to God's laws, Adam and his descendants marred His image in them, enfeebling the harmonious development of the whole being. For "man's physical powers were weakened, his mental capacity was lessened, his spiritual vision was dimmed."[1]

Christ came to restore not only one part of what Adam lost, but all aspects of his original nature. He said that His mission was to "seek and to save that which was lost" (Luke 19:10). Christ sought to restore not only our dimmed spiritual vision, but our lessened mental capacity and weakened physical powers as well. His restorative ministry dealt with the sick in mind and body as well as those sick in spirit.

Jesus came to arrest and reverse our deterioration of body, mind, and spirit, demonstrating in His own life the restoration of the whole person to the image of His Father. He lived what He taught, and that is why His life and teaching had such a life-changing influence on others. He was the gospel personified, demonstrating it, "not as a lifeless theory, but as a living force to change the life." [2]

Christ by no means lived the sedentary life of a scribe, but the rugged one of a carpenter. Using tools every day in His carpentry trade, He must have developed calluses on His hands, sweated, and experienced aching muscles from physical exertion. He must have associated often with hardy peasants and common laborers, built and repaired their tools, and given them a helping hand. After a tiring but rewarding day's honest work, He must have then slept soundly, regaining His strength for a new day. This life of "natural simplicity was favorable to the development of a *good physical constitution, and a firm, unsullied character.*" [3]

Even from childhood, Jesus did not squander His time and talents in idleness and worthless endeavors. He learned to *balance* His physical exertion with His physical growth and development. "The life of Jesus was filled with industry, and He took exercise in performing varied tasks in harmony with His developing physical strength. . . . He took no part in that which would poison the moral and lower the physical tone, but was trained in useful labor, and even for the endurance of hardship." [4]

Although He was diligent in His work, He was never what we describe today as a workaholic. He was a good steward of His health by carefully preserving and renewing His physical resources. "As Jesus worked in childhood and youth, *mind and body* were developed. He did not use His physical powers recklessly, but in such a way as to keep them in health, that He might do the best work in every line. . . . The exercise that teaches the hands to be useful and trains the young to bear their share of life's burdens gives physical strength, and develops every faculty." [5]

Moreover, as an itinerant teacher, He often walked from place to place with His disciples, stopping only to rest and meditate, and then pressed on His journey. We find no hint that He used a horse or a donkey in His travels. He must have worn out many sandals, traveling from place to place on foot for miles. His life was definitely not a lazy existence of leisure and luxury, but a vigorous and an abundant one lived to the maximum for God and humanity.

Today we know that following a program of vigorous daily walking is one of the best exercises for total fitness. To condition all the muscles, to breathe the fresh air, to enjoy the healing rays of the sun, to reduce stress, to clear the mind, to commune with God and nature, and to improve the blood circulation and every other physiological function of the body—it will do all these things for us.

In the accounts of the four Gospels our Saviour emerges as a person with a strong constitution, someone with plenty of physical stamina and endurance. It was essential for Him to be in top physical condition to shoulder all the heavy burdens and responsibilities thrust upon Him in His restorative mission to humanity. He did not want His physical health to in the slightest way hinder Him in accomplishing His sacred mission. Rather, He wanted to be in robust health so that He might most effectively serve humanity and glorify His Father.

Daily He poured out His life in wholistic restoration of others, especially in healing their diseases. He kept giving till finally He offered His healthy body and holy life as the perfect sacrifice "*without blemish* and *without spot*" (1 Peter 1:19). We may use the words of Paul to apply to Christ's supreme sacrifice of Himself on the cross. He, for our sake, presented His body unto His Father as a "living sacrifice, holy, acceptable" (Rom. 12:1).

"Jesus was an earnest, constant worker. Never lived there among men another so weighted with responsibilities. . . . Never another toiled with such self-consuming zeal for the good of men. Yet His was a *life of health. Physically* as well as *spiritually* He was represented by the sacrificial lamb, 'without blemish and without spot' (1 Peter 1:19). In *body* as in *soul* He was an example of what God designed all humanity to be through obedience to His laws." [6]

The Old Testament describes the offerings and sacrifices to God as whole and without any blemishes whatsoever. Such were the types of Jesus, the ultimate and perfect sacrifice before God in behalf of fallen humanity. If the sacrificial animals were free of all physical blemish and deformity, then "it is evident that Jesus Himself was free from *physical* deformity. . . . His *physical* structure was not marred by any defect; His *body was strong and healthy.* And throughout His lifetime He lived in conformity to nature's laws." [7]

Beholding such a pure, perfect, and priceless sacrifice, shouldn't we be driven to Calvary to offer our own bodies too as living, holy, and acceptable sacrifices to our God? In offering ourselves as living and holy sacrifices to Him, we gain Him, the living and holy sacrifice. We receive vastly much more in return, for we receive Him and all that He has to offer us.

When the body—the temple of the Holy Spirit—is open to and indwelt by God's Spirit, then God can have a profound and transforming impact on the *entire* being. It is true in both the physical realm and the spiritual that we are determined by what we eat and breathe, and how we exercise. Moreover, our physical health has a direct bearing on our mental health, which in turn directly affects our spiritual health. "Health is an inestimable blessing, and one which is more closely related to conscience and religion than many realize."[8]

To treat the body carelessly is to also regard the mind and the spirit with indifference, and whatever adversely affects our physical health adversely affects our mental and spiritual health. "Anything that lessens physical strength enfeebles the mind and makes it less capable of discriminating between right and wrong. We become less capable of choosing the good and have less strength of will to do that which we know to be right."[9]

Therefore, true spirituality takes into serious account the total aspect of our health—the physical, the mental, and the spiritual. "The sanctification set forth in the Sacred Scriptures has to do with the *entire* being—spirit, soul, and body. Here is the true idea of *entire* consecration."[10] We need to care no less about the body than about the mind and the spirit, because all three aspects of health interact with each other.

"The relation which exists between the mind and the body is *very intimate*. When one is affected, the other sympathizes. The condition of the mind affects the health of the physical system."[11] Thus the care of our bodies is not an isolated duty dealing only with our physical health, but a sacred trust and a spiritual responsibility. What affects our bodies profoundly shapes our spirituality.

Ellen White repeatedly emphasized the concept and its impact on our spiritual growth and sanctification. We simply cannot sustain or enhance our spirituality while sacrificing our bodies, the temples of the Holy Spirit, to destructive health practices.

"Let none who profess godliness regard with indifference the health of the body, and flatter themselves that intemperance is no sin, and will not affect their spirituality," she strongly attests. "A *close sympathy* exists between the physical and the moral nature. Any habit which does not promote health degrades the higher and nobler faculties. Wrong habits in eating and drinking lead to errors in thought and action. Indulgence of appetite strengthens the animal propensities, giving them the ascendancy over the mental and spiritual powers." [12]

That is why we seriously impair our capacity to "taste and see that the Lord is good" when we live intemperate and sickly lives. Also it tragically impedes our capability to delight ourselves in God's presence. For though He longs to communicate with us, a cluttered body temple and a clouded mind block His Spirit. Consequently our prayers are powerless, and our devotional life is devoid of life. It is "having a form of godliness but denying its power" (2 Tim. 3:5). Experience has repeatedly taught us that when our bodies are stressed out, when we deprive them of proper rest and adequate sleep, and when our health is run down, then we do not really want to be around people. We do not enjoy even the company of friends. Rather, we act irritable and distracted, not being able to concentrate on the task at hand. The same thing applies to our relationship with God.

Our body is "the temple of the Holy Spirit" (1 Cor. 6:19), and our mind is the only channel through which God can communicate to our souls. If everything that is destructive to our relationship with God clogs up our bodies and minds, then how is it possible to experience spiritual vitality? How can we ever grow in our spiritual life if the Holy Spirit does not find room to dwell in our body, and if God cannot reach us through our minds? Therefore, whatever affects our bodies and minds affects our spirituality.

God created us as totally integrated beings, indivisible. The body, the mind, and the spirit are so inextricably interconnected that whatever affects one affects the others. Consequently, following God's health laws by becoming good stewards of our bodies and minds is just as much a spiritual activity as are Bible study and prayer. A sick body and a depressed mind undermine our ability to respond to God, and thus our spiritual vitality and growth greatly suffer.

Our God in His love strives to reach our hearts, only to find Himself hindered by our abuse of our bodies and minds, His channels of communication with us. God is the source of the spiritual laws as well as the physical ones. His laws of nature are "as truly divine *as* are the precepts of the Decalogue," Ellen White attests. "The laws that govern our physical organism, God has written upon *every* nerve, muscle, and fiber of the body." Then she adds, "Every careless or willful violation of these laws is a *sin* against our Creator." [13]

Furthermore, "Since the mind and the soul find expression

through the body, both mental and spiritual vigor are in great degree dependent upon physical strength and activity. Whatever promotes physical health, promotes the development of a strong mind and a well-balanced character."[14] God created us as total beings, and He wants to restore us as total beings as well. And Satan fiercely fights our physical restoration because he knows that it opens the channel of the mind to God's renewing of the spiritual life.

Tragically, Satan has deceived many to think that God is only interested in the spiritual realm of their lives, and that their physical health is a separate and unrelated issue. He accuses God of being too rigid and demanding of His children in wanting them to faithfully follow His health laws. Thus many forget that the real reason He cares about our total health is because He loves us. If even loving earthly parents care about the complete health of their children, how infinitely more our loving heavenly Father cares. With Him is "the fountain of life" (Ps. 36:9), and He desires for us to have it with all its fullness.

Many, even Christians, are into thinking that their bodies are their own rightful property, and that they have the inalienable right to recklessly do with them as they please. But if God is the fountain of all life, and if in Him we "live and move and have our being" (Acts 17:28), then our total lives belong to Him. He is indeed the rightful owner twice—by both creation and redemption. In entrusting us with this inestimable investment, He desires us to be His good stewards. And that is not because He is someone severe or selfish, but because in His great love He wants us to be healthy and happy, preparing ourselves to enjoy eternity with Him. He wants us to be all that we can possibly be.

How can we so arrogantly abuse our bodies that He has fashioned by His own hands, formed after His own image, and energized by His own breath! How can we so woefully waste bodies that He purchased "with the precious blood of Christ, as of a lamb without blemish and without spot" (1 Peter 1:19)! How can we ever disfigure and destroy a priceless painting of an artist whom we greatly love and admire!

We are indeed His precious masterpiece of all creation. Through our bodies He wants to continue breathing the breath of His life and the breath of His Spirit for the total restoration of our beings. Let us not clutter or cut those channels of communication, but clear the way for the Holy Spirit to commune with us and dwell in us. Our only hope for revitalizing our spiritual lives, we should view taking care of our bodies not as an intolerable burden, but as an infinite blessing.

It is a blessing with immense spiritual benefits for us. Let us review some of them here:

1. Because we love and admire God as our Creator and Redeemer, and because health is His gift of love to us, we find ourselves motivated not to imperil it but to ensure and improve it. It gives us the capacity to live for Him and enjoy Him to the optimum to our great joy and delight. And why not? After all, don't we want to live for, and give our best to, some fellow human being whom we love and admire? God wants us to love Him with all our being—with all our heart, all our soul, all our mind, and also with all our *physical strength* (Mark 12:30).

2. The more healthy in body and mind we are, the more receptive we become to God's Spirit and truth, since the body and mind are the only mediums through which He can reach us. Thus our reception of His messages is proportional to our physical and mental health.

3. Being healthy gives us the needed physical and mental stamina and strength to carry out God's will in our everyday life. It is like what the disciples experienced in Gethsemane, when Jesus said to them, "The spirit indeed is willing, but the flesh is weak" (Matt. 26:41). In other words, even though we desire in our spirit to stay close to Jesus and pray, it may remain merely a desire unless bolstered by a healthy body. Consequently, poor health often robs us of meaningful spiritual times with Jesus.

4. A healthy mind and body helps us more easily to recognize Satan's subtle strategies, and gives us a greater sensitivity in distinguishing between the holy and the profane. Consequently, we are in a stronger position to resist and overcome temptation. Christ "presents the result of unrestrained indulgence of appetite. The moral powers are enfeebled, so that sin does not appear sinful. Crime is lightly regarded, and passion controls the mind, until good principles and impulses are rooted out, and God is blasphemed." [15]

5. Poor health will cripple our effectiveness in reaching people with the gospel. We know that spreading the gospel during the final days will take place under very difficult circumstances, thus we will particularly need vibrant health during such times.

6. People instantly notice the buoyant life of a healthy and happy Christian. It makes a powerful impression on others, and at-

tracts them to the message of the gospel. They realize that the spiritual beliefs we advocate really do work. And that is why the health message, by word and deed, is the entering wedge for the gospel.

7. Such a health message, propounded and practiced, prepares us and others to meet Christ when He comes. Thus preserving our total health, including the physical, for total sanctification has an eschatological dimension. Our belief in the urgency of His soon coming prompts us to present to Him a healthy and holy life that we live through His grace.

Notice that the apostle Paul regards health, with its spiritual, mental, and physical dimensions, as a complete and integrated unity. Observe also how he makes the connection between preserving our *whole* health and the coming of the Lord: "Now may the God of peace Himself sanctify you *completely;* and may your *whole spirit, soul, and body* be preserved blameless at the *coming* of our Lord Jesus Christ" (1 Thess. 5:23).

Realizing that Christ's second coming is close at hand, we do not carelessly sacrifice our health but carefully strive for its optimum. And we do so simply because we want nothing to hinder Christ from revealing Himself *to* us. Moreover, we do it because we want our Lord to manifest Himself so clearly *through* us that it will draw others to Him.

Ellen White declares that health reform and restoration enables Christ to manifest Himself through us to the world. "The world needs today what it needed nineteen hundred years ago—*a revelation of Christ.* A great work of *reform* is demanded, and it is only through the grace of Christ that the work of *restoration, physical, mental,* and *spiritual,* can be accomplished." [16]

Furthermore, she emphasizes the priority that studying the laws that govern our physical being should have in our lives, and how it is closely connected to our spirituality and witness. "*All* should have an intelligent knowledge of the *human frame* that they may keep their *bodies* in the condition necessary to do the *work of the Lord.* The *physical life* is to be carefully *preserved and developed* that *through* humanity the *divine nature* may be revealed in its *fullness.* The relation of the *physical organism* to the *spiritual life* is one of the *most important* branches of education." [17]

---

[1] White, *Education,* p. 15.
[2] ———, *The Ministry of Healing,* p. 99.

[3] ———, *Sons and Daughters of God*, p. 140. (Italics supplied.)

[4] ———, *The Adventist Home* (Nashville: Southern Pub. Assn., 1952), pp. 506, 507.

[5] ———, *The Desire of Ages*, p. 72. (Italics supplied.)

[6] ———, *The Ministry of Healing*, p. 51. (Italics supplied.)

[7] ———, *The Desire of Ages*, p. 50. (Italics supplied.)

[8] ———, *Counsels on Health* (Mountain View, Calif.: Pacific Press Pub. Assn., 1923), p. 566.

[9] ———, *Christ's Object Lessons*, p. 346.

[10] ———, *The Sanctified Life*, p. 7. (Italics supplied.)

[11] ———, *Counsels on Health*, p. 28. (Italics supplied.)

[12] ———, *The Sanctified Life*, p. 25. (Italics supplied.)

[13] ———, *Education*, pp. 196, 197. (Italics supplied.)

[14] *Ibid.*, p. 195.

[15] White, *Counsels on Health*, p. 24.

[16] ———, *The Ministry of Healing*, p. 143. (Italics supplied.)

[17] ———, *Christ's Object Lessons*, p. 348. (Italics supplied.)

CHAPTER FOURTEEN

HEALTH AND HOLINESS—2

When it comes to preserving and promoting our total life, one of the best ways is applying the eight natural remedies that God has given us. Through the grace of God, they enable Christ to reveal Himself fully through our humanity. So what are these natural remedies?

"Pure air, sunlight, abstemiousness, rest, exercise, proper diet, the use of water, trust in divine power—these are the true remedies. Every person should have a knowledge of nature's remedial agencies and how to apply them." [1]

Weimar Institute took this simple and sensible statement, and built their lifestyle program around it using the acronym NEW START for easy recall. It happens also that the acronym sounds a note of hope and encouragement, for God does indeed want to give us a new start. As we submit ourselves to His work of restoration, He reaches us wherever we may be, doing His best to help us have a new start in life.

Here are the basic guidelines:

1. Nutrition
2. Exercise
3. Water
4. Sunshine
5. Temperance
6. Air
7. Rest
8. Trust

As we studied the harmonious development of Christ's health in the previous chapter, we could not help thinking that He must have practiced the above eight natural remedies given by His loving and wise Father. They were definitely not a lifeless theory, but a living reality in His spiritual devotion to God and service to humanity.

Let us discuss the implications of these natural remedies, and then see how we can use them to enhance our spirituality. In this chapter we will address the first three remedies referred to by the word *NEW*, the first word in the acronym *NEW START*. The next two chapters will examine the remaining five natural remedies.

1. Nutrition. The saying "we are what we eat" not only applies to our physical health but to our spiritual health as well. And the nutrition that affects the body affects the soul. Likewise, the spiritual nourishment that affects the soul will have an impact on the body. Food is the fuel for the body, and it helps to construct all its tissues and cells and supply it with needed energy.

Our physical health reflects the quality of food we consume. Poor nutrition equals poor health, good nutrition good health. And that being the case, why not nourish the body, the most wonderful of God's creations, with the best foods available? Why do we maintain disposable machines much better than we do our own bodies, which we need for a lifetime? Strangely, sometimes we care more about the fuel we pump into our cars than the quality of the food we eat for our bodies. "The wonderful mechanism of the human body does not receive half the care that is often given to a mere lifeless machine." [2] Our health is certainly worth much more than any possession or wealth we may ever acquire.

Our Creator designed our bodies "fearfully and wonderfully" (Ps. 139:14) in every way. And when it comes to nourishing the body, He provided us with just the right food for maintaining it in optimum health. "Grains, fruits, nuts, and vegetables, in proper combination, contain *all* the elements of nutrition; and when properly prepared, they constitute the diet that *best* promotes both physical and mental strength." [3]

God certainly knows how to best sustain what He has created. He lovingly serves us with this natural, complete, and best diet, providing us with the capacity to enjoy how it looks, smells, and tastes. But sadly, we have perverted our appetites and tampered with God's perfect plan. Consequently, we are paying the highest of all possible prices for that—our health.

Although the wealthiest nation on the face of the earth, we are not the healthiest. We produce enough food to feed the world, yet it is not easy for an average American family to enjoy a wholesome meal. Too many of us consume inordinate amounts of the wrong foods. And when it comes to wholesome food, we excel in tinkering with it—processing and refining it, adding to it and subtracting from it.

So many people diligently accumulate wealth, yet carelessly squander their precious health on poor diet. It is said that as a people we are overfed but undernourished. We indulge ourselves in eating too much of the wrong foods, and hardly any of the right ones. Such harmful dietary practices contribute to all kinds of health problems. At the same time they impoverish the spiritual life, ravaging us with spiritual sickness and death.

Likewise, we need to simply feed on the unadulterated Word of God as given to us. We need to be energized by every spiritual morsel as we smell, savor, slowly masticate, digest, and assimilate it into the fabric of our spiritual being. We cannot make a rushed dash into a spiritual fast-food restaurant, but must linger in God's presence with rapturous delight, feasting on His delicious and life-giving Word. This is how we reveal His life and reflect His image as His life becomes assimilated into our lives.

2. Exercise. The eating, the digestion, and the assimilation of even the best food is not sufficient without regular exercise. Exercise affects how the body absorbs and circulates food throughout the body. And more than that, it enhances every physiological bodily function, and thus strengthens and revitalizes the whole being. God gave us the ideal diet not merely for us to enjoy it, but to give us energy to move and work and become fit and strong.

The truism that we lose what we do not use particularly applies to our physical and spiritual health. And in the physical realm it affects not only our muscles but all our internal organs and every aspect of their physiology. Diehl and Ludington attest that a "sedentary lifestyle is the quickest route to an early death. Inactivity kills us—literally." On the other hand, "greater vitality, better health, and longer life can be ours through regular, brisk physical activity."[4]

Satan has a clever counterfeit for every genuine gift of God. He defrauds people by enticing them to substitute a harmful diet for a healthful one. But when we expose his deception in this area by regularly eating healthful foods, he tries to deceive us in another important sphere. He takes advantage of all our modern conveniences to make it difficult for us to have regular exercise, knowing that motion brings life and vitality, while atrophy and death, both physically and spiritually, result from inactivity.

Take, for example, what happened to one of our two cars after months of lack of use. Trying to motivate myself to exercise every day during a long Michigan winter, I decided to park the car in the garage and walk to work. (By the way, walking outdoors is the best and most complete exercise we can have. It does not cost anything, and you can do it almost anywhere.) When spring finally arrived I was fit, but the car wasn't. I had the hardest time trying to get it to run properly. It took weeks of reconditioning to get the car to perform as well as before.

The mechanic said that there had been nothing wrong with my car to begin with, and that the culprit was simply the lack of use. Surprised that I had failed to drive the car, he commented that the only reason people own cars is to use them. One of the major problems was that as a result of the inadequate circulation of fuel gummy deposits and other impurities now clogged the system. The engine had a good supply of oil, the tank was full of gasoline, all fluids were at proper levels, and everything else seemed to be in top shape.

The mechanic tried to clear the obstructions, but he advised me to begin driving the car on long trips right away, and that is exactly what I did. It was rough going initially, but I could tell that the more I drove it, the more the problem cleared up, until eventually the car functioned as well as before. I kept active that winter, so I was fit, but the car sat in the garage, so it was unfit.

Afterward I thought to myself, *If lack of activity can immobilize a well-running car, how much more can it wreck our physical, emotional, and spiritual well-being. If this can happen to a lifeless machine, how much more to a living human being.* "Continued inactivity is one of the greatest causes of debility of body and feebleness of mind."[5]

God designed the human body to move, for the feet to walk, for the muscles to stretch, and for the joints to bend. And that is the Designer's wise way to keep the body in top shape. Ellen White tells us that we will receive spiritual benefits from exercise as well as physical ones. "Healthful exercise in the open air will strengthen the muscles, encourage a proper circulation of blood, help to preserve the body from disease, and will be a *great help in spirituality.*"[6]

Here is a summary of some of the benefits a regular physical exercise in the open air will give us:

a. Exercise strengthens the muscles and helps the bone to retain calcium and its marrow to produce red blood cells more efficiently.

b. It improves the circulation of the blood and forces it to reach all parts of the body, supplying it with proper nourishment and maintaining an adequate temperature.

c. It massages and strengthens the heart, and thus helps that organ to accomplish its needed work with less effort.

d. It stabilizes blood pressure and lowers the heart's resting rate, thus promoting the health of the heart, arteries, and veins.

e. It helps with food digestion and absorption, especially when we take walks after meals.

f. It aids in maintaining an ideal weight by building up needed muscles and burning off extra fat.

g. It makes the body more efficient in eliminating waste and impurities.

h. It strengthens the immune system to ward off disease.

i. It forces us to inhale deeply the life-giving oxygen, enabling it to permeate all the tiny air sacs in the lungs.

j. It helps the brain to produce hormones that give us good feelings, and a sense of vitality and well-being.

k. It relieves physical stress as well as emotional tension. Dr. David Nieman states that research shows that physical activity elevates alpha waves. These waves are linked to a state of tranquility and relaxation in the body, thus decreasing stress and feelings of apprehension.[7]

These are but some of the great benefits of exercise. Mobility is life, and exercise vitally affects every aspect of our existence. Like oil, it lubricates all parts of the body and makes them run much more smoothly and efficiently. We can also see how the benefits we have mentioned affect our spiritual life. How can they but enhance our relationship with God? When exercise helps our body and mind function well, then it certainly enhances our daily walk and communion with our heavenly Father.

It also aids our service to Him, for He can use us much more efficiently when we are vigorous and strong. And when we walk and work with Jesus, we experience His presence and power in our lives, and thus become more spiritually alive. Consider this statement: "Strength comes by exercise; activity is the very condition of life. Those who endeavor to maintain Christian life by passively accepting the blessings that come through the means of grace, and doing nothing for Christ, are simply trying to live by *eating without working."* [8]

We simply cannot partake of spiritual food without becoming active for Christ. For in the *"spiritual as in the natural world,* this *always* results in *degeneration and decay."* And what we do not use, we lose. It is a natural consequence because a "man who would refuse to exercise his limbs would soon lose all power to use them. Thus the Christian who will not exercise his God-given powers not only *fails to grow up* in Christ, but he *loses the strength* that he already had."* [9]

3. **Water.** Jesus took this common commodity and used it as a powerful object lesson when He depicted Himself as the water of life. The giver of this marvelous substance, the combination of two hydrogen atoms and one oxygen atom, knew the close connection between physical water and Himself, the water of life. It is fitting that He called Himself that, for without water there is no life, and without Him neither physical nor spiritual life exists.

The body is approximately 70 percent water, all of it essential for the proper function of the minutest cell to the most important organ. A person can survive longer without food than water. "In health and in sickness, pure water is one of heaven's choicest blessings." [10]

What are some of the benefits of this life-giving substance?

a. More than any other beverage, it is the best and most effective thirst-quencher.

b. It is a solvent and a dispensing vehicle for nutrients throughout the body.

c. Just as water is an effective cleanser of the body externally, so it is an excellent cleanser internally. Most people drink water very infrequently, and when they do they drink too little of it. But the body needs plenty of water to continuously bathe and flush every cell in the body and carry dissolved impurities to the skin, lungs, and kidneys, which will then excrete them. The center of this cleansing activity, the kidneys require lots of water (six to eight glasses a day) in order to adequately get rid of dissolved waste matter. The kidneys are like a washing machine that cannot clean dirty clothes well without plenty of water. We expend a lot of water in irrigating our lawns and gardens, and in washing our cars, so why not for our own bodies?

d. It has many remedial uses. Drinking plenty of pure water builds up resistance to disease and helps prevent headaches and colds, or helps get rid of them easier. Hydrotherapy stimulates and regulates blood circulation, aids in digestion, and serves as an excellent tonic. Fomentations, foot and steam baths, and hot and cold applications all aid the body in recovering from different ailments. They also stimulate the white blood cells to fight germs.

e. Water and its treatments also can soothe the nerves, reduce fatigue and stress, assist the mind to think clearly, and help us overcome irritability and anxiety.

Making good use of this wonderful gift of water, as its Giver intended it to be used, cannot help drawing us closer to Him. A body refreshed and cleansed by water, externally and internally, prepares and propels us to seek the invigorating and purifying power of the Water of Life. Absolutely no other substitute can do that for us.

Let our abundant and daily use of fresh and pure water constantly remind us of our daily spiritual need to be refreshed, cleansed, and healed by Jesus, the Water of Life. "The refreshing water, welling up in a parched and barren land, causing the desert place to bloom, and flowing out to give life to the perishing, is an emblem of the divine grace which Christ alone can bestow, and which is as the living water, purifying, refreshing, and invigorating the soul. He in whom Christ is abiding has within him a never-failing fountain of grace and strength." [11]

---

[1] White, *The Ministry of Healing,* p. 127.

[2] ———, *Counsels on Health,* p. 566.

[3] ———, *Education,* pp. 204, 205. (Italics supplied.)

[4] Hans Diehl and Aileen Ludington, *Lifestyle Capsules* (Santa Barbara, Calif.: Woodbridge Press, 1991), p. 164.

[5] White, *Testimonies,* vol. 2, p. 524.

[6] ———, *Medical Ministry* (Mountain View, Calif.: Pacific Press Pub. Assn., 1932), p. 81. (Italics supplied.)

[7] David Nieman, *The Sports Medicine Fitness Course* (Palo Alto, Calif.: Bull Pub. Co., 1986), p. 250.

[8] White, *Steps to Christ,* pp. 80, 81. (Italics supplied.)

[9] *Ibid.,* p. 81. (Italics supplied.)

[10] White, *The Ministry of Healing,* p. 237.

[11] ———, *Patriarchs and Prophets,* p. 412.

CHAPTER

FIFTEEN

———

HEALTH AND HOLINESS—3

Now that we have covered the first three natural remedies in the first word, of the acronym *NEW START,* we will discuss the remaining five remedies covered by the second word, *START,* in this chapter and the next.

4. Sunshine. As I write this we are just coming out of a very cold winter in Michigan. For weeks and months heavy clouds, freezing temperatures, and rain engulfed us, with no sunshine to break through. Everything outdoors seemed frozen and lifeless. During such cold and dreary times one wonders what would happen if warmer weather never returned and the sun never shone. What would happen to the human race without the life-giving rays of sunshine?

It is God's life and healing that we receive in the light and warmth of the sun, just as we receive the life and healing of His Son. He promised us that "the Sun of Righteousness shall arise with healing in His wings" (Mal. 4:2). Christ is the light that fills our lives with His light, driving away mental gloom and spiritual darkness. It is the warmth of His light that melts the iciness of our hardened hearts, filling them with His love and life.

Let us contemplate some of the benefits of sunshine, and how they relate to our spiritual lives:

a. Sunshine promotes healing in its important role as a disinfectant and a killer of bacteria on and around us. It also helps to increase the white blood cells that will fight these intruders when they do manage to enter the body.

b. It aids in building up the immune system so that the body can resist and overcome disease.

c. It synthesizes and builds vitamin D in the skin, enabling the body to use calcium to build and repair the bones.

d. It invigorates the body and cheers up the spirit, producing a sense of well-being and driving away the darkness of anxiety and depression.

Experiencing the benefits of the sun can lead us to Jesus the Sun of righteousness. Undoubtedly, the energizing and the healing of our body, and the lifting of our spirit, not only promote our physical health but better prepare us to bask in the light of Christ's rays of spiritual health. May the rays of the sun always remind us that He is the true life-giver and the true healer. And that only in His strength can we have a strong spiritual immune system to fight and conquer the viruses of darkness, depression, and death.

5. **Temperance.** Today, in our permissive and indulgent society, many consider temperance something outdated. After all, who wants to practice self-control in a hedonistic world, where everything calls for indulging the passions without moderation or restraint? Yet old-fashioned temperance is the very thing that our homes, churches, and society need. Most of the chaos, conflict, and moral corruption that we see all around us traces back to a lack of temperance.

And we definitely find a close connection between temperance and spirituality. Being intemperate blocks our hearts and minds against the Spirit of God. But on the other hand, practicing true temperance opens wide the human channels to respond to what is spiritual. Discipline learned in living temperate lives leads to spiritual discipline. Thus we have divine-human control in our lives rather than chaos and confusion.

So, what is true temperance? The following offers an excellent definition for it: "True temperance teaches us to dispense entirely with everything hurtful and to use judiciously that which is healthful."[1] In the New Testament the Greek word for temperance is *egkrateia*, which means "self-control." But to control one's self does not simply mean living a life of denial and deprivation. We should not approach it from a negative perspective, but a positive one.

Rather, it means that God is in control of our lives, for we belong to Him by creation and redemption. And His control enables *us* to have true self-control over our lives. It means that the Creator, who made us to be masters and not slaves of His creation, intends us also to be masters of our passions and practices, not their slaves. Temperance includes in it the wisdom to distinguish between the harmful and the helpful, and in patience and moderation to make the needed and proper application in our lives.

Usually we think of temperance in terms of controlling our appetite and passions. Of avoiding harmful practices and actuating helpful ones. Yet in the normally helpful and healthy (and even holy) activities of life we need to be careful not to go to extremes. True temperance makes an impact on *every* aspect of our lives, no matter what that aspect may be. For example, honest work is a good thing, but if that causes us to be workaholics, then it becomes intemperance. The same goes for prayer. If that is what we mostly do, not taking time to witness to others, then the time will come when we will lose interest in prayer. Our example should be that of Jesus. He was balanced in His worship and work. "The life must be like Christ's life— between the mountain and the multitude." Because "He who does nothing but pray will soon cease to pray, or his prayers will become a formal routine." [2]

Could we go overboard even in witnessing? We can when our witnessing for Christ becomes more important than our devotion to Him. Or when our service to Him becomes more consuming than our solitude with Him. True temperance covers every area of the Christian's life. It cuts in all directions, and engages us on a very practical level.

The apostle Peter uses *egkrateia* (temperance) as an important step in ascending the stairway of spiritual growth in Christ. Interestingly, he positions it after knowledge and before patience. Many would escape the misconceptions of temperance if they only learned what true temperance is all about and then patiently and prudently practiced that knowledge.

If knowledge is knowing what to do, then wisdom is knowing how to do it. Therefore, having true knowledge of something, and true wisdom as to how to do it, makes it possible for us to be temperate in all things. And being truly temperate can lead us to be patient and persevering. They are qualities that mark a seasoned and disciplined spiritual life.

Notice that Peter writes about the steps for spiritual growth and development from a spiritual context as well as from a temperance context. Having admonished us to be godly by becoming "partakers of the divine nature," he credits this to escaping "the corruption that is in the world through lust" (2 Peter 1:4, KJV). That is true temperance, isn't it? The temperance that is an integral part of holy living in every believer's life.

Then in verses 5-8 he continues: "And beside this, giving all diligence, add to your faith virtue; and to virtue knowledge; and to knowledge temperance; and to temperance patience; and to patience godliness; and to godliness brotherly kindness; and to brotherly kindness charity. For if these things be in you, and abound, they make you that ye shall neither be barren nor unfruitful in the knowledge of our Lord Jesus Christ" (KJV).

Look carefully at some of the words the apostle uses. The spiritual aim, or goal, is godliness, growth, fruitfulness, knowledge of Christ, and partaking or reflecting of His divine nature. He closely links such spiritual aspirations to escaping corruption and lust, and to diligence, temperance, patience, and perseverance.

Moreover, the apostle Paul joins living and walking in the Spirit (sanctification) with *egkrateia* (temperance) in Galatians 5:22-25, in which temperance culminates the list of all the graces of the fruit of the Spirit (verse 23). In our lives, the works of the flesh (verses 19-21) war against the fruit of the Spirit (verses 22, 23). Intemperance struggles against temperance. But "they that are Christ's have crucified the flesh with the affections and lusts" (verse 24, KJV). That means the execution or death of intemperance in its myriad manifestations. And thus through belonging to Christ, walking in the Spirit, and manifesting His fruit, we can overcome the intemperate drives and deeds of the flesh.

We learn a valuable lesson in true temperance from Christ's victory in His first great temptation in the wilderness. Satan thought that he might overcome Christ by first attacking Him with uncontrolled appetite. And Satan had a cleverly calculated reason for his strategy, because he seeks to destroy spiritual strength and sensitivity through indulgence in appetite and passion.

Christ was surely the ultimate example of true temperance. He knew that intemperance in any form would undermine His spiritual relationship with His Father, and He determined not to let that ever happen. Let us be vigilant and gain the victory over Satan in Christ and what He has done.

The devil is never satisfied unless he, through intemperance, obstructs our connection with God and our appreciation of spiritual things. For intemperance, in all its forms, can lead to "physical disease and degeneracy, *benumbing the spiritual perceptions, and lessening the sensibility to sin.*"[3] "Of all the lessons to be learned from our Lord's first great temptation *none* is more important than that bearing upon the control of the appetites and passions," Ellen White explains. "In all ages, temptations appealing to the physical nature have been most effectual in corrupting and degrading mankind," she recounts. "Through intemperance, Satan works to destroy the *mental and moral* powers that God gave to man as a priceless endowment. Thus it becomes *impossible* for men to *appreciate* things of eternal worth. Through sensual indulgence, Satan seeks to blot from the soul *every trace* of likeness to God."[4]

Intemperate persons are selfish ones, because they are self-absorbed with getting what they want and when they want it, regardless of others. They really do not care about what pleases God, but only about what pleases them and impresses others. Spending all their energies focusing on gratifying the self, they find it difficult to respond to God's voice.

As does the Bible, Ellen White connects temperance and sanctification. "We need to learn that indulged appetite is the *greatest hindrance to mental improvement and soul sanctification.*"[5] And soul sanctification in Christ is what makes us fit to be restored to Eden. Again she writes: "With our first parents, intemperate desire resulted in the loss of Eden. *Temperance* in *all* things has *more* to do with our restoration to Eden than men realize."[6]

An athlete has to practice temperance in all areas of life in order to give himself or herself the best opportunity to win a temporary prize. How much more we ourselves need to do our best to be temperate in all things, so that we may be found sanctified in Christ and gain eternal glory. Paul emphasizes this concept of total temperance: "And everyone who competes for the prize is temperate in all things. Now they do it to obtain a perishable crown, but we for an imperishable crown" (1 Cor. 9:25). Then he makes the crucial connection between total temperance and eternal life: "But I discipline my body and bring it into subjection, lest, when I have preached to others, I myself should become disqualified" (verse 27).

A truly temperate life is a seasoned life without extremes, even in good things. Such a life makes a tremendous spiritual impact on others. That is the kind of thoroughly transformed life through which

Jesus desires to reveal Himself to the world. "Those who understand the laws of health and who are governed by principle will *shun the extremes, both* of indulgence and restriction. . . . They seek to preserve *every* power in the *best* condition for the *highest* service to God and man. . . . While they do not urge their views offensively upon others, their *example is a testimony* in favor of right principles. These persons have a wide influence for good."[7]

6. **Air.** We can exist without food for a few weeks, we can endure without water for a few days, but we can survive for only a few minutes without breathing. Air is absolutely vital to life, and it is significant that Scripture links Adam becoming a living being directly to God breathing "into his nostrils the breath of life" (Gen. 2:7).

Breath of life means breath is life, and this life comes from God the Creator. Can you imagine the feeling Adam had as he inhaled his first life-giving breath breathed by God Himself? We can be certain that joy and gratitude for his Maker filled him, and that he cherished every breath he took. That is why we should also value every breath of fresh air—it is God's priceless gift of Himself to us.

Who can say that breathing the Creator's fresh air is not a spiritual act? And in breathing into us His breath of life every moment, He desires as well to breathe His Spirit in our lives with every breath we take. God's breath of life energizes our physical health, and God's breath of His Spirit energizes our spiritual health.

Air is essential to sustain life, but pure air is vital to good health. Particularly today, we need clean and fresh air to breathe because of all the many pollutants in the air. Our modern way of life compounds the problem. Millions of cars and factories spew out filthy smoke, joined by millions of people belching out foul cigarette smoke. We have made sure that we provided ourselves with all the conveniences of modern life, but at the same time we have deprived ourselves of pure air—most essential to life and health.

Many people stay indoors in the convenience of well-heated and air-conditioned homes and workplaces, robbed of the blessing of fresh air. There they can find convenient entertainment on their TV's and VCR's, and they can labor away at their computers and other modern gadgetry. In fact, opening windows for daily ventilation of stale air seems to be an outdated health practice, and often windowless buildings make it impossible.

Our God is pure, and the air He gives us to breathe needs to be pure as well. Our lungs as well as our lodgings need to be ventilated with clean air. God lined our lungs with millions of tiny air sacs that function most properly with plenty of pure air. We need not only good air quality but also a good quantity of it, for by breathing deeply, such quality air can then penetrate the lungs and fill them to full capacity.

Inhaling pure air saturated with oxygen, and exhaling used air loaded with carbon dioxide, is in many ways like praying. For as we pray to God we should breathe out to Him all our stale air of sin, and in exchange breathe in deeply His pure air of salvation. We exhale our spirit of self-centeredness and inhale His Spirit of sanctification. God wants us to inhale, not the stale secondhand air of other people's opinions, but the pure air of His own thoughts.

Just as we can never stop breathing, we are to also "pray without ceasing" (1 Thess. 5:17). We are not to merely pray once or twice, and then feel that we have done our spiritual duty for the day. Instead we are to constantly breathe out prayers whatever circumstance we find ourselves in. *"Cultivate* the habit of talking with the Saviour when you are alone, when you are walking, and when you are busy with your daily labor. Let the heart be continually uplifted in silent petition for help, for light, for strength, for knowledge. *Let every breath be a prayer."* [8]

Here is a summary of some of the healthy effects of breathing plenty of pure air, and the harmful effects of inhaling polluted air. Let us study them carefully and see their relationship to and affect on our spiritual life.

a. Fresh air helps expel toxic impurities from the blood and speeds up its circulation to every part of the body. Getting plenty of oxygen helps us to think more clearly and work more efficiently. It can also improve our memory and enhance our creativity.

b. Not only can fresh air kill germs on the outside of the body, but it can do the same thing in the lower clusters of the air sacs when we remember to breathe it fully and deeply. And there the red blood cells carry the fresh supplies of oxygen to all the cells of the body, making them vigorous and efficient.

c. When breathed fully and deeply, pure air, with its revitalizing oxygen, can refresh a fatigued mind and boost up a waning morale. On the other hand, shallow breathing can result in drowsiness of the body, dullness of the mind, and depression of the spirit.

d. Breathing clean air helps soothe ragged nerves, inducing relaxation and restful sleep. We know that when we get away to the country, for example, we calm down and sleep better. However, when we resign ourselves to breathing stale air in our homes, places of work, and shopping malls, then no wonder that we suffer headaches and feel run-down. Stale air is poor in oxygen and rich in carbon monoxide and other pollutants.

As we have seen, breathing freely and fully God's pure air relaxes the body, calms the nerves, invigorates the mind, and lifts up the spirit. Isn't this a great incentive for us to breathe God's vitalizing life and Spirit in our lives? Proper physical breathing, as the Creator ordained it to be, can be a spiritual act, for it enhances our spiritual growth and fruitfulness, and leads us to be one with the One who breathes His life and Spirit into our entire being.

---

[1] White, *Patriarchs and Prophets,* p. 562.

[2] ——, *Steps to Christ,* p. 101.

[3] ——, *The Desire of Ages,* p. 100. (Italics supplied.)

[4] *Ibid.,* p. 122. (Italics supplied.)

[5] ——, *Counsels on Diet and Foods* (Washington, D.C.: Review and Herald Pub. Assn., 1946), p. 127. (Italics supplied.)

[6] ——, *The Ministry of Healing,* p. 129. (Italics supplied.)

[7] *Ibid.,* p. 319. (Italics supplied.)

[8] *Ibid.,* pp. 510, 511. (Italics supplied.)

CHAPTER
SIXTEEN

———

HEALTH AND HOLINESS—4

It is fitting that we discuss the last two natural remedies together in this chapter because *Rest* and *Trust* in God go hand in hand. To really rest in God is to truly trust Him. Rest, be it physical, mental, or spiritual, is intertwined with trusting in God's providence.

7. Rest. Rest is related to restoration, and is the remedy for restoration. To be restored is to recover one's state of rest. And from a spiritual perspective, for us to be prepared to enter God's heavenly rest we must first enter His rest here. Not only do we need rest and restoration, but everything else does as well. For instance, the many machines that we use require tuning and repair, and they eventually wear out. Don't our weary bodies need rejuvenation too, so that they may serve us well and long? Of course they do. Our Creator knew that the bodies He had designed for us must have rest in order to survive. And to be sure that some of our most important organs do get their indispensable rest, He "built in *automatic rest,*"[1] explains Dr. Ethel Nelson.

For instance, consider the important organ of the heart "which contracts for one tenth of a second and then rests the remainder of the second. During the resting period the circulating blood nourishes it with nutrients and oxygen." Nelson goes on to give other fascinating examples of how the kidneys, liver, muscle fibers, and cells acquire such rest.

"The tiny filters in your kidneys operate in shifts: one third work, one third rest, and one third prepare for work. The cells of your liver and pancreas have cycles of work and rest. The fibers of your muscles work and rest in shifts, except when strenuously exercised. Every cell in your body follows this cycle of rest and work, and mostly without your conscious control."[2]

Our Creator, in His wisdom, ordained rest not only for the organs just mentioned but also for the entire being. Fortunately for our immediate survival, He designed a built-in and marvelous rest mechanism in them. But for our well-being in the long run, He left us with personal choices to seek rest and thus avoid overloading our system with too much work, too much eating, and too much sleep deprivation, just to mention a few dangers.

Our God believes in rest, and that is evident in the fact that at the beginning of the world "He rested on the seventh day from all His work which He had done" (Gen. 2:2). Of course, He did not get exhausted after the six days of creation, but He wanted to show humanity an example that rest from work is vital. And that we do not live merely to work, but to renew ourselves and enjoy our fellowship with Him and with others.

To have us rest in Him and with Him is a very special thing to God, because He desires to have a living relationship with us. That is why in the heart of the Decalogue He reminds us again to "remember the Sabbath day, to keep it holy" (Ex. 20:8-11). He knows that resting from our physical work ushers us into His spiritual rest of submission to Him. And He recognizes that it is easy for us to become so caught up with our busy schedules that we forget about Him, and thus destroy ourselves from lack of both physical and spiritual rest. The very commandment He asks us to remember is the very one we most often forget. No life was more demanding than the life of Jesus, yet He took time for rest and contemplation. And the way He carried Himself and related to others clearly indicates that He regularly renewed Himself physically as well as spiritually. It was the custom for Jesus, the Lord of the Sabbath, to remember to rest on that holy day (Luke 4:16). And He also made sure that He took time during the week to renew Himself from His exhaustive days of work.

As we discussed in a previous chapter, Jesus, in spite of a very demanding life, daily renewed Himself in solitude and rest with His Father. The hospitable homes of loving friends such as Martha, Mary, and their brother Lazarus provided Him with welcome opportunities to relax and collect Himself. He also rested with His disciples by slipping away to a secluded place, away from the crowds that followed Him. One time they were so busy that they did not even have time to eat because of the crush of people. Knowing the situation, Jesus invited them to "come aside by yourselves to a deserted place and rest a while" (Mark 6:31). Commenting on this incident, Ellen White writes: "Christ is full of tenderness and compassion for all in His service. . . . They had been putting their whole souls into labor for the people, and this was exhausting their physical and mental strength. It was their *duty* to rest."[3]

Then she cautions that a lack of rest causes our whole system to become overly strained, opening the avenue for Satan to exploit our vulnerability and undermine our spirituality. "It is not wise to be always under the strain of work and excitement, even in ministering to men's spiritual needs; for in this way personal *piety* is neglected, and the powers of *mind* and *soul* and *body* are overtaxed. Self-denial is required of the disciples of Christ, and sacrifices must be made; but care must also be exercised lest through their *overzeal* Satan take advantage of the weakness of humanity, and the work of God be *marred.*"[4]

Depriving ourselves of much needed rest, even in ministering to people's spiritual needs, can jeopardize our own spirituality—a fact many of us know all too well from personal experience. Although we mean well, overtaxing our systems can make us behave less like Jesus. We face the danger of becoming impatient, irritable, and impulsive, and our focus shifts from Christ to self. Instead, we need to heed Christ's invitation to come aside and rest a while.

Let us reflect on some concepts relating to rest or lack of it, and how they affect our whole being, including the spiritual dimension:

a. Rest gives us the opportunity to slow down enough in order to reflect, to unwind, to laugh, to smell the flowers, to enjoy the rising and setting of the sun—to simply live. We may think that we cannot squander the time because of all that we need to accomplish. However, by not resting we waste more time than we gain, and, more important, we squander life itself. Are we too busy making a living that we forget to make a life? And forgetting to make a life leads us to forget the Lord.

b. In our task-oriented society, rest from our work gives us the chance to invest in our families and friends—in people. And in the long run it will prove to be the most sound and lasting investment. A survey once asked a group of retired executives living in a retirement village what they regretted most not doing in their earlier years. Most of them felt that it was not spending time with their loved ones and friends.

Position and prestige pass away, money and material possessions lose their luster, but our investment in people always endures. Such investment in worthwhile relationships with others instead of only things makes us more receptive to investing ourselves in a spiritual and enduring relationship with God. A hectic lifestyle, without much time to rest and to enjoy living, cannot help undermining our relationship with Him. If we do not take time to unwind and rest so that we may enjoy those in our lives whom we do see, how can we ever enjoy a meaningful relationship with the One whom we see not?

Modern society does not put much emphasis on human relationships. Many try to substitute for that lack by amassing money, power, or other substitutes. But, for example, how much money is enough? Enough to buy and do more and more things, only to discover that we are still empty for something we still do not have? "One of the most fruitful sources of shattered constitutions among men is a devotion to the getting of money, an inordinate desire for wealth. They narrow their lives to the single pursuit of money, sacrifice rest, sleep, and the comforts of life to this one object."[5]

c. To be always on the run not only keeps us from enjoying our family members and friends but also may prevent us from investing ourselves in a relationship with God. We become so used to receiving our security and worth from our work and wealth that it blinds us to God, the real source. Thus we overlook developing a spiritual relationship with Him.

d. Regular and sufficient nightly sleep is the most effective means for obtaining our needed rest. When we do not take some time to rest because we have become so engrossed in our work, our sleep may suffer. Coupled with an unhealthy lifestyle, the problem compounds as we become more anxious and uptight. Watching late TV while snacking does not help matters either.

For example, we push beyond our endurance by studying or working late at night because we ignorantly suppose that we will get ahead that way. But in reality we do not get ahead—rather, we fall behind. "As a rule, the labor of the day should not be prolonged into the evening. . . . I have been shown that those who do this often *lose much more than they gain,* for their energies are exhausted, and they labor on nervous excitement."[6]

I know this fact from personal experience. For example, in trying to complete this book, I pushed myself to stay up late at night in order to meet certain expectations I had placed on myself. Late that evening I went to bed thinking that I had really progressed in my writing. But in reality I had only set myself up for disappointment, for the next day was almost wasted, and my writing regressed instead of progressing. You see, I did not give my brain enough rest to recharge itself, and did not allow my body to rebuild itself, and the results were clearly apparent when I woke up the next morning. During such days one feels wiped out. Exhaustion leaves us more touchy and easily upset and destroys our desire for close communion with God.

e. Adequate sleep is a great restorer, for it rebuilds the cells throughout the entire body. It refreshes our minds and bodies, making us more alert, efficient, and calmer.

f. Restful sleep is a healer, for it helps in our recovery from infections, sickness, and trauma, and it improves the immune system's ability to ward off disease.

g. "It does not pay to 'go into debt' on sleep. Nervous breakdowns, depression, and organ failures happen all too often because overly ambitious, and even successful people feel they don't have time to rest."[7] Moreover, "there are many professing Christians who are *anxious and depressed,* many who are so full of busy activity that they cannot find time to *rest* quietly in the promises of God, who act *as if* they could not afford to have peace and quietness."[8]

Some of us may, unfortunately, feel that because we have not met our expectations or finished our work, we have no right to rest until we do finish. But let us be realistic. Unfinished work is a part of human existence. God said that in "six days you shall labor and do all your work" (Ex. 20:9). But don't we often come to the end of a week of even diligent work and feel that we haven't finished all that we had set out to accomplish? Of course we do.

Then does that mean that if we are unable to "do *all* our work" we cannot enter the Sabbath rest that we so desperately need? No, because only God could perfectly finish all His work (Gen. 2:1) and perfectly merit His rest. But He knows our limitations, and while doing our best to finish all our work may not be good enough for ourselves or others, it is sufficient for Him. Thus after doing what we reasonably can in six days, God invites us to rest on the seventh day anyway. He urges us to enter into His own rest.

196

It is *His* rest that we enter into, not *ours.* And that is the only true rest that restores us into His likeness, body, mind, and spirit. Such rest is indeed His act of grace toward us: we rest in His rest, for He Himself has already finished His work of creation and work of redemption in our behalf. Thank God for His abundant grace.

Abraham Heschel, in his book *The Sabbath,* makes an insightful comment on our text in Exodus 20:9: "Six days you shall labor and do all your work." "Is it possible for a human being to do all his work in six days? Does not our work always remain incomplete? What the verse means to convey is: Rest on the Sabbath *as if* all your work were done."[9]

It is Jesus who invites us: "Come to Me, all you who labor and are heavy laden, and I will give you rest" (Matt. 11:28). The rest that He offers is the kind that we really need—a rest for the entire being. He freely offers it to us. And it is the kind of rest He alone can give.

"The love which Christ diffuses through the whole being is a vitalizing power. Every vital part—the brain, the heart, the nerves—it touches with healing. By it the highest energies of the being are roused to activity. It frees the soul from the guilt and sorrow, the anxiety and care, that crush the life forces. With it come serenity and composure. It implants in the soul joy that nothing earthly can destroy—joy in the Holy Spirit—health-giving, life-giving joy."[10]

8. **T**rust. This involves trust in God's divine power. The previous natural remedy has a close connection to our final one. In *trust* we accept Christ's invitation to go to Him, and there in His healing presence exchange our heavy burdens for His renewing *rest.* The more we rest in Christ, the more we trust Him, and the more we trust Him, the more we want to rest in Him. In other words, rest leads to trust and trust leads to rest—each reinforces the other. But we can find and place such rest and trust only in Christ. Loved ones and good friends can offer their help, but the best that they can give us is still quite limited compared to His limitless supply.

The world has a crisis of faith. People need to place their trust in something or someone, and they do. Unfortunately, their trust is often misplaced or betrayed. Our ultimate trust must be rooted in God's divine power, as our eighth remedy points out. It is *His* power that makes us strong; it is *His* strength that makes us healthy; and it is *His* life that makes every cell of our being throb with life and vitality.

I believe it is fitting that the eight natural remedies we have been looking at conclude with our need to trust in divine power. This trust, then, serves as the solid foundation in which the preceding remedies anchor themselves. We trust His divine power to help us apply every one of His natural remedies. As a result, we have strong confidence that divine power enables us to apply these remedies in our everyday life, helping us to become more healthy and holy, and thus better reflectors of Christ's likeness.

Because of the hectic world we live in, it is not always easy to implement the eight natural remedies. Expecting instant results, people do not have the patience for long-term outcomes. It takes faith, effort, discipline, and sacrifice—things many of us are not so willing to exercise. But for whatever we expend in renewing our total health, we will receive a hundredfold in return. It will give us abundant life in this world and eternal life in the world to come.

Just after she mentions the eight natural remedies, Ellen White gives practical counsel on how we can avoid becoming discouraged as we try to follow them: "The use of natural remedies requires an amount of care and effort that many are *not* willing to give. Nature's process of healing and upbuilding is *gradual,* and to the impatient it seems slow. The surrender of hurtful indulgences requires *sacrifice.* But in the end it will be found that nature, untrammeled, does her work *wisely* and *well.* Those who *persevere* in obedience to her laws will *reap* the *reward* in health of body and health of mind." [11]

Personal experience teaches us that it takes effort and patience to prepare healthy food, to exercise, to be temperate, and to use nondrug therapy. It is easy to give up sometimes, because so many other easier alternatives constantly beckon us. For example, it is much simpler to take some pills to treat the symptoms of a common cold than to use hydrotherapy to help the body actually overcome the infection. Hydrotherapeutic treatments can be involved and take time and patience, but they bolster and condition our body's immune system to fight disease—something that pills do not do. The treatments strengthen our bodies to ward off future disease when it comes, and we will be much better off for it in the long run.

This is just one example. And if we trust God to give us His divine power, and with patience and discipline put to practice His all-natural remedies, we will be much better prepared to experience a solid spiritual life. A stable religious life is hard to achieve if we condition ourselves to take short cuts, cut corners, take the easy way out, and impatiently opt for instant gratification. "Godliness does not conflict with the laws of health, but is in harmony with them." [12]

Another thing that we need to be fully aware of is that Satan seeks to defeat us on the spiritual front by overwhelming us on the physical and mental fronts. He knows too well that if we neglect to practice God's natural remedies, he has a better chance of undermining our spirituality. By subtly counterfeiting each natural remedy, he can wage his vicious war against our spiritual life on many fronts. For example, he uses intemperance with all its forms to lower our inhibitions, dull our senses, weaken our resistance, and plague us with tension and depression.

And in essence we can call this a spiritual war, because the devil does not merely seek to destroy the body but, more important, the soul along with the body. "Evil angels are striving for the dominion of every human being. Whatever injures the health not only lessens physical vigor, but tends to *weaken* the mental and moral powers. Indulgence in any unhealthful practice makes it *more* difficult for one to discriminate between right and wrong, and hence *more* difficult to resist evil. It *increases* the danger of failure and defeat." [13]

But we must not allow the evil one to have mastery on any front in this warfare, for our eternal destiny depends on it. That is why we must let God take full control of our lives, and trust in His divine power to help us follow His laws of health, so that we may fortify every aspect of our lives against the devil's assaults. We can define faith as "trusting God—believing that He loves us and knows best what is for our good." And through trust in Christ, "every deficiency of character may be supplied, every defilement cleansed, every fault corrected, every excellence developed." [14]

As we place our trust in Christ, let us remember that He was the model of how to put trust in His Father. As we discussed earlier, He trusted Him in every detail of His life from beginning to end. Christ trusted God for His words, for His guidance, and for His power. He did nothing without His Father's divine power although Satan constantly tempted Him to trust His own strength.

In Gethsemane, though God's wrath against the sin He was to bear pierced His soul and threatened to crush His life, He nevertheless trusted implicitly His Father's will for His life: "Not as I will, but as You will" (Matt. 26:39). And as He breathed His last on the cross, His final words were ones of unshakable trust in His Father: "Father, into Your hands I commend My spirit" (Luke 23:46).

As Christ uttered His unswerving trust in His Father, He forever defeated Satan. The devil had constantly sought to undermine Christ's trust in His Father. After all, he had defeated the first Adam, and he marshaled all his hellish forces to overwhelm the Second Adam the same way: through distrust of God. Shortly before Jesus breathed His last, Satan tried through some of the Jewish leaders to shake His Father-Son relationship of trust. But even Christ's human enemies had to admit that He trusted His Father. "He trusted in God; let Him deliver Him now if He will have Him; for He said, 'I am the Son of God'" (Matt. 27:43).

Finally, let us go over some of the benefits we receive when we follow Christ's example of trusting God. And as we review them, let us remember that trust in His divine power empowers us to accomplish His will in our own lives. Such trust, "instead of our own, . . . leads us to choose His way. In place of our ignorance, it accepts His wisdom; in place of our weakness, His strength; in place of our sinfulness, His righteousness. Our lives, ourselves, are already His; faith acknowledges His ownership and accepts its blessing." Moreover, "if we are willing to do His will, all His strength is ours." [15]

a. A person who places His trust in the loving and caring God is a healthier individual. Trust, contentment, joy, and other positive emotions increase the number of hormones that bolster the immune system and allow its mechanism to function more effectively. Trusting in God, who loves and guides us, helps promote our health and happiness.

Some may hold that "spirituality is a detriment to health," but such a view is but the "sophistry of Satan." For the "religion of the Bible is not detrimental to the health of either body or mind." And the "influence of the Spirit of God is the *very best* medicine for disease." [16] Solomon recognized that "a merry heart does good, like medicine, but a broken spirit dries the bones" (Prov. 17:22).

Placing our trust in what God is like and in what He can do for us is an indispensable ingredient to our health and well-being. "Health and fitness are not enough," assert Drs. Diehl and Ludington. "The ultimate lifestyle includes spiritual growth and development. It brings a contentment in which we learn that if we are not satisfied with what we have, we will never be satisfied with what we want." [17]

b. Thoughts of distrust, and suspicion, and other negative emotions increase the production of hormones that weaken the immune system, making its defenses less effective in warding off disease. That is why it is "a positive duty to resist melancholy, discontented thoughts and feelings—as much a duty as it is to pray." For "nothing tends more to promote health of body and of soul than does a spirit of gratitude and praise." [18] Again Scripture declares, "Anxiety in the heart of man causes depression" (Prov. 12:25).

c. We must saturate our minds every day with wholesome thoughts, for whatever we think affects how our bodies function. We must constantly fill our minds with the thoughts of Christ, because in our world we are continuously bombarded with the most negative thoughts. In a society in which it is in style to expose the mind to the most wretched ideas under the guise that everyone needs to be informed, we desperately need to heed Paul's relevant counsel: "Finally, brethren, whatever things are true, whatever things are noble, whatever things are just, whatever things are pure, whatever things are lovely, whatever things are of good report, if there is any virtue and if there is anything praiseworthy—meditate on these things" (Phil. 4:8).

Listen to what Norman Cousins says about how our thoughts and feelings affect the condition of the immune system and other bodily functions: "The immune system is a *mirror to life,* responding to its joy and anguish, its exuberance and boredom, its laughter and tears, its excitement and depression, its problems and prospects. Scarcely anything that enters the mind doesn't find its way into the workings of the body." [19]

d. Trusting in God removes fear and anxiety, because we know that He takes up our cause. We do not worry about what may happen to us now or in the future, because we have entrusted our lives to Him who holds us and the world in the palms of His hands. Genuine peace results from our minds and hearts dwelling on Jesus and trusting in Him. Isaiah writes: "You will keep him in perfect peace, whose mind is stayed on You, because he trusts in You" (Isa. 26:3). And Peter exhorts us: "Casting all your care upon Him, for He cares for You" (1 Peter 5:7).

The reason we sometimes worry and become anxious is that we find it difficult to entrust ourselves to God's care. It is true that "many who profess to be His followers have an anxious, troubled heart, because they are afraid to *trust themselves with God.*" [20] Consequently, they go to others to fill their need to trust instead of entrusting themselves to the all-trustworthy Jesus.

However, no human being can take the place of God in meeting such a need. God knows when His people are inclined to substitute trust in Him for trust in others. Then in His great love to draw us to Himself, He "often permits those in whom we place confidence to fail us, in order that we may learn the folly of trusting in man and making flesh our arm." Therefore, "let us trust fully, humbly, unselfishly in God." [21] So when those in whom we have placed our confidence fail us, we can instead view it as a divine incentive to place our ultimate trust in the all-trustworthy God. He alone will never fail us or betray our trust.

But why, then, are we so afraid to trust Him? It is because we forget that He is our best and never-failing friend, and in His love He is constantly doing His best for our welfare. "Keep your wants, your joys, your sorrows, your cares, and your fears before God. You cannot burden Him; you cannot weary Him. . . . His heart of love is touched by our sorrows, and even by our utterances of them. Take to Him everything that perplexes the mind. Nothing is too great for Him to bear, for He holds up worlds." [22]

God is the Lord of new beginnings. If we entrust ourselves to Him, He will take us where we are and transform us into the likeness of His Son. His great mercies are "new every morning" (Lam. 3:23). If we will only appropriate them, they can help our entire being to renew itself. Although Satan has had his way in undermining our health, happiness, and holiness, and although he has managed to shake our trust in God, "the Father's mercy and love have not ceased to flow earthward in rich currents. If human beings would open the windows of the soul heavenward, in appreciation of the divine gifts, a flood of healing virtue would pour in." [23]

Let the rich currents of God's love and mercy flow in your life. Let your soul open heavenward so that the surging floods of His healing and restoration may pour into your whole being. And let God give you a NEW START.

---

[1] Ethel R. Nelson, *Eight Secrets of Health* (Bangkok, Thailand: Thailand Pub. House, 1991), p. 221.

[2] *Ibid.*

[3] White, *The Desire of Ages,* p. 360. (Italics supplied.)

[4] *Ibid.,* p. 362. (Italics supplied.)

[5] ———, *Temperance* (Mountain View, Calif.: Pacific Press Pub. Assn., 1949), p. 140.

[6] *Ibid.,* p. 140. (Italics supplied.)

[7] Nelson, p. 222.

[8] White, *Counsels on Health,* p. 251. (Italics supplied.)

[9] Abraham Joshua Heschel, *The Sabbath* (New York: The Noonday Press, 1975), p. 32. (Italics supplied.)

[10] White, *The Ministry of Healing,* p. 115.

[11] ———, *Counsels on Health,* p. 90. (Italics supplied.)

[12] *Ibid.,* p. 627.

[13] White, *The Ministry of Healing,* p. 128. (Italics supplied.)

[14] ———, *Education,* pp. 253, 257.

[15] *Ibid.,* p. 253.

[16] White, *Counsels on Health,* p. 28. (Italics supplied.)

[17] Diehl and Ludington, *Lifestyle Capsules,* p. 196.

[18] White, *The Ministry of Healing,* p. 251.

[19] Norman Cousins, *Head First: The Biology of Hope* (New York: E. P. Dutton, 1989), pp. 35-37. (Italics supplied.)

[20] White, *The Desire of Ages,* p. 330. (Italics supplied.)

[21] ———, *The Ministry of Healing,* p. 486.

[22] ———, *Steps to Christ,* p. 100.

[23] ———, *The Ministry of Healing,* p. 116.

———

OUR MIGHTY PETITIONER

Daddy, but you promised to pray for him!" my 4-year-old daughter suddenly blurted out when she realized that I had concluded family worship without mentioning that particular prayer request. "You remember, yesterday you promised that man you would pray for him," she persisted. She was right. I had forgotten to include his name on my prayer list. Thanking her for reminding me, we knelt down again and offered a special prayer for him.

"When we say to people 'I will pray for you,' we make a very important commitment," writes Henri Nouwen. "The sad thing is that this remark often remains nothing but a well-meant expression of concern. But when we learn to descend with our mind into our heart, then all those who have become part of our lives are led into the healing presence of God . . . because God's heart has become one with ours." [1]

Reflecting on that incident later that morning, I thought of how much our hearts need to throb with our Lord's spirit of intercession. Jesus, a perfect petitioner, never forgets to pray for us, for "He ever lives to make intercession" (Heb. 7:25) in our behalf before the Father. Christ is ready to pray for us every moment. Adolph Safir explains how life and prayer are one in Christ. He writes that "in the Lord Jesus Christ we see most clearly the union of prayer and life." [2] His whole existence has always been constant communion with His Father. And He has been including humanity in such communion ever since the creation of our first parents.

Even now, with you and me always on His mind, He gives Himself to intercessory prayer with the Father. Christ's enduring engagement in living and praying for us clearly confirms that He loves us and cares deeply for us. Just listen to His moving words of intercession in behalf of His people recorded in Isaiah 62:1: "For Zion's sake I will not hold My peace, and for Jerusalem's sake I will not rest, until her righteousness goes forth as brightness, and her salvation as a lamp that burns."

A few verses later the preincarnate Christ even calls on His watchmen to ally themselves with Him in His intercession to the Father. In other words, He will not cease His intercession for His people, neither will His ministers rest until heaven has completely restored them. Listen to His passionate appeal: "I have set watchmen on your walls, O Jerusalem, who shall never hold their peace day or night. You who make mention of the Lord, do not keep silent, and give Him no rest till He establishes and till He makes Jerusalem a praise in the earth" (verses 6, 7).

Later on we will discuss our sacred privilege of joining Christ in His intercession for the salvation of others. For now let us focus on His intercession. Our Intercessor is so devoted to our welfare, and so determined to restore us to Himself, that He employs a three-pronged strategy in His intercession. He involves Himself, His watchmen [angels], and the Father. First, He Himself does not rest in His efforts to save us. Second, He calls on all His watchmen not to rest. And third, He requests them not to give the Father any rest, as it were, until His glorious purposes are accomplished in His people.

Christ's entire life on earth served as a living sacrifice and mighty intercession. And as the "priest forever" He offered His intercession with infinite intensity and tremendous fervor. For He, "in the days of His flesh, when He had offered up prayers and supplications, with vehement cries and tears to Him who was able to save Him from death, and was heard because of His godly fear" (Heb. 5:7).

What helps me get a glimpse of the intensity and perseverance of Christ's intercessory prayer is the example my mother showed in her prayers for me. As a child I would often hear her crying to God, and I would see and sense the intensity of emotion on her face and in her voice. She seemed to be in living connection with Him, experiencing His very presence as she would pour out her heart to Him as to her best friend. Often she would agonize and shed tears as she prostrated herself before Him. And God did answer her prayers and petitions.

Ellen White wrote: "When with earnestness and intensity we

breathe a prayer in the name of Christ, there is in that very intensity a pledge from God that He is about to answer our prayer 'exceeding abundantly above all that we ask or think.'"[3] If God delights to answer such human prayers, how infinitely more He is willing to respond to the prayers of His Son Jesus, who stands at the His right hand making intercession for us (see Rom. 8:34).

As I witnessed her living demonstration of intercessory prayer, I found myself compelled to ask my mother to show me also how to pray. And she did, but it was something not merely taught but caught. Often the disciples witnessed their Master absorbed in prayer, and they longed to emulate His example. They became so convinced that His exemplary life and mighty works had a direct relationship to His prayer life that they asked Him, "Lord, teach us to pray" (Luke 11:1). It deeply moved them as they observed that His "face was irradiated with a celestial brightness." Moreover, "He seemed to be in the very presence of the Unseen, and there was a living power in His words as of one who spoke with God."[4]

Christ's dynamic prayers vastly differed from the stale prayers of the Pharisees. His words were full of faith, love, and power. Sometimes the disciples witnessed Him pray for them all night, pouring out "His supplications with bitter agony and tears."[5] Jesus' powerful example strongly convicted them that here was the way to pray and to prevail with God. He "supplicated the throne of God, till His humanity was charged with a heavenly current that connected humanity with divinity."[6] How much we need such living models in supplication, those who agonize and pour out their hearts to God as did Jesus!

"God's cause creeps forward timidly and slowly when there are more *organizers* than *agonizers,* more workers than prevailing prayer warriors," asserts Wesley Duewel. "We need prayer warriors who have seen the heart of God, who have experienced the power and the glory of the cross."[7] Of course, we need to be both, the agonizers as well as the organizers, the warriors as well as the workers, and in that order. But unfortunately, all too often we put organization and work over prayer.

"We would rather work for God than pray," Duewel continues. "We would rather attend another service than pray. We would rather watch TV than pray. May God forgive us!"[8] And we may add that we would rather attend a prayer meeting, or even participate in a seminar on how to effectively pray than just to simply pray. Isn't it about time that we realize that the best and only way to pray is to actually do it? And isn't it time that we become convicted that to downplay or push off to the side our prayer life means to cut off our lifeline with the Divine, and to spiritually self-destruct?

In some of the theology classes that I have taught I discovered with my students the great spiritual blessings God had in store for us as we interceded in behalf of our class members and others in need. We were interested in more than just beginning the class with prayer or simply talking about prayer. Bringing specific needs before God, we opened our hearts and availed ourselves of what He had in mind for us. Not demanding anything, we simply interceded along with Christ and the Spirit for God's will to be done in another person's life.

As we shared reports of answered prayers, the Spirit of God brought spiritual unity and power among us. Others in the class, inspired by the tangible evidences of the reality of God's presence and power, felt impressed to share their own prayer requests. The experience reminded us of Andrew Murray's pertinent and challenging words: "He [God] looks to the thousands of young men and young women in training for the work of ministry and mission, and gazes longingly to see if the church is teaching them that intercession . . . must be their *first* care, and in seeking to train and help them to it." [9]

We would rather do many other spiritual things than pray and intercede, because it calls for us to give up ourselves to God and invest in others. In fact, we would rather give up anything than self. In this regard, Bishop J. C. Ryle explained: "We spend our spiritual strength and forget to renew it. We multiply engagements and curtail prayer. . . . We work when we ought to pray, because to an active mind work is far easier than prayer. . . . The servant whom the Holy Spirit is to use must resist the tyranny of overwork. He must resolve to be alone with God even if the hours spent with Him appear to rob his fellowmen of his service." [10]

Throughout His life and ministry Jesus exemplified His need to pray and prevail. Prayer guided all His steps. He conceived all His important decisions in prayer. Whether it was His choice of disciples, His teachings, or His miracles—all resulted from prevailing prayer. Jesus began His ministry in such prayer at the river Jordan, and culminated it in intercession on Golgotha. Christ lived, moved, taught, healed, and died praying. His life was prayer. Prayer that was *per-*

petual and *prevailing* in its nature, and *pervading* all things in its scope. "In the Lord Jesus Christ we see most clearly the union of prayer and life, the harmony and continual interpretation of the two spheres of life." [11]

"Those who are unwilling to deny self, to agonize before God, to pray long and earnestly for His blessing, will not obtain it. Wrestling with God—how few know what it is! How few have ever had their souls drawn out after God with intensity of desire until every power is on the stretch. When waves of despair which no language can express sweep over the suppliant, how few cling with unyielding faith to the promises of God." [12]

The apostle James assures us that the "effective, fervent prayer of a righteous man avails much" (James 5:16). Ponder the tremendous impact of this promise when we apply it to Jesus praying for us. He is indeed righteousness embodied, for He is "The Lord Our Righteousness" (Jer. 23:6). Christ is the righteous Son of man who prays fervently, and whose fervent prayers are extremely effectual. And this mighty Petitioner longs to pray for us! Have we been making the most of His petitions in our behalf, or have we been recklessly disregarding them?

Jesus prayed for others as well as for Himself. "In the hour of distress He [Jesus] turned to His Father" in fervent intercession. Although He could perform all miracles and accomplish all mighty deeds, "yet He prayed, often with strong crying and tears. He prayed for His disciples and for Himself, thus identifying Himself with human needs. He was a mighty petitioner. As the Prince of life, He had power with God, and prevailed." [13] Note that Jesus never wavered in His intercessions even till the end of His life. In fact, they intensified shortly before His crucifixion. The Gospels record that on four different occasions during this brief time He offered memorable prayers of intercession:

1. He prayed for Peter that his faith might remain strong (Luke 22:31, 32).

2. He prayed for Himself, for His disciples, and for all believers (John 17:1-26).

3. He prayed for Himself and all lost humanity in Gethsemane (Matt. 26:36-42).

4. He prayed for His enemies who were crucifying Him (Luke 23:34).

208

Peter was so devoted to Jesus that when he heard Him say to him "when you have returned to Me" (see Luke 22:31, 32), he probably wondered how Jesus could say such a thing if he never left or planned to leave Him. Was Jesus hinting that he was not committed or loyal enough? Thus he instantly replied that he would never leave His sight. In fact, he was not merely going to stay with Him, but he was ready to go to prison and even to death with Him.

The confident reaction sounds familiar, doesn't it? Peter vowed never to leave Him, but he denied Him three times. On another occasion He asked Jesus to depart from him, yet he clung to His feet, unable to part from Him. Also when Jesus tried to wash his feet, the disciple said that he would never let Him do that, yet as soon as he heard that such a refusal would affect their relationship, he begged Him to wash all of him.

That was Peter. He meant well, yet in His love and devotion to Christ, he needed to maintain his constant focus on Him who would keep him from falling. Christ knew that Satan was after Peter. "Satan has asked for you" (verse 31). And today Satan is never satisfied until he also has our souls. If we assume otherwise, we do it at the peril of our eternal destiny.

Christ came not only to warn Peter of Satan's impending attack, but also to assure him of His own intercessory prayers for him. I like the conjunction "but" at the beginning of verse 32, implying that Satan may do what he wants, but Christ wages a counteroffensive against him in our behalf. "But I [Jesus] have prayed for you [Peter]." Christ spent entire nights interceding for Peter and the other disciples as well, that their faith would not fail.[14]

Although Satan will do everything he can to destroy us, Jesus wants to have us too, and He has been fervently praying for us. And when we totally avail ourselves of His mighty intercession, focusing more on what Christ can do and less on what Satan can do, then we have victory in Christ. "There is *no* power in the whole satanic force that can disable the soul that trusts, in simple confidence, in the wisdom that comes from God. . . . Satan could do *nothing* against the all-powerful intercession of Christ. And the prayer that Christ offered for Peter He offers in behalf of *all* who are humble and contrite in heart."[15]

While we must be realistic and recognize Satan's subtle strategies against us, at the same time we must always view everything from a position of strength in Jesus. When we see it from the perspective of what Christ is capable of doing, Satan's power and strongholds crumble. Look for a moment at Christ's strategy as compared to the enemy's in the fierce battle for our eternal destiny:

1. Satan is a fallen angel who accuses us every moment, but Christ is the Lamb of God slain from the foundation of the world for our salvation. And in giving Himself completely for our redemption, He neither slumbers nor sleeps (Ps. 121:4).

2. Satan specializes in accusation, but Christ is the expert in salvation—He Himself *is* salvation. While Satan can rely only on deception, accusation, and death, Christ is the truth and the life, and He has all of heaven's resources at His total disposal to save us.

3. Satan knows that he is a defeated enemy, and that none of the facts of the struggle between him and Christ are in his favor. Thus he can do nothing in the face of Christ the all-triumphant commander of heaven's forces, except to refine his falsehoods.

4. Satan is total darkness, and Christ is absolute light. The devil is utter defeat, and Christ is all-powerful and gloriously victorious. And in the presence of Christ's light and power Satan trembles and flees. In fact, one word of Christ's intercession in our behalf makes him shake like a reed with fear. Why, then, do we ever give Satan any chance to overcome us! Why not let our prayers continuously blend and ascend with Christ's prayers as we avail ourselves of His light and power? (In chapter 19 we will discuss further the wrestling and warfare levels of prevailing prayer.)

As we look back at Peter, we see that for his faith not to fail he needed to closely and constantly cling to Christ instead of trusting in his own ability. In his rashness and self-sufficiency he became vulnerable to the devil's devises. Alone, in his feeble power, he was no match for Satan's deceptions, even though he meant well and his intentions were good. But in such spiritual struggle good intentions are not enough—we must be ever vigilant and persevere alongside of Christ.

Right after Christ's warning to Peter to stay strong in his faith, the disciple succumbed to Satan as the devil dulled his senses with paralyzing physical and spiritual stupor. There in Gethsemane, where he desperately needed to respond to Christ's prayers for him by praying with Him, he slept instead. "Had those hours in the garden been spent in watching and prayer, Peter would not have been left to depend on his own feeble strength. He would not have denied his Lord." [16]

Even Christ's mighty prayers in his behalf Peter needed to respond to and appropriate them in his life. Yet Christ did not leave Peter discouraged and desolate, but in His great love and forgiveness drew him back to Himself. And ultimately Christ's prayers for his victory received their answer, for he came back humble and transformed, ready to strengthen others and feed Christ's sheep (see Luke 22:32; John 21:15-19).

The apostle James, who testified about the effectiveness of the righteous man's fervent prayers in James 5:16, also told us the secret of how to overcome the enemy in James 4:7: "Therefore submit to God. Resist the devil and he will flee from you." First and foremost, we must humbly and trustingly and constantly *submit* ourselves to Christ in prayer and devotion. Then being with Christ and becoming one with Him, we can successfully *resist* the devil together. And the result is Satan's rout before this formidable divine-human front. Satan indeed will *flee* away from us instead of us retreating from him. Let us never forget that resistance without submission to Christ spells defeat. We are never fit to resist unless we first submit.

Someone once asked a young girl who daily submitted herself to Christ in prayer and supplication, "What do you do when Satan comes knocking at your heart's door?"

"As soon as he knocks I ask Jesus, who is always with me, to answer the door," she wisely replied. "Then when he sees Jesus at the door, he says as he leaves, 'Sorry, I've got the wrong address.'" The child's simple trust and humble submission is indeed the secret to appropriating Christ's mighty petitions for us. "An appeal to heaven by the *humblest* saint is *more dreaded* by Satan than the decrees of cabinets or the mandates of kings."

And the good news is that Satan does more than say "Sorry, I've got the wrong address." For he "trembles and flees before the weakest soul who finds refuge in that mighty name [of Jesus]." Moreover, "Satan *cannot endure* to have his *powerful rival* [Jesus] appealed to, for he fears and trembles before His strength and majesty. At the *sound of fervent prayer,* Satan's whole host trembles." [19]

That is what Satan fears the most, for he knows that when we pray with Christ and in His mighty name, we possess a living connection to His power. And that is why he fights such prayer life the fiercest, for he fears it the most. Then why do we ignore the very thing that Satan so dreads? Why do we brandish every weapon but the one that can mortally wound him? "Satan dreads nothing but prayer," asserts Samuel Chadwick. "The *one concern* of the devil is to keep the church from praying. He fears nothing from prayerless studies, prayerless works. . . . He laughs at our toil, mocks our wisdom, but trembles when we pray." [20]

Satan takes prevailing prayer most seriously. He dreads it far more than even our most noble deeds and sacred duties. The devil simply does not know how to deal with it except to discourage us from praying. "Satan is more afraid of your praying than of your pure life or zealous witness. One's life may be a beautiful witness that cannot be silenced, but prayer is a *militant force* that has the potential of *defeating* Satan, *destroying* his works, and *driving him out* of places and lives he claims for his own." [21]

Then why don't we pray, or why do we pray so feebly and sporadically? Don't we realize that such prayerlessness exposes us to great spiritual dangers? If we are genuine followers of our praying Jesus, perpetual prayer and petition will feed and fashion us. Then we will know from personal experience that our very spiritual survival and vitality depend on this lifesaving spiritual reality.

We will also know that we simply cannot afford to be sporadic and casual in our prayer, because "the light and strength of one day is not sufficient for the trials and conflicts of the next." Moreover, "Satan is continually changing his temptations. Every day we shall be placed in different circumstances; and in the untried scenes that await us we shall be surrounded by fresh dangers, and constantly assailed by new and unexpected temptations." [22]

When we neglect the privilege of praying with Jesus, we are essentially telling Him (as well as the devil) that we do not really want to be close to Him, and that we do not really love Him that much. Is this really the message we want to convey to Christ and to Satan? Our best Friend, Christ, who longs to encircle us with His light and life, and our worst enemy, Satan, who desires to enclose us with his darkness and death.

It must baffle the angels to see us so recklessly neglect our only link to spiritual power, especially considering Satan's wiliness and subtleties. They must watch in amazement as we so carelessly disregard the highest possible privilege of conversing with the God of the universe. Samuel Chadwick writes: "It would seem as if the biggest thing in God's universe is a man who prays." Then he adds that "there is only one thing more amazing, that is, knowing this, he should not pray." [23]

212

Then let us, by all means, never allow him to keep us from praying. Let us continuously pray with Jesus and let the sound of such fervent prayers ever reverberate heavenward, filling Satan with dread and forcing him to tremble and flee.

Christ's parting words to His disciples, which commenced in the upper room and continued on His way to the Garden of Gethsemane, took the form of intercessory prayer. His longest and most profound prayer, in it He desired His disciples to enter into intimate intercession with His Father in His behalf (John 17:1-5), in their behalf (verses 6-19), and in behalf of all believers (verses 20-26). In our own intercessory prayer we need to include ourselves as well as others.

It is important to note that Jesus felt the need to pray for Himself as He prayed for others. In Gethsemane He even longed to have His disciples watch and pray with Him as He prayed for Himself, for them, and for the salvation of fallen humanity (Matt. 26:36-46). We are told that "hitherto He had been as an intercessor for others; now He longed to have an intercessor for Himself."[24] During His intense suffering He yearned for the sympathy and supplications of His beloved disciples, and "He longed to know that they were praying for Him and for themselves. . . . Had He found them praying, He would have been relieved. . . . He would have been comforted by their steadfast faith."[25]

Christ's experience gives a glimpse of how vital it is for us to be reciprocal in our intercessions. Jesus was, and we also need to be. There, alone in the garden, while His inner circle of disciples slept soundly, Jesus poured out His soul in supplication to His Father. "My soul is exceedingly sorrowful, even to death" (Matt. 26:38), He uttered in agony. Yes, He interceded for Himself, but He interceded for the ultimate purpose of saving humanity through His death on the cruel cross. "O My Father, if it is possible, let this cup pass from Me," He petitioned. But He added, "Nevertheless, not as I will, but as You will" (verse 39).

He repeated His petition three times (verses 42, 44), but always concluded it with His submission to His Father's will. Jesus abhorred the terrible thought of becoming separated for the first time ever from His Father. The sins of humanity and the wrath of God pierced and heavily burdened His soul. "The humanity of the Son of God trembled in that trying hour. He prayed not now for His disciples that their faith might not fail, but for His own tempted, agonized soul. . . . The

213

fate of humanity trembled in the balance." [26]

But—praise God!—in His great love to His Father and lost humanity, He completely submitted to His Father's will and not His own. If we are ever tempted to demand something of God according to our will and not His, let us remember Gethsemane. Whenever we make our requests known to God, and we become displeased because He does not answer in just the way we want, let us ponder Christ's words: "Not as I will, but as You will."

Our supreme example Jesus, whose perfect will had ever been in perfect harmony with His Father's will, humbly condescended to submit His will to that of His Father. How much more we need to submit our imperfect will to His perfect will, knowing that whatever He wills is the best for our lives and something we would have chosen for ourselves had we known how to. And how much more we need to trust Him with all the affairs of our lives—lives redeemed by the precious blood of His Son. "He who did not spare His own Son, but delivered Him up for us all, how shall He not with Him also freely give us all things?" (Rom. 8:32).

As we contemplate Calvary, we become powerfully persuaded that the God who had gone to the extreme extent of giving us His only beloved Son will now give us whatever is best for us. And when we turn our gaze to the cross, we know that God has already answered our greatest need by giving us the Saviour and salvation. There can be absolutely no greater answered prayer than having Jesus and the eternal life He gives us.

Although God always responds to our prayer requests according to His will, let us suppose for the sake of the argument that He does not. We are still of all people the most fortunate for having Jesus. God delights in us and honors our faith when He sees that we love Him the giver much more than any and all other gifts. But it greatly pains Him when the gifts that He intended to draw us closer to Him the giver, on the contrary, lead us away from Him.

If we are not worshiping the Giver, then we are worshiping His gifts. Blessed is the one who not only seeks an answer to prayer, but first and foremost diligently seeks the One who gives the answer. Calvin Miller states that "our ultimate motivation for prayer should not be that we want something from God, but that *we want God*." [27]

Christ delights when we have the experience of Paul in testifying: "What things were gain to me, these I have counted loss for

Christ. But indeed I also count all things loss for the excellence of the knowledge of Christ Jesus my Lord, for whom I have suffered the loss of all things, and count them as rubbish, that I may gain Christ" (Phil. 3:7, 8). When He sees that we put Him first and foremost above all things, and that we are full of gratitude to Him for who He is, then what Jesus said in Matthew 6:33 becomes actualized in our lives: "But seek first the kingdom of God and His righteousness, and all these things shall be added to you."

Indeed, when we contemplate Calvary, we sense the unsurpassable worth of having Jesus Himself as our Saviour and Lord of our lives. There, hanging on that cruel cross, He did not just die for His friends, but His most bitter enemies as well. Despite His acute anguish and agony, He interceded with His Father for embittered enemies who delighted to see Him slowly suffer and die. Breathing His last, He looked upon His vengeful tormentors, not with hate and vengeance, but with love and pity. "Father, forgive them," He interceded, "for they do not know what they do" (Luke 23:34).

Only a heart bursting with love and sympathy could have uttered such words. Jesus longed to be their Advocate too before His Father. In His amazing intercession in their behalf, He seemed to be trying hard to find even a small sign of hope in their darkened and evil hearts. To find some way, so that by any means possible He could save them. In His loving supplication, He chose to focus on the consideration that they may not have known what they were doing. That is what Jesus the true Intercessor is capable of doing. He takes His mind off His indescribable anguish and directs it to His torturers, trying desperately to somehow find some way to save them from themselves.

Christ breathed His last gasps with this kind of intercession on His heart and lips! We stand in awe of His large and heroic heart. It is the literal application of what Jesus said about loving and praying for our enemies and not just our friends. He certainly was the perfect embodiment of His teaching: "You have heard that it was said, 'You shall love your neighbor and hate your enemy.' But I say to you, love your enemies, bless those who curse you, do good to those who hate you, and pray for those who spitefully use you and persecute you'" (Matt. 5:43, 44). That is what the Son of God is like, and that is also what we are to be like as true sons and daughters of God.

[1] Henri Nouwen, *The Way of the Heart* (New York: The Seabury Press, 1981), p. 87.

[2] Adoph Safir, *Our Lord's Pattern for Prayer* (Grand Rapids: Kregel Publications, 1984), p. 87.

[3] White, *Christ's Object Lessons,* p. 147.

[4] ———, *Thoughts From the Mount of Blessing,* p. 102.

[5] ———, *The Desire of Ages,* p. 379.

[6] ———, *Education,* pp. 80, 81.

[7] Wesley L. Duewel, *Mighty Prevailing Prayer* (Grand Rapids: Francis Asbury Press, 1990), p. 23. (Italics supplied.)

[8] *Ibid.,* p. 311.

[9] Andrew Murray, *The Ministry of Intercession* (New York: Fleming Revell, 1898), pp. 168, 169. (Italics supplied.)

[10] Cited in Duewel, p. 312.

[11] Safir, p. 25.

[12] White, *The Great Controversy,* p. 621.

[13] ———, *Gospel Workers,* p. 256.

[14] ———, *The Desire of Ages,* p. 689.

[15] ———, *Sons and Daughters of God,* p. 91. (Italics supplied.)

[16] ———, *The Desire of Ages,* p. 714.

[17] *The SDA Bible Commentary,* Ellen G. White Comments, vol. 2, p. 1008. (Italics supplied.)

[18] ———, *The Desire of Ages,* p. 131.

[19] ———, *Testimonies,* vol. 1, p. 346. (Italics supplied.)

[20] Cited in Harold L. Calkins, *Master Preachers* (Alma Park, Great Britain: Stanborough Press Ltd., 1986), p. 129. (Italics supplied.)

[21] Duewel, p. 233. (Italics supplied.)

[22] White, *Gospel Workers,* p. 257.

[23] Samuel Chadwick, *The Path of Prayer* (Kansas City, Kans: Beacon Hill, 1931), pp. 11, 12.

[24] White, *The Desire of Ages,* p. 686.

[25] *Ibid.,* pp. 687, 688.

[26] *Ibid.,* p. 690.

[27] C. Miller, *The Table of Inwardness,* p. 68. (Italics supplied.)

Chapter Eighteen

PARTNERS IN
HIS PETITIONS—1

We can have no mightier intercessor than to have Jesus praying with us and for us! Just look at Gethsemane and Calvary to see the glorious blessing of having Christ as our mighty petitioner. What greater reassurance can we have than to know that our fervent prayers ever ascend along with His fervent prayers! That He intercedes with and for us with deep emotion filled with "vehement cries and tears" (Heb. 5:7).

No greater honor and privilege awaits us than to join Christ in His tears of intercession for others, in becoming His special participants in petition. For as Jesus lives to make intercession for humanity, we know that the Father in His boundless love "raised us up together [with Christ], and made us sit together in the heavenly places in Christ Jesus" (Eph. 2:6). "Blessed are they also who weep with Jesus in sympathy with the world's sorrow and in sorrow for its sin," Ellen White writes. "All who are followers of Christ will share in this experience. As they partake of His love they will enter into His travail for the saving of the lost." [1]

Wesley Duewel depicts the awesome and glorious responsibility we have of sharing in Christ's intercession for others. "There is no more Christlike role than to be a cointercessor with Christ for the priorities upon His heart. . . . Prevailing prayer is glorious because it unites you with the heartbeat of Christ. It is glorious because in prevailing prayer you share the vision of Christ. . . . The Spirit shares with you Christ's passion until you are convulsed by the same heart-cry as the Son and the same groanings as the Spirit (Rom. 8:26)." [2]

As Jesus intercedes for us at the right hand of the Father, He invites us to unite with Him in His ministry of intercession and reconciliation. Shall we not accept His invitation? After all, He united Himself with us and the Father. "As we approach God through the virtue of the Redeemer's merits, Christ places us close by His side, encircling us with His human arm, while with His divine arm He grasps the throne of the Infinite."[3]

Enveloping us with His intimate presence and placing us close to His heart, He joins us in our prayers, defective as they may be, and blends them with His perfect petitions to the Father. That is what we must ever keep in mind whenever we pray. His petitions mingled with ours will make them truly efficacious, transforming them to be His own before God, who always responds to Him. For "as the sinner's sincere, humble prayers ascend to the throne of God, Christ *mingles* with them the merits of His own life of perfect obedience. Our prayers are made *fragrant* by this incense."[4]

When we become engaged in such glorious ministry of prayer and intercession for ourselves and others, Christ Himself takes up our cause. And just like a very competent attorney who does not accept a case to lose it, but to win, Jesus our great Advocate is infinitely more committed to winning *our* case. He puts Himself on the line, making our petition His own petition. If we continue trusting Him, we have His ironclad guarantee to decisively win our case.

"No sooner does the child of God approach the mercy seat than he becomes the *client* of the great Advocate. At his first utterance of penitence and appeal for pardon Christ *espouses* his case and makes it *His own,* presenting the supplication before the Father as *His own request.*"[5]

Does a sobering sense of our own sins sometimes cause us to shrink from participating in Christ's intercession? Do the terrible transgressions of others put us off? Does our abhorrence of both our sins and their sins keep us away from reaching out to God in intercession with Jesus? "When we feel the *least* inclined to commune with Jesus, let us pray the *most*. By so doing we shall break Satan's snare, the clouds of darkness will disappear, and we shall realize the sweet presence of Jesus."[6]

Whenever we feel least inclined to pray for our sinful selves and intercede for other sinners—ones who may even hate and hurt us—let us remember Calvary. As He died on the cross, Jesus included

Himself with all transgressors of all ages, and the weight of their sins crushed His life. "He [the coming Jesus] poured out His soul unto death, and He was numbered with the transgressors, and He bore the sin of many, and made intercession for the transgressors" (Isa. 53:12).

It is much easier to pray for the ones who love us and care about us than it is to pray for those who hate and hurt us. How can we pray for them? Remember Calvary when Jesus interceded with His Father for those who hated Him to death. "Let us pray not only for ourselves, but for those who have hurt us, and are continuing to hurt us. Pray, pray, especially in your mind. Give not the Lord rest; for His ears are open to hear sincere, importunate prayers, when the soul is humbled before Him."[7]

Samuel, recognizing all the great sins of his people, realized that in failing to intercede for them he would be himself sinning against God. One of their sins particularly affected this caring and righteous leader personally, for they had rejected his rulership over them. (At the same time God recognized that in spurning Samuel they were in fact turning away from Him [see 1 Sam. 8:8, 9]). Yet for Samuel it was a high privilege as well as a sacred duty to continue in his intercession for them in spite of themselves. "As for me, far be it from me that I should sin against the Lord in ceasing to pray for you" (1 Sam. 12:23).

And in calling us to join Him in His intercessory prayers, Jesus summons us to share holy ministry with the glorious company of the Father and the Holy Spirit. "For through Him [Jesus] we both have access by one Spirit to the Father" (Eph. 2:18). Judson Cornwall, an expert on prayer, suggests that prevailing prayer always involves four or more persons. The first Person is God the *Father,* who is the *"provider."* He is the vast and rich storehouse that supplies all our needs. The second Person participating is *Jesus,* the *"intercessor."* He unceasingly intercedes for us, reveals the Father's will to us, and calls on us to approach God in His name.[8]

The third Person is the *Holy Spirit,* the *"implementor."* Conveying and carrying out God's will in our lives, He is the one who illuminates our minds, convicts our hearts of God's will, and implements God's commands in our behalf. Finally, we have the *angels,* who are the *"activators"* of answered prayer. They serve as God's mobilized troops to do His bidding with any person or in any place.[9]

The apostle Paul tells us that the third person of the Godhead joins Jesus in such intercession with deep groanings impossible to express in words (Rom. 8:26). Indeed, we are never alone when we pray. Jesus and the Spirit are always beside us, interceding with us and for us, and They petition with passion and power. They yearn to possess us ever more completely so that They may pray through us ever more powerfully. The Holy Spirit "has ordained to bring His will to pass through your prevailing prayer, joined to the prevailing intercession of *both* God the Son on heaven's throne of grace and God the *Spirit.*"[10] Furthermore, "In a truly blessed sense the Holy Spirit gives birth to His petitions within us, and He kindles faith within us."[11] And in the words of Thomas Payne in his book *The Greatest Force on Earth,* such prevailing prayer conceived by the Holy Spirit "has the almightiness of God linked to it. It reaches round the world. It can touch the highest heaven or shake the lowest hell."[12]

"Likewise the Spirit also helps in our weaknesses. For we do not know what we should pray for as we ought, but the Spirit Himself makes intercession for us with groanings which cannot be uttered. Now He who searches the hearts knows what the mind of the Spirit is, because He makes intercession for the saints according to the will of God" (Rom. 8:26, 27).

Then in his Epistle to the Ephesians Paul admonishes us to persevere in prayer and supplication *in the Spirit* for all the saints and for himself. "Praying always with all prayer and supplication in the Spirit, being watchful to this end with all perseverance and supplication for all the saints—and for me" (Eph. 6:18, 19). The apostle was not merely satisfied to teach such counsel, but he put it into practice himself. Despite his spiritual stature as an apostle, he did not feel that he was beyond needing others to minister to him in prayerful intercession.

In Romans 1:9-12 he not only affirms the believers' faith in his continuous prayers for them, but he seeks their affirmation of his own faith as well. "For God is my witness . . . that without ceasing I make mention of you always in my prayers" (verse 9). In this regard notice the remarkable spirit of mutuality and humble reciprocity in verses 11 and 12: "For I long to see you, that I may impart to you some spiritual gift . . . that is, that I may be encouraged together with you by the mutual faith both of you and me."

Paul did three things: He interceded for others, he interceded for them without ceasing, and he asked them to intercede for himself and others. To the Ephesian believers he declared: "[I] do not cease to give thanks for you, making mention of you in my prayers" (Eph.

1:16). Furthermore, he informed the Colossian believers: "[I] do not cease to pray for you" (Col. 1:9). And to the Romans he assured: "For God is my witness . . . that without ceasing I make mention of you always in my prayers" (Rom. 1:9).

Let us go back to Romans 6:18 and 19 and find out what it means to pray in the Spirit. First, we need to submit to the wise will and perfect purpose of God for us. For our prayer Partner, the Holy Spirit, knows the divine will and purpose perfectly. "For the Spirit searches all things, yes, the deep things of God" (1 Cor. 2:10). Second, God knows perfectly the mind of the Holy Spirit, thus there exists perfect communication between the persons of the Godhead.

Third, the Holy Spirit sympathizes with our weaknesses and understands that we do not know what to pray for. That is why He Himself helps us in stirring us to pray, in speaking through us, and in speaking for us. The verb to "help" in Greek means to stand by someone, or to hold someone as we face something together. Yes, He constantly stands by us, holding us as He prays with, in, and for us.

Fourth, the Holy Spirit makes just the right type of intercession for us, and in just the proper way. He accomplishes it in His own special divine language of "groanings" that we could never utter. Happily, as the Spirit testifies to our own spirit, He takes our deficient groanings and mingles them with His own in their ascent to Heaven. "The simple prayers *indited* by the Holy Spirit will ascend through the gates ajar, the open door which Christ has declared: I have opened, and no man can shut. These prayers, *mingled* with the incense of the perfection of Christ, will ascend as *fragrance* to the Father, and answers will come." [13]

Oh, how much we need to experience this kind of prayer! For we know, especially in retrospect, how foolish some of our own prayers have been, although offered with the best of intentions. In fact, we are grateful that God in His love answered them in His own way and not the way we ourselves wanted. It is a great blessing to know that the Holy Spirit is right there, holding us and totally engaged in our prayer life! May we always avail ourselves of such blessing in the Spirit according to God's will.

This helps us to understand why God seems sometimes not to answer our prayers. "In the future life the mysteries that here have annoyed and disappointed us will be made plain. We shall see that our seemingly unanswered prayers and disappointed hopes have been among our *greatest blessings.*"[14] Sometimes He purposely delays His answer, and when He does respond, He does so not necessarily in the particular way we want, because He desires to do only the most and best for us.

Therefore, we should not let any seeming delay frustrate us, for in His perfect wisdom and love He is totally committed to do His utmost best for us in every respect. In submitting ourselves to our perfectly wise and loving God, we are to constantly cling to Him no matter what happens.

After all, in cleaving to Him we are clinging to the very One who is on our side, and who has taken up our cause in His heart. We can fully trust our God, for He "is *too wise to err,* and *too good to withhold* any good thing from them that walk uprightly. Then do not fear to trust Him, even though you do not see the immediate answer to your prayers."[15]

Even though God may not answer our prayers in the exact way and time we desire, we can still trust His great love and infinite wisdom. For His will for us is vastly much better than our own. Again Ellen White states that "God is *too wise and good* to answer our prayers always at just the time and in just the manner we desire. He will do *more and better* for us than to accomplish all our wishes. . . . Our desires and interests should be lost in His will."[16]

Finally, knowing what the Holy Spirit does to help us in our prayers will move us to continuously commune with God so that we may avail ourselves of whatever blessing He has in mind for us. And as mentioned earlier, Jesus joins the Holy Spirit in praying for us. What mightier Intercessors can we ask for! May we always remember this spiritual reality whenever we pray, for it humbles us, energizes us, and boosts our confidence in our God.

Let us always remember to keep in mind that Jesus and the Spirit, who love us and want our best, are both there interceding for us, in us, and through us. That They mingle their fervent and forceful prayers with our feeble prayers, making them prevail mightily. Moreover, this is what makes our prayers pleasing to God as they ascend to Him like the sweet fragrance of incense in golden bowls. "We must not only pray in Christ's name, but by the inspiration of the Holy Spirit. . . . Such prayer God delights to answer."[17]

Entering into such special experience of intercession brings us close to the heart of God, and unites us intimately with the ministry of Christ and the Spirit. Moreover, our joyous privilege of participating in united intercession with Christ leads us to sense even more deeply that it is also our sacred duty. How is it ever possible to be near to the heart of God without sharing His love, passion, and burden to save humanity! Sharing the ministry of intercession makes us ever more Christlike, and ever more Spirit-filled.

Most of the time it is difficult to get access to important people. We try to contact them by telephone, only to get a busy signal or to hear a recorded message on their answering machine. Perhaps we call to make an appointment, and the secretary tries to squeeze us in. Sometimes we wonder if we are bothering or burdening them with our business. But we do not have to ever wonder about God's constant and instant availability to us. Through Christ and in the Spirit we have direct and unrestricted access to the very throne of the King of kings of the whole universe.

"Let us therefore come boldly to the throne of grace," Paul assures us, "that we may obtain mercy and find grace to help in time of need" (Heb. 4:16). Duewel states that we are loved and constantly awaited and welcome at God's throne. Then he suggests five succinct ideas to help us as we approach God in prayer: We need to come to it, first, as "a throne of grace;" second, with "confident boldness;" third, with "openness and sincerity;" fourth, with "faith," and, finally, with "love and joy." [18]

Furthermore, Duewel presents us with seven progressively intensifying levels of prayer, suggesting that we apply any or some of these levels to suit particular situations. Instead of becoming discouraged at the first level of *asking,* for example, we become more determined to delve gradually into one or more intensified levels as outlined below. There exists no demarcation line as such between these different levels, and we may find ourselves moving from one to another without being aware of it. [19]

We must be careful not to become bogged down analyzing what level we are engaged in and at what time, but rather avail ourselves completely of the Spirit's guidance. Thus we may pray freely in the Spirit and according to His mind. Experiencing such levels of prayer not only helps us to prevail but also enables our prayer life to become authentic, our spirituality alive and growing. Here are the seven levels listed in order of intensity:

The first level is to *ask,* the second level is to *seek,* the third level is to *knock,* the fourth level is to *fast,* the fifth level is to bring to God a prayer *burden,* the sixth level is to *wrestle* in prayer, and the seventh level is to wage *warfare* in prayer. Ellen White explains that the prayer of faith is a science that we all need to understand. "Prayer and faith are closely allied, and they need to be studied together," she writes. "In the prayer of faith there is a divine science; it is a science that everyone who would make his lifework a success must understand." [20]

In the following chapter we will discuss each of these important levels of intercessory prayer.

---

[1] White, *Thoughts From the Mount of Blessing,* pp. 12, 13.

[2] Duewel, *Mighty Prevailing Prayer,* pp. 27, 28.

[3] White, *Testimonies,* vol. 8, p. 178.

[4] ———, *Sons and Daughters of God,* p. 22. (Italics supplied.)

[5] ———, *Testimonies,* vol. 6, p. 364. (Italics supplied.)

[6] ———, *Historical Sketches* (Basle, Switzerland: Imprimerie Polyglotte, 1886), p. 146. (Italics supplied.)

[7] *The SDA Bible Commentary,* Ellen G. White Comments, vol. 3, p. 1141.

[8] Cornwall, *Praying the Scriptures,* p. 147.

[9] *Ibid.,* p. 148.

[10] Duewel, p. 210. (Italics supplied.)

[11] *Ibid.,* p. 222.

[12] Cited in Duewel, p. 222.

[13] White, *Testimonies,* vol. 6, p. 467. (Italics supplied.)

[14] ———, *The Ministry of Healing,* p. 474. (Italics supplied.)

[15] ———, *Steps to Christ,* p. 96. (Italics supplied.)

[16] ———, *The Ministry of Healing,* p. 231. (Italics supplied.)

[17] ———, *Christ's Object Lessons,* p. 147.

[18] Duewel, pp. 45, 46.

[19] *Ibid.,* pp. 17, 18.

[20] White, *Education,* p. 257.

CHAPTER
NINETEEN

PARTNERS IN HIS PETITIONS—2

Jesus said: "Ask, and it will be given to you; seek, and you will find; knock, and it will be opened to you. For everyone who asks receives, and he who seeks finds, and to him who knocks it will be opened" (Matt. 7:7, 8). Let us begin with these first three levels of prayer, and then we will go on to the remaining four:

1. *Ask.* Our prayer life of prevailing intercession begins with asking, and is engaged in it at all its levels of intensity. For example, if we desire to find an old friend that we have lost track of, then we start our quest by asking about him or her. Jesus often invites us to ask in our petitions. Consider, for example, Luke 11:9-13 which begins: "And I say to you, ask, and it will be given to you; seek, and you will find; knock, and it will be opened to you" (verse 9). The entire brief passage has Jesus making six specific references to asking. The Scriptures often mention asking. Clearly God wants us to ask.

In John 15:7 Jesus clarifies that the asking in our prayers needs to spring forth from an abiding, or resting, in Him and His words. "If you abide in Me, and My words abide in you, you will ask what you desire, and it shall be done for you." John affirms that, having confidence in Him, "if we ask anything according to His will, He hears us" (1 John 5:14). Moreover, "if we know that He hears us, whatever we ask, we know that we have the petitions that we have asked of Him" (verse 15).

2. *Seek.* But we do not become discouraged and give up at this first level if we do not see an immediate answer. We must do more than ask. If we are hunting someone, we go on to seek that friend wherever he or she may be found. Seeking is a more intense activity

than asking. We find the person's address and follow the directions to the city, neighborhood, street, and door, while all along inquiring of others along the way. Again, Jesus often admonishes us to "seek, and you will find" (Luke 11:9). The Scriptures resound with God's invitation for us to seek Him. "When You said, 'Seek My face,' my heart said to You, 'Your face, Lord, I will seek'" (Ps. 27:8). "Seek the Lord while He may be found, call upon Him while He is near" (Isa. 55:6).

And just as we ask according to God's will, we also seek Him with all our being. "But from there you will seek the Lord your God, and you will find Him if you seek Him with all your heart and with all your soul" (Deut. 4:29). The psalmist echoes this thought when he says, "Blessed are those who keep His testimonies, who seek Him with the whole heart!" (Ps. 119:2). Our deep desire to let Him transform our hearts, and our firm commitment to forsake our own way and to follow His way (Isa. 55:7), propel us to seek Him.

This leads to thorough heart searching to find out if we have any hindrances that we need to remove, or any other areas in our lives that God wants us to submit to Him more fully. We examine our motives to see how earnest we are in seeking after God. Do we seek after Him because we truly love Him more than anything else? Do we reflect the spirit of David when he declared, "My soul thirsts for You; my flesh longs for You in a dry and thirsty land where there is no water" (Ps. 63:1)?

All too often we seek human greatness much more than we do heavenly glory. We strive valiantly to succeed in business, trade, or other temporal endeavors, but why don't we show the same dedication and intensity in our search for God? "God will be to us everything we will let Him be. Our languid, halfhearted prayers will not bring us returns from heaven. Oh, we need to press our petitions! . . . Be in earnest in the matter. Seek God with all the heart. . . . With intense earnestness *learn the trade* of seeking the rich blessings that God has promised."[1]

3. *Knock.* Staying with our analogy, when we finally find the door of our old friend, we proceed to knock at it, waiting for a response. And if necessary we knock again and again till someone hears us. Knocking is a more urgent and bold form of prayer. Just prior to Christ's words "knock, and it will be opened to you," He told the parable about the persevering friend knocking at midnight to borrow food (Luke 11:5-8).

It was already quite late at night, but the man's unexpected traveling friend was hungry, and he desperately needed some bread to serve him. Hospitality and food were mandatory in the biblical world. He did not get up, walk across town, and disturb his sleeping friend at such a late hour, only to leave empty-handed. Instead he had determined to keep knocking until he got the three loaves of bread.

Having obtained God's sure promises, why do we knock so faintly and infrequently? Knowing that God is never asleep or disturbed at our knocking (He invites us to knock), are we as bold as the man in the parable to knock loudly and persistently at heaven's gates until God blesses us with the bread of life? Christ wants to get across to us the message that sometimes it is not merely enough for us to ask or seek, but that we must go to God in holy boldness, knocking at heaven's door.

This level of prevailing prayer of faith reminds us of the woman of Canaan who came to Jesus asking Him to heal her daughter. No matter how the disciples treated her, or what seemingly discouraging words Jesus said to her, she kept on pressing her case. She kept on knocking again and again. Christ responded to her first request with the statement that He "was not sent except to the lost sheep of the house of Israel." And again He replied to her repeated entreaty by saying that "it is not good to take the children's bread and throw it to the little dogs" (Matt. 15:24, 26).

The woman could have become discouraged and defensive, but she kept on knocking as if she could not be denied. Of course Jesus wanted to help her, but He was testing her faith and teaching His disciples a valuable lesson at the same time. He honored her request when she, in her valiant faith, responded, "True, Lord, yet even the little dogs eat the crumbs which fall from their masters' table" (verse 27). "O woman, great is your faith!" Jesus declared. "Let it be to you as you desire" (verse 28). She had genuine faith in Christ—the kind of faith that pleases God.

Jesus related the parable of the persistent widow because He knows that we "always ought to pray and not lose heart" (Luke 18:1). Then He concluded the parable with the probing question "When the Son of Man comes, will He really find faith on the earth?" (verse 8). It is a parable about relentless faith. While we have absolutely no reason to worry that God may ignore our petitions, the real concern is that we ourselves, in our impatience, weariness, and discouragement, may give up first.

In our petitions the Lord wants us to exercise our faith in Him and not lose heart or yield to discouragement. Even the unjust judge, who "did not fear God nor regard man" (verse 2), eventually gave the woman what she needed in order to rid himself of her. For his own selfish motives, he grudgingly relented before her repeated knocks at his court, finally avenging her of her adversaries. Despite his questionable motives, he still granted her request. And God actually longs to help us.

Therefore, our greatest reason for not becoming disheartened in our petitions to God is God Himself. Jesus contrasts the perfectly loving, merciful, and just Judge we have with the selfish, cruel, and unjust judge the widow had. If that kind of cruel and corrupt judge eventually responded to her petitions despite selfish motives, how infinitely more will our God answer our petitions because of loving motives! Yes, will He not "avenge His own elect who cry out day and night to Him, though He bears long with them? . . . He will avenge them speedily" (verses 7, 8).

What about this seeming paradox between "bearing long with them," and "avenging them speedily"? Slowness and swiftness? Why does our God who loves to answer us swiftly sometimes respond so slowly? First of all, we must recognize that "God will not delay one moment longer than is absolutely necessary. He will do everything in His power to hasten the answer." [2] While we may wonder why God has not done anything *yet* about our situation, He has *already* been working on our case. Although from our limited knowledge nothing seems to be transpiring, at the same time He has already set in motion just the right dynamics to accomplish His wise will for us.

His miracle of producing and ripening a fruit has already been in motion even before the fruit is ready to be harvested. As we mature spiritually, we learn to fully trust that our loving and wise God simply knows what He is doing. As a child I remember being so impatient in waiting for the first fruits in our orchard to ripen that I would pick them prematurely. Hurriedly biting into the fruit, I would be disappointed with its tart taste. And my father would admonish me that I should have waited more patiently for it to ripen.

Likewise, our young daughter longed to try certain tasks more appropriate for older persons. Of course we wanted her to participate in such adult tasks, and we set things in motion for the future. Yet we and she waited for the right time. That is how we may understand our heavenly Father's slowness as well as His swiftness in answering our petitions. Let us confidently trust Him, for He knows all things, and He knows what is for our best from beginning to end.

God takes many things into consideration that we may not be aware of. Possibly He is correcting some condition in our characters. Perhaps He is waiting for some circumstances to come together in the right way. Maybe He is considering helping others in the process of helping us. Whatever the reason for the seeming delay, we may be sure that persevering faithfully in our prayers will certainly be rewarded in the best way possible. "Real faith cannot be disappointed," affirms Andrew Murray. "It knows that to exercise its power, it must be gathered up, just like water, until the steam can come down in full force."[3] Let Him gather us up in His hands, and let Him enfold us in His arms so that His Spirit may fill us in full force.

Consider Peter in prison, waiting to be executed by Herod. The disciple's fellow believers knocked at heaven's gate with "constant prayer" (Acts 12:1-19). And when an angel miraculously freed him from prison, Peter came to the house of Mary, "where many were gathered together praying" (verse 12). There in the middle of the night they were *continuing* to intercede for him. The fact that Peter found them praying when he arrived at their door unexpectedly, and the fact that it was late in the night, indicates that they were having a continuous prayer vigil for him.

Although Peter now knocked at their door, they could not believe that God had actually answered their prayers. *Too good to be true!* they thought. But Peter "continued knocking" (verse 16) till they finally came to the door and welcomed him in. It is interesting to note that while they were persistently knocking at heaven's door, Peter was persistently knocking at their house's door! God's answer to their knocking was in Peter's knocking, right there and then.

4. *Fasting.* Charles Stanley defines fasting as "more than mere self-denial or abstinence, but it does involve both." Moreover, he asserts that "it is abstinence with a spiritual goal in mind. Fasting is abstinence from anything that hinders our communion with God."[4] There are crucial times and circumstances when we especially need to free ourselves to become totally absorbed in communion with God. Trying times and difficult situations when we particularly need to be alert to discern God's will.

The spiritual discipline of fasting can never substitute for living out the spirit of the law in true obedience. We must never try to use it to impress God with our piety. Neither must we presume to manipulate God, or in some way earn His special favor with it. Nor is it for public display that we may awe others with our supposed spirituality. Jesus linked faithful fasting to personal prayer as something between us and God. Just as we need to pray in secret, we also need to fast in secret (Matt. 6:6-18).

Our Saviour did not make fasting a rigid requirement for His disciples, but taught them how to truly fast when they felt the need to do so. He instructed them to pray and fast in private before God, and not publicly so as to gain hypocritical recognition. In His teaching about fasting Jesus apparently considers it a given that His disciples would sometimes fast as they would pray.

In Matthew 6:5, 7 He discusses with them not whether they should pray, but how to properly do so. Likewise, in verses 16 and 17 He admonishes them not how they ought to fast, but how to do it faithfully. "But you, when you pray" (verse 6) and "But you, when you fast" (verse 17). Christ's use of the conjunction "but" is significant in this context, because it contrasts His true way of fasting with the ritualistic way of the hypocrites He describes in the preceding verse.

A number of Jewish leaders made fasting so legalistic, showy, burdensome, and gloomy that it became an abhorrence to God. It certainly lay behind Christ's comment about not fasting but rejoicing while He, the Bridegroom, was still with them. It is quite unlikely that He intended that they would never fast under any circumstances.

After all, Jesus Himself fasted and prayed for 40 days in the wilderness in His spiritual preparation to overcome Satan's temptations (Luke 4:1-13). Remember the incident when the disciples failed to cast the evil spirit out of a boy? Then when Jesus healed the child, His disciples asked Him, "Why could we not cast him out?" Jesus replied: "This kind can come out by nothing but prayer and fasting" (Mark 9:28, 29). Furthermore, He told His disciples that there would be trying times when they would need to fast. "The days will come when the bridegroom [Jesus] will be taken away from them; then they will fast in those days" (Luke 5:35; cf. Matt. 9:15).

After the ascension of Jesus, persecution and even execution threatened the early believers. And today, just prior to Christ's second coming, we confront enormous problems and terrible dilemmas both from within and from without. Certainly we cannot adequately deal with some of them except through prayer and fasting. Therefore, in as much as the disciples especially needed to fast after Christ ascended to heaven, so we too need to fast as we await His soon return to earth.

Now, we want to be careful never to be rigid or legalistic. Whether we fast or not and how and to what extent is a personal matter between us and our God. And if He convicts our hearts to fast, it must be for His glory and the deepening of our relationship with Him. We must also take into consideration our circumstances, our spiritual growth and maturity, and our health needs.

Generally, however, genuine and prudent fasting can produce highly positive spiritual results. Here are a few helpful ideas for our careful consideration:

a. We may fast for one meal a day, or for a whole day once a week or once a month, or twice or more a year. Also, we may fast from eating rich and unhealthy foods, which we need to do anyway for the sake of our health. Fasting can give our overworked stomachs the needed opportunity to rest, and our tired minds the clarity to focus on the spiritual.

b. The problem in our society is not usually fasting, but feasting. We often snack and indulge ourselves in overeating. To fast sometimes can be quite helpful to us for our total health. Also, the money we save from not overeating we can use to feed others who do not have enough to eat.

c. We fast in order to yield our total being—body, mind, and spirit—in total humility and submission to God, so that we may become particularly open to Him.

d. We fast in order to free ourselves from the many daily distractions, making God and spiritual matters our focused attraction. Usually we think of fasting only in the context of eating, but we may also think of it as fasting from other activities that divert us from focusing on God. In self-denial we give the spiritual realm the opportunity to rule over the physical.

e. When we fast, we do it primarily for the special purpose of freeing and devoting ourselves to meditation, prayer, and Bible study. True fasting is not merely abstaining from food. Such fasting is actually feasting on His Word. That was Christ's kind of feasting while fasting in the wilderness of temptation: "Man shall not live by bread alone," Jesus responded to Satan, "but by every word that proceeds from the mouth of God" (Matt. 4:4). Such fasting can deepen and intensify our spirituality, shifting our hunger from our physical food to our heavenly Father.

f. Fasting is linked to prayer and intercession in seeking God's will and intervention in specific situations. We fast when confronted with crises, life-threatening illnesses, tragedies, and attacks from Satan.

g. We fast when we need to seek God's inspiration and guidance in ascertaining and understanding a particular doctrine or facet of truth in the Scriptures.

h. We fast because we sense our need for God's grace and power to help us obey Him more faithfully and to serve Him more effectively.

5. *Prayer Burden.* All of us sometimes experience a certain burden to pray for someone or about something. We sense the Holy Spirit tugging at our hearts to intercede for an urgent need. Duewel describes such a prayer burden as a "spiritual concern on the heart of God that is imparted by the Holy Spirit to someone whose intercession the Holy Spirit desires to use."[5] However, we must include ourselves too as being the subjects of such prayer burdens. In other words, the Holy Spirit places a heaviness on our own hearts about a certain unconfessed sin, a specific act of disobedience, or a particular deed He wants us to carry out. In such a case, we must confess the sin, abandon the disobedient action, and carry out God's will.

Moreover, Duewel affirms that Jesus and the Holy Spirit are the source of such a prayer burden, and are always involved in it. Yet They choose to include us in it. "Jesus has been interceding for this need, and now the Spirit needs you to join with the intercession of Jesus. It is a specially sacred level of prayer intensity and prayer responsibility. It is always a special trust committed to you from the Lord, a special call of the Spirit for faithful intercession. It is an indication of the Lord's priority for you."[6]

It is a great and sacred honor to be impressed by the Holy Spirit with a prayer burden, and to share this holy privilege with Him and Jesus! One time, as I was concluding my morning devotions, I suddenly felt struck with the conviction to pray urgently for a particular family. Throughout that day I interceded for the members of that family, not knowing the particular crisis they were confronting. Later that month I spoke with the family and learned how God had miraculously intervened to save them from a terrible situation that day I felt convicted to pray for them.

As we enjoy a continuous communion with Jesus, and as we live and walk in the Holy Spirit, They give us specific burdens to intercede for. When I come under conviction of any prayer burdens, I write them down in my prayer notebook. Then during my prayers I focus on my list of specific prayer burdens. For example, as we witness for Christ, we sometimes find ourselves struck with the clear conviction to start praying for a particular person's salvation. Ellen White writes that "in times past there were those who fastened their minds upon one soul after another, saying, 'Lord, help me to save this soul.' But now such instances are rare."[7] Furthermore, she admonishes: "Let the workers grasp the promises of God, saying, . . . 'I must have this soul converted to Jesus Christ.'"[8] May God lay on our hearts prayer burdens for those who desperately need His salvation. And may we, in their behalf, pour out our hearts to God in focused intercession.

God's Spirit, in honoring our faith, moves in a special way in the particular situation we have been burdened to pray for, and does something He would not have done otherwise. He, who even sent His only Son to die for fallen humanity, is most assuredly willing to help us guide a lost person to Him. Indeed, in His love and wisdom, God often causes things to work out in such a providential way that we are brought together with the specific persons whom He wants us to help.

"It is a part of God's plan to grant us, in answer to the prayer of faith, that which He would not bestow did we not thus ask."[9] Charles Finney wrote that "prayer is not to change God, but to change us. Prayer produces such a change in us, and fulfills such conditions in us as to render it consistent for God to do as it would not be consistent for Him to do otherwise."[10]

The faith of the one whom we are interceding for may be too feeble to hold on to God. Ellen White urges such a person: "If you cannot rely upon your own faith, rely upon the faith of others. We believe and hope for you. God accepts our faith in your behalf."[11] Remember the incident when Jesus brought spiritual and physical healing to the helpless paralytic? His friends lowered him from the roof to where Jesus was. "So when He [Jesus] saw their [the friends'] faith, He said to him [the paralytic], 'Man, your sins are forgiven you'" (Luke 5:20). It is true that he believed with his loving and loyal friends, yet Jesus referred to *their* faith on his behalf.

Charles Stanley, in one of his television sermons, outlined nine requirements for us to follow in joining Christ in the ministry of intercession for others. Remember that not all such requirements necessarily apply at any one time. It will all depend on the kind of prayer burden God entrusts us with. The requirements include:

a. *Awareness.* To be sensitive to people's needs, and to become acquainted with what is happening in their lives.

b. *Availability.* To be available for God to use us to pray for certain individuals or situations.

c. *Advocate.* To become fellow intercessors with Christ in behalf of others. To go in their place and plead their case. We do not have to know all the details, for God knows everything.

d. *Acceptance.* Sometimes God places people on our hearts to pray for, whom we happen not to like. Instead of trying to change them, let us pray for them and sympathize with them, and see how God is able to change them (as well as us in the process).

e. *Abandonment.* Abandonment in terms of relinquishing ourselves to God, giving up our time and self-interest in joining Jesus in His intercession. It is losing sight of self in becoming caught up with God and in doing His will.

f. *Agonizing.* Satan hates to see us persevere in our prayers for others, and tempts us to become weary and give up. But as we see their lostness, feel their pain and hopelessness, the Spirit helps us to persist in agonizing for them. Imagine how many more would be saved if we had more ardent agonizers before God's throne.

g. *Authority.* When we are in the right relationship with God, we may press our petitions with boldness and authority. We should have no fear or timidity as we do so. Of course, we are not worthy in ourselves to have such authority, but in Jesus we do.

h. *Armor.* Perseveringly pressing our petitions before God greatly angers Satan. Therefore, we must put on the *full* armor of God discussed in Ephesians 6. We must not leave the devil any opening, for in his wrath he may attack us and the ones we are agonizing for.

i. *Accountability.* When God places a burden on our hearts to pray for someone, we become responsible before Him for that trust. With His help we will be accountable for whom He has entrusted us with.

6. *Wrestling Prayer.* This level of prayerful intercession is intense, and endures for only a limited segment of time. It is usually physically demanding and spiritually draining, hence the reason for its shorter duration. And also the reason why only a few are willing or capable of experiencing it. "Wrestling in prayer enlists all the powers of your soul, marshals your deepest holy desire, and uses the

perseverance of your holy determination. . . . You reach beyond the visible to the very throne of God. With all your strength and tenacity you lay hold of God's grace and power." [12]

Certainly Christ's very intense wrestling in prayer in the Garden of Gethsemane is the best example in the Bible. "And being in agony, He [Jesus] prayed more earnestly. And His sweat became like great drops of blood falling down to the ground" (Luke 22:44). The Gospel account describes Christ as being in *agony*, a term that captures what it means to wrestle in prayer. We will never be called upon to come close to the intensity of Christ's experience, but at times in these last days we will need to wrestle with God as did Jacob, Moses, Daniel, and others.

Jacob's experience is a good example of what it means to wrestle with God in prayer. All night Jacob struggled with the Angel [Christ] without letting Him go until He blessed him. "And He [Christ] said, 'Let Me go, for the day breaks.' But he [Jacob] said, 'I will not let You go unless You bless me!'" (Gen. 32:26). "Such will be the experience of God's people in their final struggle with the powers of evil." [13]

Christ, with whom Jacob wrestled and prevailed, seemed to want to escape him: "Let Me go . . ." But Jacob held on to Him, refusing to release Him. Christ desires to stay with us much more than we do. Then why this paradox? Because in His love He tests our faith and purifies our hearts, so that we may fully appreciate Him and what He blesses us with. Therefore, He sometimes remains silent, or seems to turn away from us. He is simply trying to draw us even nearer to Him with greater consecration. Our lack of appreciation confirms our self-centeredness, and if He were to grant us our wishes in that state, we would become even more entrenched in our independence of Him.

Andrew Murray writes: "Blessed is the man who is not staggered by God's delay or silence or apparent refusal." [14] Then he explains why God comes across that way sometimes: "God holds Himself back, and tries to get away from us, until what is of flesh, self, and sloth in us is overcome, and we so prevail in Him that He can and must bless us." [15] The Lord wants to refine the weak as well as the strong. He even tested His faithful prophet Elijah when he had to pray seven times before God sent the rain.

One cannot help wondering why God waited until the seventh time before granting His prophet's request. After all, shortly before hadn't God immediately answered His prayer for fire the first time? (See 1 Kings 18:36-40.) But now Elijah went back up Mount Carmel to pray again. Why did God wait until the seventh time before responding this time? (See verses 41-46.) Could it be that He in His love for His prophet desired to cleanse Him from any pride, potential or actual, about the mighty and glorious miracle He had recently wrought through him? Could it be that God wanted to make sure that His prophet felt His nothingness without Him?

"The servant watched while Elijah prayed. Six times he returned from the watch, saying, there is nothing, no cloud, no sign of rain. But the prophet did not give up in discouragement. He kept reviewing his life, to see where he had failed to honor God. . . . As he searched his heart, he seemed to be less and less. . . . It seemed to him that he was nothing, and that God was everything; and when he reached the point of renouncing self, while he clung to the Saviour as his only strength and righteousness, the answer came." [16]

Patiently God waits to get our attention. So when He finally receives it, He is not merely satisfied to grant us what we ask for, but, more importantly, He wants to teach us the invaluable lesson of putting Him ahead of all things. In His great love for us He knows that it is His opportunity to help us feel our nothingness without Him. He has probably been trying to do this for a long time already, but we never gave Him a chance. Now He hopes that this time we finally will respond and learn.

God desires through all of this to "have all our interests interwoven with His interests, and then He can *safely* bless us; for we shall not then take glory to self when the blessing is ours, but shall render all the praise to God." Furthermore, "God does not always answer our prayers the first time we call upon Him; for should He do this, we might *take it for granted* that we had a right to all the blessings. . . . Instead of searching our hearts to see if any evil was entertained by us, any sin indulged, we should *become careless,* and fail to realize our dependence upon Him." [17]

When I first arrived in the United States many years ago, it took me a while to get used to the new culture of my adopted country. When some of my classmates would invite me home for a meal, I would initially resist, saying, "No, thank you, I don't want to burden you," while at the same time really wanting to eat with them. I would hope that they would look beyond my initial no and see my potential yes. Inside, I would hope that they would not give up on me the first time, or the second, but that they would persevere a bit more.

What I really wanted to know was that they genuinely wanted me in their home, and that it was not merely an empty or a dutiful gesture on their part. Their persistence in spite of my initial resistance would prove two things to me: that I really wanted to eat with them, but for the right reason, and that they in their persistence were really interested in being with me as a person. At least that is the way I used to look at it.

In a similar way, God may initially say no, may seem to hide His face or run from us. But that is a proof that He really longs for us to pursue Him more passionately and persistently with all our hearts. Is it because He is timid or passive? No, not at all. Rather, it is because He yearns for us to love Him genuinely. He ardently hopes that we will not become disheartened over His seeming aloofness, but will diligently seek Him.

The Lord will never spurn such passionate and persistent persual of Himself, but will produce clear evidence in our lives that He will accomplish what He desired to do all along. "Never a prayer is offered, however faltering, never a tear is shed, however secret, never a sincere desire after God is cherished, however feeble, but the Spirit of God *goes forth* to meet it," Ellen White assures us. Furthermore, "Even *before* the prayer is uttered or the yearning of the heart made known, grace from Christ *goes forth* to meet the grace that is working upon the human soul." [18]

Returning to Jacob's experience, we learn that as the Lord blessed him He changed his name to "Israel," saying to him, "You have struggled with God and with men, and have prevailed" (Gen. 32:28). His new name "Israel" means the one who strives with God. Apparently, God wanted this striving with Him to be an integral part of his life and mission. We too will prevail with the Almighty as Jacob did when we also strive and agonize with Him.

"Jacob prevailed because he was persevering and determined. His experience testifies to the power of importunate prayer. It is now that we are to learn this lesson of prevailing prayer, of unyielding faith. The greatest victories . . . are not those that are gained by talent or education, by wealth or the favor of men. They are those victories that are gained in the audience chamber with God, when earnest, agonizing faith lays hold upon the mighty arm of power." [19]

7. *Warfare Prayer.* Here we encounter the highest level of intense, militant, long-term prayer. It is battling the forces of evil in Christ's mighty name and through His shed blood. In total submission to Christ we resist such forces, not giving up until the devil is decidedly defeated, dislodged, and driven away, and Christ's reign has become supreme.

Throughout His life and ministry Christ battled Satan's vicious attacks. Submitting to His Father's will and depending on His power, Jesus gained the decisive victory. And we may too through His mighty name. Paul used the term "wrestle" when he described our spiritual warfare against evil. It is what he had in mind when he wrote that "we do not wrestle against flesh and blood, but against principalities, against powers, against the rulers of the darkness of this age, against spiritual hosts of wickedness in the heavenly places" (Eph. 6:12).

Then he tells us the real Source of our power for winning in this struggle, and the spiritual weapons that God provides us. Paul writes: "Finally, my brethren, be strong in the Lord and in the power of His might. Put on the whole armor of God, that you may be able to stand against the wiles of the devil" (verses 10-18).

"Keep up your prayer offensive. Mobilize all your prayer resources. Fasting prayer is heavy artillery in your arsenal. Prayer burden is powerful bombardment of Satan's territory. Wrestling prayer sends mighty guided prayer missiles to destroy Satan's works. Satan is always vulnerable to the prevailing prayer of God's intercessors. He cannot stop prayer or escape your prayer. Press on. God's power is available and unlimited. It is released with devastating effect on Satan's forces as you militantly prevail." [20]

---

[1] White, *Our Father Cares,* p. 99. (Italics supplied.)

[2] Murray, *With Christ in the School of Prayer,* p. 120.

[3] *Ibid.,* p. 119.

[4] Charles F. Stanley, *Handle With Prayer* (Wheaton, Ill.: Victor Books, 1982), p. 30.

[5] Duewel, *Mighty Prevailing Prayer,* p. 200.

[6] *Ibid.,* pp. 200, 201.

[7] White, *Gospel Workers,* p. 65.

[8] ——, *Medical Ministry,* p. 244.

[9] ——, *The Great Controversy,* p. 525.

[10] Quoted in Richard E. Day, *Man of Like Passions* (Grand Rapids: Zondervan Pub. House, 1942), pp. 126, 127.

[11] White, *Testimonies,* vol. 2, p. 319.

[12] Duewel, pp. 210, 211.

[13] White, *Patriarchs and Prophets* (Mountain View, Calif.: Pacific Press Pub. Assn., 1958), p. 202.

[14] Murray, *The Ministry of Intercession* (Pittsburgh, Pa.: Whitaker House, 1982), p. 36.

[15] *Ibid.,* p. 44.

[16] White, *Our Father Cares,* p. 100.

[17] *Ibid.* (Italics supplied.)

[18] White, *Christ's Object Lessons,* p. 206. (Italics supplied.)

[19] ——, *Patriarchs and Prophets,* p. 203.

[20] Duewel, p. 233.

RECOGNIZED BY HIS AROMA

As I write this we have just returned home from attending the memorable funeral service of a saintly mother in Israel, Helen Economou. Along with her daughter Elly, a professor of religion at Andrews University, she had been known by many for her deep devotion to God, which she expressed in unusual kindness and hospitality. Helen and Elly exemplified what a loving relationship a mother and a daughter can have. And this love in their lives spilled over to others around them. Generously they opened their heart and their home to so many.

Trying to comfort grieving Elly at the committal service, Pastor Dwight Nelson reminded her of a childhood experience with her mother that Elly recounted in her book *Beloved Enemy*. As a little girl Elly had searched the fields around her house for just the right beautiful flower to offer her mother.

"'Mama, Mama, look what I found.' The little girl, Elly, ran in from the garden, leaned against her mother's knee, and slowly opened her hand to reveal a tiny crushed flower. 'Oh, Mama.' Her eyes filled with tears. 'I loved it too tight. The poor little flower is broken.' Mother looked compassionately at the child, smoothed the dark hair, and drew the little girl into her arms. 'Smell it, dear. It smells so nice when you hold it tight. Even if you crush it, the sweet perfume still comes out.' Elly held the broken blossom to her nose for a long time." [1]

Yes, events can snuff out the lives of saints, but nothing can block the fragrance of their godly lives. It is indestructible and will endure forever. Their godly and fragrant works are not dead and buried, but make a lasting impact on others. "Then I heard a voice from heaven saying to me, 'Write: "Blessed are the dead who die in the Lord from now on."' 'Yes,' says the Spirit, 'that they may rest from their labors, and their works follow them'" (Rev. 14:13).

About 2,000 years ago another flower was crushed, the Rose of Sharon, and its sweet perfume still continues to saturate the atmosphere. Yes, Satan and evil broke the life of Christ on the cross, but its fragrance has ever since pervaded the world through the lives of His faithful followers. Think of the time when Mary came beforehand to anoint Christ's body for burial, breaking the alabaster jar and pouring on Him its precious nard (see Mark 14:3-9). In this moving account of love and devotion we find spiritual parallels between the alabaster jar filled with nard and the body of Jesus.

1. The alabaster jar symbolizes the body of Christ.

2. The broken alabaster jar correlates with the broken body of Christ.

3. Mary's great love for Christ led her to break the precious alabaster jar. And it was Christ's supreme love for fallen humanity that compelled Him to allow His holy body to be broken on the cross.

4. The sweet fragrance of nard filled Simon's entire house. And the sweet aroma of Christ's gospel flowed out from the cross to saturate the whole world. Jesus associated the loving act of Mary spreading the nard with the advance of the gospel. "Assuredly, I say to you, wherever this gospel is preached throughout the whole world, what this woman did will also be spoken of as a memorial to her" (verse 9).

Commenting on Mary's act of devotion, Ellen White draws a similar correlation. "As the alabaster box was broken, and filled the whole house with its fragrance, so Christ was to die, His body was to be broken; but He was to rise from the tomb, and the *fragrance of His life* was to fill the earth." [2]

Nothing can stop the spread of such sweet fragrance. Simon hoped to, for he thought Mary would simply say something to Christ and leave, and things would return to normal. But whenever there is such great love and devotion to Christ it issues a sweet fragrance. In Simon's house the fragrance of nard and love simply could not be confined to a corner, but it overpowered his whole house. "When the love of Christ is enshrined in the heart, like sweet fragrance it *cannot be hidden.* Its holy influence will be felt by all with whom we come in contact." [3]

It is the fragrance of *His* life that makes *our* lives fragrant. For if we do not let His aroma saturate our lives, then we can only reek with the stench of our own selfishness. The apostle Paul affirms that it is the fragrance of His knowledge that we diffuse around us: "Now thanks be to God who always leads us in triumph in Christ, and through us diffuses the fragrance of His knowledge in every place" (2 Cor. 2:14). In His incarnation, Jesus was the aroma of God to the world. The fragrance of what the Father is like freely emanated from His life and ministry.

We too, as disciples of Christ, are called to become the perfume of Christ to God and to the world. "For we are to God the fragrance of Christ among those who are being saved and among those who are perishing" (verse 15). Notice the progressive degree of our relationship to that powerful scent as we compare verses 14 and 15 in our passage. Paul moves from telling us that we diffuse the fragrance of Christ to our becoming that fragrance of Christ.

But how is that ever possible when we consider our depraved human condition? How is it possible for us, failing human beings, to acquire such a sacred honor of becoming the aroma of Christ? The answer is right there in verse 14: when we have the spirit of gratitude and humility to submit to God's triumphant leadership in our daily lives. When we are united with Christ. When He fills our lives with His Spirit and surrounds us with His presence. Or, as Paul put it, when we are "in Christ."

Therefore, from our "in Christ" experience springs forth the "through us" experience. Whatever is in must come out. For when Christ is saturating our lives He diffuses His fragrance through us. In fact, we become so intimately associated with the diffusion of Christ's fragrance and become so much like Him in our lives and witness that others see Him clearly in us. After all, it is the fragrance of Christ that diffuses through us. Our lives and witness must give others a clear portrait of what Christ is like.

The historical background of Paul's powerful analogy of spreading fragrance goes back to the Roman festival that the NIV renders a "triumphal procession" (verse 14). And that is what it was. A victorious Roman general would enter the gates of Rome riding on his chariot. With his right hand he held a staff of authority, and on his head he wore a wreath of victory. Going to greet him from the capital were, among others, senators, trumpeters, and persons carrying ornate censers brimming with pungent burning incense. Its fragrance would permeate the city and drift beyond its walls to herald the sweet smell of victory.

Likewise, we are marching with our victorious Commander Jesus, spreading the fragrance of His knowledge. But when and where do we diffuse such fragrance? Again Paul provides the answer: "Always," and in "every place" (verse 14). When we are in Christ we breathe out His fragrance, and we are surrounded by it as well. It is to spiritual life what breathing is to physical existence.

Just as we are what we eat, we also smell like what we eat and what surrounds us. In other words, we can only breathe out the fragrances that we breathe in, and we can transmit only those fragrances that permeate and encircle us. Thus in order to "smell" sweet like Jesus, we must continuously partake of His fragrant life and be surrounded by His fragrant presence. Such an experience with Christ causes others to notice that, spiritually speaking, our fragrant breath and atmosphere are those of Christ Himself.

When one is thus refreshed and energized with this kind of genuine relationship with Jesus, then such a person "will be *surrounded* with an *atmosphere* of light and peace. The life will *breathe out fragrance,* and will reveal a divine power that will reach men's hearts."[4] On the other hand, if we feed on and surround ourselves with the things of the world, then we breathe out its worldliness.

For example, some years back I remember giving weekly Bible studies to a large family in their tobacco-smoke-filled home. As we would gather around the kitchen table, several of the family members would smoke incessantly, and by the time I was ready to leave I knew that I was totally saturated with tobacco odor. Then as I would enter my home, my wife would draw away from me, repulsed by the offensive odor surrounding me.

When we were missionaries in Africa, our then 3-year-old daughter, Marla, and I really enjoyed eating papayas off our papaya tree. Our little family ritual was that whenever a papaya would ripen we would pick it and eat it together. One day I came home from work quite tired and hungry, and found my family gone for the evening. Noticing that one big papaya on the tree was turning yellow, I decided to pick it and have it ready to eat with my daughter when she returned.

But when the delay was much longer than expected, I thought that perhaps I could peel the papaya and slice it, getting it all ready to share with Marla when she did arrive. As I watched the many luscious and mouthwatering slices filling the bowl, my appetite got the best of me. I figured that if I could just eat a couple of slices, nobody would be able to notice anyway. But before I knew it I had devoured the whole thing. Feeling satiated and refreshed, yet a bit guilty, I wiped the table clean, threw away the peelings, and covered up any telltale signs.

I hoped that my daughter would not notice what I had done, but she certainly did. No sooner had she arrived than she asked about the missing papaya, and who possibly could have stolen it. Distracting her inquisitive mind to other things, I managed, to my relief, to get her preoccupied playing with her toys. However, when it came close to her bedtime, she wanted me to play with her. As we played together, her face got near to mine, and she abruptly stopped and asked me to move my face even closer. When I obliged, she pulled my cheeks toward her and directed me to open my mouth.

I could hardly believe what happened next. She actually stuck her tiny nose in my mouth and took a deep breath. "Daddy!" she exclaimed. "You are the one who ate the papaya, aren't you?"

"How could you blame daddy for doing such a thing, especially since you did not see me do it?" I teasingly demanded. "What proof do you have?"

"Daddy, I don't need any proof," she shot back, exasperated that I did not seem to catch on. "You are full of papaya, and its sweet smell is coming from inside of you."

Wisdom comes from the mouths of children just as guilt may come from the mouths of parents. The incident was a profound lesson about partaking of Christ's life! The only way to breathe out the fragrance of Christ is to feed on Him. And the only way to smell like Christ is to be filled with Christ. There is no short cut to such a spiritual experience. It is something that we can never pretend to have, for it must become a living reality in our lives. As someone aptly put it, we must not merely talk the talk but, more important, walk the walk.

We may eloquently preach about God's love to lost humanity, and we may valiantly try to add new members to our church, but unless we truly love each other in our homes and churches, we will never draw others to our Christianity. They catch on that we are not authentic, that we do not possess what we profess. For if the fragrance of Christ possesses us, then others will see His life, His love, and the transforming power of His gospel in how we relate to those close to us. They will be able to recognize us as authentic Christians, living in our everyday lives the love that we tell them about.

Jesus says to us, His present-day disciples: "By this all will know that you are My disciples, if you have love for one another" (John 13:35). Such love takes place only as we first experience how much Christ Himself loves us. It is the indispensable and reciprocal connection that He establishes, in the previous verse, between our love for Him and our love for one another. It is not something that we wear outwardly to impress others, rather it is experiencing an inner spiritual transformation to please God. But such an authentic and inward spiritual reality has a fresh and a spontaneous outward flow, bringing glory to Him.

The fragrance of such love is never self-generated. We need to particularly stress this because of all the overemphasis today on self-love. "You've got to love yourself," we often hear. Loving one's self seems to be the first and foremost commandment in our society. But it was not to Jesus. Some suppose that Jesus gave such a commandment in Matthew 22:34-40, but in fact He did not.

Jesus gave only two commandments in response to the lawyer's testy inquiry, "Teacher, which is the great commandment in the law?" (verse 36). "The first and great commandment," Jesus said, is "You shall love the Lord your God with all your heart, with all your soul, and with all your mind" (verses 38, 37). And "the second is like it," He added. "You shall love your neighbor as yourself" (verse 39).

The only two commandments that Jesus gave, they have to do with loving God and loving one's neighbor. Christ presented no third commandment of loving one's self. True and proper self-love is the natural by-product of obeying the first two. The stipulation immediately following each commandment is the "how to" obey it. In other words, the first commandment asks us to love God. And the question is *How* do we do that? With all our being. The second commandment asks us to love our neighbor. And the question again is *How* do we do that? As ourselves.

According to Jesus, the thrust of the two great commandments is to genuinely love God and our neighbor, and from such love springs forth our proper love of self. "We love Him because He first loved us" (1 John 4:19), John writes. And if someone claims to "love God" but "hates his brother, he is a liar" (verse 20). God is the only source of all true love, and without Him, self-love degenerates into self-worship.

Therefore, we become fragrant with God's love because Christ's fragrant love first permeates and surrounds our lives. That is the only way others will know that we are indeed His loving disciples. Ellen White refers to this dynamic spiritual reality as "the badge of Christianity," which is not "an outward sign, not the wearing of a cross or a crown, but it is that which reveals *the union of man with God.* By the power of His grace manifested in the transformation of character the world is to be convinced that God has sent His Son as its Redeemer. No other influence that can surround the human soul has such power as the influence of an unselfish life. *The strongest argument in favor of the gospel is a loving and lovable Christian."* [5]

"If you always say you are as fragrant as a rose, how come when I get near you, you smell like a skunk?" someone once confronted a nominal Christian. It is true that, in a spiritual sense, we all stink like a skunk without the sweet fragrance of Christ transforming our lives. Would others be drawn to Christ by His sweet aroma exuding from our lives? Or would they be repulsed away from Him by our own stench of selfishness?

The world reeks with the intoxicating odors of sin and selfishness, but we are to be "distinguished from the world because God has placed His seal upon us, because He manifests in us His own character of love." [6] A few verses after Paul calls us the aroma of Christ (2 Cor. 2:15), he refers to us as "an epistle of Christ" that reveals His distinctive character because it is "written not with ink but by the Spirit of the living God, not on tablets of stone but on tablets of flesh, that is, of the heart" (2 Cor. 3:3).

Someone once wondered that if we were ever taken into custody for being Christians, would they find enough evidence to convict us? Or would they have to let us go free for lack of it? May there always be enough evidence in our lives to render us guilty of being like Christ. A vital union with Him results in a noticeable transformation in the lives of His followers. However, "when persons profess to be Christians, and their religion does not make them better men and better women in all the relations of life—living representatives of Christ in disposition and character—they are none of His." [7]

The enemies of Peter and John recognized that they had been with Jesus, for they spoke and acted like Him (see Acts 4:13). Of course, this does not just all happen overnight. It takes walking with, learning from, and adhering to Christ from day to day. As Dietrich Bonhoeffer put it: "When we are called to follow Christ, we are summoned to an *exclusive attachment* to His person."[8] Yes, it takes continuous submission and training to become like Him, and to be recognized as having been with Him. And this is what Jesus had in mind when He said: "A student is not above his teacher, but everyone who is fully trained will be like his teacher" (Luke 6:40, NIV).

To be with our Teacher, to learn from Him, and to become like Him is what genuine spirituality is all about. It must comprise our perpetual praise, prayer, and passion, and give our relationship with Him intimacy and freshness. "When this is in truth the experience of the Christian, there will be seen in his life a simplicity, a humility, meekness, and lowliness in heart, that show to all with whom he associates that *he has been with Jesus* and *learned of Him.*" Furthermore, "In those who possess it, the religion of Christ will reveal itself as a vitalizing, pervading principle, a living, working, spiritual energy. There will be manifest the freshness and power and joyousness of perpetual youth."[9]

This is what it really means to diffuse the fragrance of Christ. To be like our Teacher is the greatest accomplishment and the most distinguished recognition we can ever have. People who interact with us will then recognize that we have been with Jesus, because we diffuse His distinct fragrance as a spontaneous expression of His presence in our lives, whenever and wherever. In other words, it is the divine and glorious act of Jesus spiritually reproducing Himself and His character in us in such a miraculous way that others who see us will observe a beautiful reflection of Himself.

Like a sweet perfume, it can permeate us in such a natural, unconscious, and unobtrusive way. The fragrance of Christ in our lives has an inherently pervasive and spontaneous quality. It does not need to be wafted about in a forced or brazen manner. J. B. Phillips has an interesting way of paraphrasing 2 Corinthians 2:14: "Thanks be to God who leads us, wherever we are, on Christ's triumphant way and makes our knowledge of him spread throughout the world like a lovely perfume!"

The panel members of a particular television program were blindfolded and asked to recognize a mystery guest. "On one occasion, as soon as the guest stepped onto the stage, one of the panelists, in harmony with the rules of the program, immediately disqualified himself, indicating that he knew without question who the mystery guest was. It was his wife. After the blindfolds were off, everyone wanted to know how the panelist knew that the mystery guest was his wife. 'It was really very simple,' he explained. 'I recognized her by her perfume.' " [10]

No accomplishment can ever become more important than reflecting Christ in our lives. No higher position can we ever reach than learning at His feet. "Nothing is more needed in our work than the practical results of communion with God. We should show by our daily lives that we have peace and rest in the Saviour. His peace in the heart will shine forth in the countenance. It will give to the voice a persuasive power. . . . Men will take knowledge of us, as of the first disciples, that we have been with Jesus. This will impart to the worker a power that nothing else can give. Of this power he must not allow himself to be deprived." [11]

It takes a lot of our energy to try to be noticed, to promote ourselves. Let Jesus take care of all of that, and let us instead focus our precious resources on sitting at His feet and walking in His footsteps. You see, when we abandon ourselves to Christ we are no longer "anxious to have the highest place," Ellen White affirms. "We have no ambition to crowd and elbow ourselves into notice; but we feel that our *highest place* is at the feet of our Saviour." [12]

We have already mentioned Mary's love and devotion to her Master. As her broken alabaster jar spread the sweet fragrance of nard, so her humble and broken life also wafted the sweet fragrance of Christ. Such sweet aroma exudes only from a life that is truly humble, a transformed life that glories in Christ, not self.

In contrast to Simon, the host, Mary humbly showed her devotion to Him in simple acts that did not escape His notice. For at the time of Christ (and to some degree still today) in the Middle East it was customary for a host to show love and appreciation to a guest by washing the feet, anointing the head with olive oil, and kissing the cheeks. Mary's humble acts of devotion toward Christ revealed how unworthy she felt yet how grateful she was to be at His feet.

In that world's culture, as we mentioned previously, the head signified the best and most noble part of the body, but the feet represented the worst and most base. We notice how Mary by her actions showed that her best (her head) was not even worthy of her Master's feet. Yet she knew it was the highest position for her to be in. Since she was not the hostess at Simon's house, she had no basin, but she had her eyes. She had no water, but she had her tears. And while she had no towel, she did have her long hair. Although she felt unworthy to kiss Jesus' cheeks, she did not cease to kiss His feet.

Jesus noticed her acts of devotion and humility. Mary used her eyes, her tears, her hair, and her lips—all in the head—to minister to His feet. A Christ-centered life—humble, transformed, and devoted as Mary's—is what we need today to radiate the sweet aroma of His love and knowledge in the world. It is the highest honor we can have. Why would we, then, crave the attention of mere mortals when we have the attention, acceptance, and love of Christ Himself! Humbly sitting at His feet, we find the highest honor. Absorbed in such devotion to Him, we freely express *His* fragrant life through our own lives.

"If you are rightly devoted to the Lord Jesus, you have reached the sublime height where no one ever thinks of noticing you, all that is noticed is that the power of God comes through you all the time," writes Oswald Chambers. "The test of the life of a saint is not success, but faithfulness in human life as it actually is . . . the aim is to manifest the glory of God in human life, to live the life hid with Christ in God in human conditions." [13]

Of course, this spiritual process is not something instantaneous, but rather something gradual. Let us look again at how Christ worked on Peter. Lovingly and patiently Jesus helped him to grow in spiritual maturity throughout the three and a half years of His earthly ministry. And thanks to Christ's love and patience, Peter continued to make advances in his spiritual development. But even following His third and last appearance after the Resurrection, when Jesus commissioned His converted disciple to "feed My sheep" and to "follow Me" (John 21:15-17, 19), the disciple started again to compare himself with John instead of focusing on Christ.

"But Lord, what about this man [John]?" (verse 21) he asked, wondering how John was going to fare in comparison to himself. Jesus steadfastly and lovingly redirected his focus from others and onto Himself. "If I will that he [John] remain till I come," Jesus responded, "what is that to you? You follow Me" (verse 22). He was trying to tell Peter that his first priority was to be faithful in fully following Him and totally trusting Him, regardless of what others might or might not do. To be recognized by Christ, and to be recognized by others as Christlike, is all that really matters.

After all, what can ever compare with the recognition that God Himself extends to us? And if we are truly caught up in His recognition, we will not be so concerned about how others regard us. But if we focus on what others think of us, we falter in following our Master. "For we dare not class ourselves or compare ourselves with those who commend themselves," the apostle Paul cautions. "But they, measuring themselves by themselves, and comparing themselves among themselves, are not wise" (2 Cor. 10:12). Furthermore, "But he who glories, let him glory in the Lord" (verse 17).

David Powlison of Westminster Seminary, interviewed in *Christianity Today* about inner motives in contrast to external behavior, stated that "an idol is anything that replaces God. Let us say that I'm a preacher and what is controlling me and giving me ulcers is 'What are my peers going to think of me?' What you could ask that preacher is 'Who is in the place of God?' Well, those people. I'm living my life in their eyes, by their approval and rejection." And in response to a follow-up question, he explained that "it is not just that I am anxious about giving a speech, where I pray, 'Lord, help make those anxious feelings go away.' It's the very fact that God doesn't like what is on my mind, and God has something to say about it. My prayer becomes, 'Lord, forgive me for being ruled by what someone else thinks of me.' " [14]

And when the Holy Spirit reveals our real inner motives for our actions, we can have hope, as did Peter, when we repent and redirect our focus onto Christ. "How many today are like Peter!" Ellen White interjects. "They are interested in the affairs of others, and anxious to know their duty, while they are in danger of neglecting their own. It is our work to *look to Christ and follow Him.* . . . Beholding Him, we shall become transformed." Moreover, "It is the duty of everyone to follow Christ, without undue anxiety as to the work assigned to others." [15]

We can truly say that Joseph exemplified in his daily life what it really means to become the aroma of Christ wherever he was. And the powerful fragrance of his reputation permeated all his surroundings. Yes, he was a loving, peaceable, and courteous person, yet in his pure and solid character he valued honoring God more than anything else in the world.

Daniel's righteous life ever diffused the fragrance of Christ all around him, and yet he was recognized for his unbending allegiance to God. Pleasing his God was much more important to him than all the power of Babylon. "He [Daniel] sought to live in peace with all, while he was unbending as the lofty cedar wherever principle was involved." Moreover, "The *approval of God* was *dearer* to him than the favor of the most powerful earthly potentate—*dearer* even than life itself."[16]

Daniel's three Hebrew friends, too, considered God's recognition of them as the highest possible acknowledgment. They felt greatly honored to be known for their intimate relationship with their God and their obedience to His will. Their daily lives were fragrant with genuine sanctification. Commenting on their exemplary character, Ellen White states that "true Christian principle will not stop to weigh consequences. It does not ask, What will people think of me if I do this? or, How will it affect my worldly prospects if I do that? . . . The Lord has made ample provision that the hearts and lives of all His followers may be controlled by divine grace, that they may be as burning and shining lights in the world."[17]

Jesus showed us the same clear example in His life. He emptied Himself, "and in all that He did, self did not appear."[18] This was because "in the heart of Christ, where reigned perfect harmony with God, there was perfect peace." Consequently, "He was never elated by applause, nor dejected by censure or disappointment. Amid the greatest opposition and the most cruel treatment, He was still of good courage." However, "many who profess to be His followers have an anxious, troubled heart, because they are afraid to trust themselves with God."[19]

Our Saviour could forget about Himself because He always remembered His Father. He could be steady in His spiritual life regardless of circumstance because He anchored Himself in God's abiding trust. Self-forgetfulness is a virtue that each one of us needs to especially foster and value. Ellen White describes it with such superlatives as the "most beautiful" and the "most essential" for us. "[It] imparts to the life such an unconscious grace. Of all excellences of character this is one of *the most beautiful,* and for every true life-work it is one of the qualifications *most essential.*"[20]

Sometimes, however, we find it impossible to forget or lose sight of self. For, "though professing to be converted, we carry around with us a bundle of self that we regard as altogether too precious to be given up."[21] But the remedy for this malady of self-unforgetfulness is to never forget Jesus, and the remedy for the malady of self-centeredness is to die to self. For when we make Christ our focus, crucifying self, then in Him we possess abundant and eternal life. Yes, when we contemplate Christ in Gethsemane, and when we gaze upon Him crucified, then we realize that our "bundle of self" is not too precious for us to give up for Him. And "self will no longer clamor to be recognized." [22]

Indeed, when our minds dwell on His sacrifice of Himself for our sake, we view things differently. Contemplating what He did convicts us that *His* was the sacrifice that was altogether precious, *not ours.* We find ourselves driven by His Spirit to die to self so that He may be raised in our lives to ever live and reign supreme, manifesting His beautiful character in and through us. "When Christ dwells in the heart, the soul will be so filled with His love, with the joy of communion with Him, that it will cleave to Him; and in the contemplation of Him, *self will be forgotten.* Love to Christ will be the spring of action." [23]

The sweet fragrance of such sanctified character is the most precious asset we may ever acquire in this world, and the only one that will accompany us to heaven. Consider how often we squander most of our lives to acquire all kinds of possessions, and only invest a little, if anything, in obtaining the most precious and enduring possession. "A character formed according to the divine likeness is the *only* treasure that we can take from this world to the next. . . . And in heaven we are continually to improve. How important, then, is the development of character in this life." [24]

Of all the possessions, position, prestige, power, and other projects that consume our entire lives, the one and only thing that we will ever take with us is the character fashioned in the likeness of Christ. The fragrance of such character is imperishable. Death can only enhance its enduring value and influence. And the resurrection will launch it into higher and higher realms for eternity.

Are we prepared "for the communion of heaven" resulting from experiencing heaven in our hearts now? [25] The true spirituality that Jesus wants us to have involves our total beings now and for eternity. For in desiring us to become more like Him, He ever has in mind to save us to "the uttermost." He longs to grant us total and complete salvation and restoration in Him.

Once I witnessed a heated theological discussion on which has primacy—justification or sanctification? The arguments went back and forth for some time without any apparent resolution. Then I interrupted them with a question, trying to get them off dead center. "What about the primacy of glorification by faith?" I asked. That did it, for it helped shift the focus onto our *complete* salvation and restoration in Christ. True spirituality through justification and sanctification in Christ must lead us to glorification in Christ at His coming.

Every one of these three aspects is of primary importance, because they are all of Christ and they all together lead to complete salvation and restoration in Him. For the sake of illustration, what good would justification, or sanctification, or glorification be without every other one of them and all of them together? That must be our emphasis in spirituality—complete salvation and restoration in Christ. We living in Christ and Christ living in us, then when He comes again we will continue living with Him in glory.

In a previous book, *Portraits of the Messiah,* I discussed this important subject in more detail. Suffice it to give a brief comment here. There, in the analysis of Zechariah's vision of Joshua the high priest (Zech. 3:4-8), we see how justification, sanctification, and glorification complement each other in the context of Christ our righteousness. We can summarize salvation and restoration in three phrases: "(1) *the covering,* symbolizing justification, (2) *walking here,* signifying sanctification, and (3) *walking there* among the angels in heaven, signifying glorification." [26]

In conclusion, let us prayerfully ponder the poignancy of the following two statements. Then let us faithfully walk with Jesus in our daily spiritual lives, so that when He comes again soon we will continue walking with Him in glory.

"As the people looked upon Jesus, they saw a face in which divine compassion was blended with conscious power. He seemed to be surrounded with an atmosphere of spiritual life. While His manners were gentle and unassuming, He impressed men with a sense of power that was hidden, yet could not be wholly concealed." [27]

"To His faithful followers Christ has been a daily companion and familiar friend. They have lived in close contact, in constant communion with God. Upon them the glory of the Lord has risen. In them the light of the knowledge of the glory of God in the face of Jesus Christ has been reflected. Now they rejoice in the undimmed rays of the brightness and glory of the King in His majesty. They are prepared for the communion of heaven; for they have heaven in their hearts." [28]

[1] Elly Economou, *Beloved Enemy* (Boise, Idaho: Pacific Press Pub. Assn., 1968), pp. 5, 6.

[2] White, *The Desire of Ages,* p. 563. (Italics supplied.)

[3] ——, *Steps to Christ,* p. 77. (Italics supplied.)

[4] ——, *The Desire of Ages,* p. 363. (Italics supplied.)

[5] ——, *The Ministry of Healing,* p. 470. (Italics supplied.)

[6] *Ibid.,* p. 37.

[7] ——, *The Sanctified Life,* p. 55.

[8] Bonhoeffer, *The Cost of Discipleship,* p. 63. (Italics supplied.)

[9] White, *Christ's Object Lessons,* pp. 129, 130. (Italics supplied.)

[10] Mansell, *New Every Morning,* p. 21.

[11] White, *The Ministry of Healing,* p. 512.

[12] ——, *Thoughts From the Mount of Blessing,* p. 15. (Italics supplied.)

[13] Oswald Chambers, *My Utmost for His Highest,* p. 321.

[14] David Powlison, "Needs and Idols," *Christianity Today,* May 16, 1994, p. 21; interviewed by senior writer Tim Stafford.

[15] White, *The Desire of Ages,* p. 816. (Italics supplied.)

[16] ——, *The Sanctified Life,* pp. 20, 21. (Italics supplied.)

[17] *Ibid.,* p. 39.

[18] White, *Thoughts From the Mount of Blessing,* p. 14.

[19] ——, *The Desire of Ages,* p. 330.

[20] ——, *Education,* p. 237. (Italics supplied.)

[21] ——, *Testimonies,* vol. 9, p. 189.

[22] ——, *The Desire of Ages,* p. 439.

[23] ——, *Our Father Cares,* p. 40. (Italics supplied.)

[24] ——, *Christ's Object Lessons,* p. 332. (Italics supplied.)

[25] ——, *Christ's Object Lessons,* p. 421.

[26] Philip G. Samaan, *Portraits of the Messiah* (Hagerstown, Md.: Review and Herald Pub. Assn., 1989), p. 47.

[27] White, *The Ministry of Healing,* p. 51.

[28] ——, *Christ's Object Lessons,* p. 421.

Also by Philip Samaan

Christ's Way of Reaching People

Philip Samaan focuses on six progressive steps Christ used in witnessing and shows how we can follow this pattern to bring God's love to those around us.

Discover listening skills that enable you to detect people's needs and desires. Learn how to develop meaningful friendships that create trust and a yearning to associate with Jesus. And gain helpful ideas on how to share your personal testimony and use intercessory prayer.

Christ's Way of Reaching People helps take the anxiety out of witnessing and enables you to find the joy, spontaneity, and success that come from genuinely loving people and having a vibrant connection with Jesus.

Paper, 160 pages. US$9.99, Cdn$14.49.